Writing Women's Communities

The Politics and Poetics of
Contemporary Multi-Genre Anthologies

CYNTHIA G. FRANKLIN

The University of Wisconsin Press

The University of Wisconsin Press
2537 Daniels Street
Madison, Wisconsin 53718

3 Henrietta Street
London WC2E 8LU, England

Library of Congress Cataloging-in-Publication Data
Franklin, Cynthia G.
    Writing women's communities : the politics and poetics of contemporary
multi-genre anthologies / Cynthia G. Franklin.
    280 pp.   cm.
    Includes bibliographical references and index.
    ISBN 0-299-15600-1 (cloth: alk. paper).
    ISBN 0-299-15604-4 (pbk.: alk. paper)
    1. American literature—Women authors—History and criticism—Theory, etc.
2. Literature publishing—Political aspects—United States—History—20th century.
3. Politics and literature—United States—History—20th century.   4. Women and
literature—United States—History—20th century.   5. Community in literature.
6. Literary form.   I. Title.
PS151.F73   1997
810.9'9287'09045—dc21   97-9460

Writing
Women's Communities

For my grandparents,
Elsie and Melvin Franklin

Contents

Acknowledgments

This book, which takes writing women's communities as its subject, itself depends upon the women who have served as my mentors, and upon the communities at the University of California at Berkeley and the University of Hawai'i which have sustained me intellectually and emotionally, and shaped this study at its every stage.

At UC Berkeley, I was lucky to have wonderful teachers and advisors. I am particularly grateful to Elizabeth Abel for giving me direction and confidence in my scholarship, and for rigorous, probing, and practical criticism and generously given insights at every stage of this project. I also am deeply indebted to Susan Schweik, who gave me the idea for this project, and then guided me through it with the right questions, warm encouragement, and crucial advice. Thanks also to Norma Alarcón, for challenging insights and support.

Also at UC Berkeley, Kristina Brooks and Kimberly Drake helped this book evolve from its sketchiest, messiest form with copious comments, exacting editing, and unfailing enthusiasm. I am grateful as well to the members of my dissertation group—Kate Brown, Sarah Cole, Teresa Fulker, Jane Garrity, Kristina Hauk, Alisa Klinger, Leila May, and Irene Tucker—for helpful questions and criticisms, and for making the writing process so much fun. I especially would like to thank Jane, for always making me laugh, and for being a wonderfully supportive reader, and Irene, whose hard questions, astonishing intellect, and loyal friendship mean more to me than I can say. My deepest thanks also go to Jacqueline Shea Murphy, for reading this manuscript from its earliest drafts to its final form with unwavering faith and formidable intelligence; for knowing what I'm trying to do better than I do; and for helping me see how to do it, both in Berkeley and then from across the Pacific via countless emails and phone calls. Anne Goldman's astute and incisive readings of chapters of this book have made the entire project a stronger one, at the same time that her acerbic wit, generosity, and friendship have been sources of sustenance and pleasure. I also would like to thank Lauren Muller, Cynthia Schrager, and Theresa Tensuan, for invigorating responses to chapters of this study.

At the University of Hawai'i, my colleagues have provided me with a supportive environment, and with intellectual awakenings that have enriched this book. My largest debt is to Laura Lyons, for fast and deep friendship, brilliant insights, and unshakable integrity, and for talking through with me—and articulating—so much of this manuscript on a daily basis. I also am immeasurably grateful to Beth Tobin, for friendship and mentoring and for tireless willingness to provide sensitive feedback on exhaustingly large chunks of this study. My thanks go as well to Paul Lyons, who read this manuscript in its entirely with his characteristic wit, energy, and intelligence. Ruth Hsu's care and thoughtfulness have made the parts of this work that she read stronger. Thanks, too, to Candace Fujikane, for scrupulous and expert commentary and advice, and to Ruth Dawson, for being a wonderful mentor and teaching companion. For generously given cites and insights both global and Local, I would like to thank Rob Wilson. And mahalo to my students at the University of Hawai'i, whose questions, comments, and anthologizing practices have helped to bring this book into focus.

Other people in Honolulu and the San Francisco Bay Area whose friendship and support have enabled this project in sometimes intangible but nevertheless crucial ways include: Cristina Bacchilega, David Baker, Kathy Dee Kaleokealoha Kaloloahilani Banggo, Erica Benson, Tammy Carroll, Mahealani Dudoit, Sherry Haber, Anne Jennings, Mary Lucasse, Glenn Man, Robin Martin, Rodney Morales, Caroline Mulder, Rico Orias, Kathy Phillips, Ron Rebholz, Alison Regan, Francesca Royster, Susan Schultz, Alix Schwartz, Saul Steier, Donna Tanigawa, Joe Tobin, Cindy Ward, Val Wayne, John R. Wilkins, and John Zuern.

At the University of Wisconsin Press, I especially would like to thank Mary Elizabeth Braun, for her interest in this manuscript, and for seeing it into print with humor and intelligence; Raphael Kadushin, for guiding this project through the editing and production process so skillfully; and Sylvan Esh, for extraordinarily perceptive and attentive copyediting. I also have benefited from valuable criticism from Deborah Carlin and an anonymous reader for the University of Wisconsin Press, and from the suggestions of Dale Bauer.

A version of chapter 4 of this book, "The Making and Unmaking of Asian American Identity: *Making Waves* and *The Forbidden Stitch*," appears under this same title in *Hitting Critical Mass* (3.3 [winter 1995]: 93–129); a version of chapter 3 is forthcoming in *MELUS, The Society for the Study of Multi-Ethnic Literature of the United States* (22.1)—thanks to these journals for allowing me to reprint these works here.

My most long-standing debt of gratitude is to my family. I would like to thank my mother, Elaine Franklin, for unfailing belief in me and for generosity and support; my father, Shel Franklin, for lost buttons and love without strings; my brother, Bob Franklin, for unmatchable sweetness, and for actually reading portions of this manuscript; my sister, Julie Franklin, for healing powers, weekly phone calls, and unflinching hospitality in the face of broken pottery and other acts of toddler terrorism; my grandparents, Elsie Franklin and Melvin Franklin, whose love and support underwrite every line of this book; Nancy Meyers and, okay, the "boys" (I draw the line at "brothers") who pass as bulldogs; the Leon and Landy families; and Gerry and Racine Murdock and the rest of the Murdock and Klueger families, especially Jackie and Daniel Klueger, who kept track of the page count. My deepest thanks of all go to Marc Murdock, for crossing an ocean for me, for generosity, humor, patience, parenting, partnership, and delicious meals, and for the gifts of love and time. Finally, I am grateful to Jesse Franklin-Murdock, for anchoring me insistently and joyfully to a world outside of academia, and for singing to me with only a trace of mockery his exuberantly composed and timely song of celebration and lament, "All My Thoughts Are Gone."

Writing
Women's Communities

1

Introduction

Writing across Communities

What is more is that identity is always in part a narrative, always in part a kind of representation. It is always within representation. Identity is not something which is formed outside and then we tell stories about it. It is that which is narrated in one's own self.
—Stuart Hall, "Old and New Identities, Old and New Ethnicities," p. 49

Our writings are our visibility and our community. They are our survival.
—C. Chung, A. Kim, and A. K. Lemeshewsky, *Between the Lines*, p. 6

Caminante, no hay puentes, se hace puentes al andar (Voyager, there are no bridges, one builds them as one walks).
—Gloria Anzaldúa, foreword to *This Bridge Called My Back*, p. v

When I was studying for my oral examinations as a Ph.D. candidate in English literature, I was particularly drawn to *This Bridge Called My Back*. With the isolation of studying for orals and the pressure to prove myself an insider to the academy, I was struck by this anthology's emphasis on community, and its resistance to the academy's elitism. The women in *This Bridge* were staging the rebellion I fantasized about, finding alternative modes of writing and community to the ones that, in the academy, I often felt were exclusionary and full of posturing and self-importance. I identified with the anger of its contributors. Accompanying these feelings were my longings for an academic community in which I would be at home, and my envy that this particular community was, quite decidedly, closed to me, even invalidating or rendering suspect the points of identification I felt between myself and its contributors: as a white woman, and an (aspiring) academic, I was precisely part of what *This Bridge* contributors were resisting and defining themselves against.

3

Not only did the identity politics of *This Bridge* delegitimate my feelings of connection to it, the academy did so as well. I was told that this work did not belong on either my twentieth-century American literature list, or on my feminist theory list, the lists of works that I needed to master to prove myself capable of certification for an academic career. *This Bridge*, given its contemporaneity and indeterminacy of genre, fit canons neither of theory nor literature, yet it was clearly responding and at least partially addressing itself to the academy, particularly to academic feminists. And it was clearly having an impact, as a hovering presence in footnotes and asides in academic feminist journals and as catalyst to student-based movements, conferences, and publications.[1]

I began to think seriously about what *This Bridge* was doing to my understanding of literature and theory, and of the academy and activism. Could it perhaps offer me a bridge between these usually opposed categories, despite my position as an outsider in the communities it constitutes? Could it offer me a way to negotiate my own uncertainties about the academy, and my criticisms of its elitism, its competitive individualism, its exclusivities, in a way that would be respectful to, perhaps even build alliances with, women marginalized by race, class, sexuality? These questions have remained central to the course of this project.

In a less directly personal but no less political way, this project also has involved thinking about the (ethno)poetics and politics of anthologies. Anthologies serve in the academy as crucial agents in the creation and teaching of periods and definitions of literature; they often determine what literature teachers include on their syllabi and how they present it. To put it more broadly, anthologies are instrumental in defining cultural traditions in U.S. society. Despite their importance, and despite the explosion in recent years not only of literary anthologies, but also of mixed-genre and critical or theoretical ones, little critical work exists on anthologies. At most, one finds a scattering of remarks in the works of cultural critics such as Henry Louis Gates, Jr., or Henry Giroux, or an occasional forum on *The Heath Anthology of American Literature*. With the exception of a recent article by Barbara Christian and Jane Gallop's *Around 1981*, no sustained, in-depth criticism exists that reads anthologies with the seriousness that they deserve.[2] Furthermore, while much attention has been paid of late to the way multiculturalisms are being deployed in universities, anthologies as such seldom figure in the discussion, despite their constituting sites in which cultural identities are being constructed.[3] In their role of defining—and, often, resisting— multiculturalism, anthologies offer a unique vantage point for engaging questions about multiculturalism and identity politics.

As I began reading anthologies, I was overwhelmed by the sheer volume of newly published ones thematizing particular identities. In particular, I found that multi-genre anthologies by marginalized groups of women were proliferating rapidly, and that they were becoming a privileged site for marginalized groups of women intent on theorizing and putting into practice communities founded upon a powerful but inherently unstable politics of identity. *Nice Jewish Girls, Home Girls, Gathering of Spirit, Gathering Ground, Tribe of Dina, Between the Lines, Compañeras: Latina Lesbians, The Common Thread, Charting the Journey, The Forbidden Stitch, Making Waves, Sowing Ti Leaves, Third Woman, Calling Home, Making Face, Making Soul/Haciendo Caras*—these represent but a partial listing of this kind of anthology published during the 1980s.[4] Reading them, I became impressed by the way their crossings of generic boundaries enabled the unfixing of other boundaries as well.

In giving voice to theories of women's communities which its construction enacts, such an anthology crosses the boundary between theory and activism, and unsettles other boundaries separating academia and "the real world." While production of these anthologies is enabled by the university and by academic feminism, and while the anthologies may address themselves to academic communities, they simultaneously spring from and strive to reach specific, targeted communities of women outside universities. In doing so, they point to the reductiveness of seeing academic and non-academic communities as wholly distinct.

The ability of these anthologies to cross so many boundaries is largely unprecedented. As someone who has witnessed the challenges to, and to a large extent the breakdown of, white feminist communities in the university, I find new possibilities for feminism being created by and for marginalized communities of women in these anthologies. I am struck, however, by the writers' difficulties in establishing communities that do not deny or exaggerate our differences from one another, that are not based upon the oppression or exclusion of groups of women, or that, while theorizing sisterhood, do not engage in practices that contradict their theorizing. Thus, these anthologies delineate both the possibilities and the limitations of writing women's communities based upon a politics of identity.

Exposing the Master's Tools

As these anthologies circulate beyond the confines of the academy and forge new models for feminist communities, they also reflect on and issue challenges to the academy's literary centerpiece—the canonical anthology. Anthologies serve in English departments to shape bodies of literature and the definition of literature itself. They often dictate not only the material a literature course will include, but how this material will be taught. That a recent forum in *American Literature* (June 1993), entitled "What Do We Need to Teach," focused almost exclusively on anthologies (*The Heath Anthology of American Literature* in particular) is but one indicator of the close alliance between anthologies and the teaching of literature. As Henry Louis Gates, Jr., notes, "A well-marked anthology functions in the academy to *create* a tradition, as well as to defend and preserve it. A Norton anthology opens up a literary tradition as simply as opening the cover of a carefully edited and ample book."5

Editors of canonical anthologies often attempt to erase the ideological construction of these anthologies by presenting them as "natural and neutral objects."6 In "The Problem of Anthologies, or Making the Dead Wince," Kenneth Warren addresses "the palpable weight of a tradition in the form of an anthology whose making is removed from the site/sight of the classroom."7 A quick perusal of anthologies such as the Norton, Harpers, and Heritage editions of American and English literature confirms the way in which these anthologies are represented as objective presentations of a body of literature. Each editor proclaims the anthology's completeness and self-sufficiency as a culmination of American or English literary history, with revisions of previous editions resulting not from ideological flux or pressures but from the possibility of more accurate and complete coverage (including, in the last fifteen years, women and people of color). For example, M. H. Abrams, the editor of the 1986 edition of *The Norton Anthology of English Literature*, states that his anthology has achieved its goal of self-sufficiency; in the completeness of its selections of literature and its organization of and commentary on this literature, it serves effectively "to free the student from dependence on a reference library, so that the anthology may be read anywhere—in the student's room, in a coffee lounge, on a bus, or under a tree."8 This set of images advertises the range of freedoms this anthology offers to students—to read in the privacy of their own room or in the cool of a coffee lounge, etc.—but these freedoms assume— and depend upon—students who have the time, place, and space for lounging. The privilege of the reader addressed here (in terms of time and money) contrasts strikingly with the economic deprivation of Anzaldúa's reader in *This Bridge,* whom she urges to write when in the bathroom or on the welfare line (170). The revised Norton thus supports a point made by Hazel Carby—that a multicultural curriculum does not necessarily lead to, and in fact may even serve to avoid or displace the need for, a more equitable society.[9]

Furthermore, most recent editions of canonical anthologies, all of which proclaim their success in correcting the short shrift previously given to women and minorities, reveal the relatively few changes the pressures of multiculturalism or "political correctness" have actually produced even at the level of curriculum. Editors list the additions of women (usually white) and ethnic or racial minorities (mainly black men) alongside their announcements about improved typefaces, and the two forms of additions in fact prove to be equivalent, with both amounting, finally, to merely cosmetic changes. The first volume of the 1991 *Heritage of American Literature,* edited by James E. Miller and featuring cover photos of Ralph Waldo Emerson, Herman Melville, Margaret Fuller, Louisa May Alcott, and Frederick Douglass, provides a particularly clear example of this. While white women and a black man appear to have joined the ranks of the most prominent figures in American literature, the number of pages Miller devotes to each of these prominently displayed authors is telling: Emerson receives 177 pages; Melville, 189; Fuller, 19; Alcott and Douglass, 13 each. Miller's preface suggests the nostalgic and conservative longings that fuel his project despite its superficial claims to a revised canon: he explains that his work on the anthology began "some five years ago because I suddenly had a yearning to see the field in its totality or wholeness, and in depth, as I had once glimpsed it years ago as a graduate student."[10] Perhaps it is no accident that Miller's yearning for the good old days becomes so intense around 1985, which Elizabeth Abel marks as "the watershed year in white feminists' engagement with questions of racial location."[11] Miller's anthology—which contains virtually all white men, with a sprinkling of black men and white women (most of the latter appearing in the short section "Emerging Feminist Perspectives"), and which gives only seven of its approximately two thousand pages over to black women—constitutes not an exception, but rather the starkest illustration of the tokenism that a page count of any one of the major anthologies of American and British literature quickly reveals, particularly with respect to periods preceding WWII.[12] Similarly, headnotes to recently revised anthologies often cast the writing of newly included or even more established writers into traditional paradigms and then find the work wanting. In Nina Baym's 1985 Norton, for example, Bernard Engel patronizes Marianne Moore and dismisses her challenges to a masculinist modernism as feminine frivolity. His headnote introduces

Moore to the reader as a poet "fussy in her endless revising and fondness for exact detail."[13]

The most significant exception to such generalizations is *The Heath Anthology of American Literature.* Paul Lauter and the anthology's thirteen other editors express their intent to correct the white male bias of other anthologies. *The Heath Anthology* presents American literature much more inclusively in terms of race and gender than do other canonical anthologies, and provides accounts of the identities of the authors it includes. Lauter connects the anthology's ethnic diversity to its inclusion of songs and chants, genres generally not presented in literary anthologies. Furthermore, the anthology differs by acknowledging its ideological purposes and influences, and, in the preface, by detailing the history and process of its production. Moreover, in this process it departs from that of other canonical anthologies in the extent of its collective and collaborative work, and in the diversity, in terms of institutional affiliation as well as race and gender, of the editors and scholars chosen to write its headnotes and introductions. However, as Lauter acknowledges in his reflection on the anthology in the *American Literature* forum, the anthology does adhere to certain traditional paradigms for American literature. It follows a periodizing logic, for example, one that leaves the definition and centrality of modernism intact. Lauter's anthology and others like Henry Louis Gates, Jr., and Nellie McKay's *Norton Anthology of African American Literature* are working to broaden the literary canon, but from places within the traditional English department. In doing so, these anthologies tend to preserve and promote the possibility of an objective and comprehensive rendering of a body of literature.

The anthologies featured in this study have few direct intersections with canonical anthologies (*The Heath* included) in terms of the contributors they include or their intended audiences. Like canonical anthologies, they present themselves as teaching tools, but they aim for inclusion in ethnic studies and women's studies classes, and they target groups of women located outside of university communities. These anthologies receive no mention in canonical anthologies, nor do they present themselves as engaging with or commenting upon canonical anthologies. Nevertheless, from their positions in the margins, they exert pressure and arguably have a transformative effect on canonical anthologies by working to redefine literature, by challenging and exposing its ideological underpinnings, and by offering a form of multiculturalism that, as it insists on the power differentials between groups, maintains a critical edge. Whether the intent is to open up the literary canon (as Janet Zandy strives to do in *Calling Home,* an anthology of working-class women's literature) or to create an alternative or counter canon (as Barbara Smith does for black lesbian literature in *Home Girls*), the editors of these anthologies resist and make evident the racial, ethnic, class, sexual, and gender biases of canonical anthologies, and make visible the women these anthologies leave out.

Furthermore, rather than proclaim their self-sufficiency and completeness, as canonical anthologies do, these anthologies mark their incompleteness, and they call attention to and detail the process of their making. The comment by Mitsuye Yamada and Sarie Sachie Hylkema, the editors of *Sowing Ti Leaves: Writings by Multi-Cultural Women*, is typical of these anthologies. After detailing their process of putting together the anthology, they state, "We hope that our process as well as the product, the collection itself, will be useful" to readers.[14] Instead of presenting their anthologies as the culmination of a body of literature, editors continually mark the provisionality of their efforts and send out calls for the next anthology, one that will extend their project or reconfigure it entirely by letting in new voices. While canonical anthologies are marketed on the basis of their supposed mastery of a field, the anthologies in this study, despite their more circumscribed subject matter, call into question the very notion of mastery.

The emphasis in these anthologies is on their social function, on their ability to constitute new communities of and for women who share the identities to which the anthologies give voice. In the introduction to *Between the Lines: An Anthology by Pacific/Asian Lesbians of Santa Cruz, California*, one that takes the form of a letter to "Cristy" (one of the editors), one of the other editors proclaims: "And now Together, You and I write and gather writings by other Pacific/Asian Lesbians, to create an anthology, a community. . . . Our writings are our visibility and our community. They are our survival" (6). In a similar vein, *A Gathering of Spirit* editor Beth Brant addresses other Native American women in her introduction: "Can I tell you how lonely I have been for you? That my search for the spirit had to begin with you?"[15] In fact, the titles of many others too, such as *Gathering Ground, Calling Home,* and *Home Girls,* reflect their editors' emphasis on these anthologies as places to find or create homes or communities.

The criterion for admission to these anthologies is not literary excellence or influence, as in canonical anthologies, but the contributor's elaboration of the identity the anthology is constructing—or, in some cases, the issues or contradictions a contributor raises about this identity. In making this distinction, I do not mean to suggest that the category of the aesthetic becomes irrelevant in relation to identity-based anthologies, but rather that these anthologies are based upon an aesthetic that is usually not recognized as such. Conversely, that which canonical anthologies promote as "aesthetic" cannot be—but often is—understood apart from the politics that informs this understanding. We need to rethink the concept of the aesthetic. As Eric Sundquist puts it, "Justice and value . . . must be recognized to be aesthetic as well as philosophical terms, to have literary as well as legal application."[16]

The anthologies in this study advance an aesthetics that is inextricably related to their editors' concerns with identity and community. Their titles often equate the anthologies with a specific community of women (as in *Home Girls, Nice Jewish Girls,* and *Tribe of Dina*), and editors' introductions establish them as places for women to write their particular identities. As co-editor Jo Cochran states in her introduction to *Gathering Ground: New Writing and Art by Northwest Women of Color,* "Writing is a way to know ourselves, to come to be strong in ourselves, and to tell the truths of our realities and visions, and as women of color to fill in our side of the story and world."[17] The structure of these anthologies typically reflects this emphasis on the anthologies as a place to construct and express a positive (communal) identity for contributors. Editors generally begin with a section focused on contributors' experiences of oppression. They then create sections in which contributors assert and celebrate their identities, and they conclude with a section that predicts and explores ways the community they have created can lead to social change or revolution. They carefully craft the anthologies to highlight the interconnections between narrative, identity, community, and activism.

Anthologies like these make their agendas explicit, and insistently locate contributors' viewpoints. In contrast, canonical anthologies practice an identity politics that is covert or unconscious. And while it might seem obvious to claim that canonical anthologies are identity-based and political, the extent to which canonical anthologies continue as staples in literature courses, and the degree to which they perpetuate business as usual under the guise of a cheerful pluralism also suggests the need to discuss rigorously their ideological function, both in the classroom, and in our scholarship. The anthologies in this study provide one way to do so: they both point to the exclusions of canonical anthologies and, with their insistence on their constructedness, provisionality, and politics, provide a language for, and a way of thinking about, canonical anthologies. However, a more dubious connection exists between the opening of the canon and the diversification of a university's student body and faculty: it is not enough simply to celebrate the entry of "new voices" in texts or to unmask the operations of a politics of dominance. To do so is to remain within the covers of anthologies. This is precisely the sort of containment the anthologies in this study begin to counter when they blur "real" and textual voices, and "real" and textual communities. In the end, such blurring may not knock down academic walls, but neither, I would argue, does it simply reinforce those walls or leave them the same. Instead, what these anthologies extend is the invitation to practice a critical multiculturalism that engages the identity politics of the academy's center as well as its margins.

The Seven-Headed Monster and the Many-Headed Demon

As these anthologies expose—and work to depose—canonical anthologies as the tools of hegemony, they also work to overturn white middle-class models of feminism of the 1970s and early 1980s. In fact, the anthologies position themselves directly against white middle-class models of community based on women's sameness.[18] Since that time, of course, such models have been thoroughly critiqued by white women as well as women of color for their erasure of differences among women, and for their unspoken assumption that "woman" constitutes a white and middle-class category.[19] In *Around 1981*, a study of anthologies of American academic feminist literary criticism, Jane Gallop finds that feminist models of community in the early 1980s privilege women's similarities. To gain insight into "the collective unconscious" of academic feminism in the 1980s, she offers a "symptomatic reading" of The Dartmouth Collective's 1981 special edition of *Yale French Studies, Feminist Readings: French Texts/American Contexts (YFS 62)*. The Dartmouth Collective opens *YFS 62* with the announcement: "This is a very unusual issue of *Yale French Studies*, in that its guest editor is a seven-headed monster from Dartmouth."[20] Gallop argues, "The monster represents the collectivity, a new kind of being in which seven individuals are neither totally merged nor totally separate."[21] She finds that this monster's monstrosity signals, despite the Dartmouth Collective's celebration of their harmonious relations, that its members find their lack of autonomy terrifying and stifling in the same way that the inadequately differentiating mother-daughter relationship is. As Gallop summarizes her argument, "The formation of groups of women draw upon the permeability of female self-boundaries. The collectivity reactivates the mother-daughter bond. One monster cannot be separated from the other" (51).

YFS 62 shares its 1981 publication date with *This Bridge Called My Back*. And while Gallop's generalization about collectivity might hold true for white middle-class academic feminists, the women in *This Bridge* approach the idea of collectivity from a different position altogether. If Gallop and the Dartmouth Collective confront their monster in the mirror, for the women in *This Bridge*, the alien other resides not within themselves; rather, as Gloria Anzaldúa puts it, third world women "are especially vulnerable" to a "many-headed demon of oppression," and the contributors' own collectivity is not the monster, but the means by which they resist the monster.[22] Furthermore, white academic feminists can be said to make up one of the demon's many heads. The demon of oppression that women of color face is thus, at least in part, the very monster the Dartmouth Collective and Gallop face in the mirror.

To counter this demon constituted by the homogeneity of white middle-class models of feminism, marginalized groups of women have created a new literary movement of multi-genre anthologies that enable them to announce their identities (individual and communal), participate in textual conversations and communities, and celebrate their differences (from white feminists, and from one another).[23] Contributors to these anthologies use a mix of creative and polemical writings to express and directly address their cultural differences, encompassing a variety of voices, languages, forms, and writing styles, so that different pieces of writing often contradict each other and highlight the writers' diverse identities and concerns. As Barbara Smith comments in *Home Girls*, multi-genre anthologies "bring together many voices [and so] seem particularly suited to the multiplicity of issues of concern to women of color."[24] The multi-genre format is intimately connected to the contributors' minority status: it presents a way to include a diversity of contributors, as well as a way to cross boundaries between different communities of women.[25]

Contributors use the anthologies' multi-genre form—from journal and diary entries, letters, notes, and transcribed conversations to fiction, essays, and poetry—not only to express and unify across their differences, but also to embody an implicit critique of, and alternative to, what they define as academic feminist writing. They present themselves as non-elitist, and the editors work to empower women without educational and economic privilege to think of themselves as writers. Anzaldúa says that in putting together *Haciendo Caras*, she "made a special effort to work with women who do not consider themselves writers, or at least not yet."[26] In *This Bridge*, she tells women, "Forget the room of one's own—write in the kitchen, lock yourself up in the bathroom. Write on the bus or the welfare line, on the job or during meals, between sleeping or waking. I write while sitting on the john" (170). Writing can, should, and must take place anywhere, anytime, since leisure to write is a luxury many of the contributors and their intended audiences cannot afford. The anthologies' format opens up the definition of what constitutes publishable material as it narrows the gap between public and private, between professional and non-professional writing, and between oral and written expression. Yet, in my exploration of these anthologies, I also question the limits to this form's openness: Just how accessible is it? How much difference can these anthologies accommodate? Whom do they exclude and why? How far outside the academy can they reach? Are the anthologies being appropriated by the academic feminists they often define themselves against?

In making the multi-genre form and an identity politics perspective the focus of my study, I am differentiating these anthologies from those feminist anthologies which, although they might employ a multi-genre approach, emerge directly out of the academy and do not attempt to break the bounds of an academic discourse, nor to highlight contributors' identities. For example, while I do not see an anthology such as *Conflicts in Feminism* as entirely distinct from the anthologies featured in this study, neither is it explicitly organized around a specific identity that the contributors share. *Conflicts* could be organized this way, since the contributors are all academic feminists, and their academic status operates powerfully as an organizing force. However, because the editors and most of the contributors occupy a dominant position within feminist discourse, they are able to leave their position unmarked. And although *Conflicts in Feminism* does experiment with breaking down distinctions between academic and other forms of writing (it contains diary and journal entries, letters, dialogues, fantasy, and fiction), and in this way resembles and perhaps takes its inspiration from anthologies such as *This Bridge,* its language remains predominantly academic. For example, while Gloria Anzaldúa in *This Bridge* turns to the letter form as a way explicitly to counter academic discourse, to unlearn "the esoteric bullshit and pseudo-intellectualizing that school brainwashed into my writing" (165), in "Parisian Letters: Between Feminism and Deconstruction," *Conflicts* contributors Peggy Kamuf and Nancy Miller employ the letter form in a self-consciously critical and literary way: Miller worries about the letter form being "received as irretrievably precious (in the French sense) and hence ridiculous,"[27] then eventually decides her exchanges with Kamuf are "more reminiscent of the reply-structure of critical response" (128). To take a more recent example, in *Feminism Beside Itself* the academy stands as the unmarked center for feminism and its divisions, and for contributors' exchanges. Thus, editors Diane

Elam and Robyn Wiegman enact their pronouncement that, "The editors . . . are divided against themselves." The two editors, in individual narratives that run in side-by-side columns, "find feminist gestures toward unity, collective and otherwise, more politically problematic than they often appear."[28] Rather than transgress academic boundaries, however, this format, in its evocation of Kristeva and Derrida, reinforces them. Even as its contributors attribute the reconfiguration of feminism to anthologies such as *This Bridge* and *Nice Jewish Girls* (see esp. Susan Stanford Friedman's "Making History: Reflections on Feminism, Narrative, and Desire") and demonstrate traces of their influence, *Feminism Beside Itself*, along with other academic feminist anthologies of the 1980s and 1990s, seems distinct from the anthologies under consideration in this book. And rather than focus on the interrelations between these types of anthologies, my main purpose here is to probe the defining characteristics and differences among those women's anthologies that are organized around a consciously deployed and critically articulated politics of identity.

Identity Politics: All the Rage

In the 1980s, identity politics was "all the rage," as Jenny Bourne bitingly notes in her 1987 critique of this politics.[29] During this period, identity politics—and multi-genre anthologies—thrived in the U.S. academy alongside, and in tension with, "high" poststructuralist theory imported from Europe (especially France).[30] Identity politics and poststructuralism were often placed in opposition to one another, a binary relationship that proponents of poststructuralism as well as of identity politics helped to establish and have been largely content to leave intact. To schematize this binary relationship in the broadest of terms, one could say that advocates of identity politics charged poststructuralists with operating in rarefied air and failing to address material conditions and concerns (namely, racism, sexism, homophobia, class discrimination), while proponents of poststructuralism dismissed identity politics as essentializing, reductive, and theoretically naive.

If the stakes in maintaining the differences between identity politics and poststructuralism often prove real enough, many of the differences themselves do not. Just as poststructuralism and identity politics have been shown to rely upon forms of essentialism, identity politics and poststructuralism both depend on conceptions of difference, however differently located, employed, and articulated.[31] Identity politics, especially as promoted in the anthologies under consideration here, is not essentializing in any simple way, but multiple, and often strategic, critical, complex and contradictory. However, the concepts of multiple identity and difference these anthologies put forth are not assimilable to Lacanian or Derridean poststructuralism: if the anthologies do not adhere to a belief in a coherent or singular self, neither do they abdicate the concept of a knowable identity. Additionally, the anthologies stress differences *among* as well as within individual women, and see these differences as interlocking rather than disparate or hierarchically ranked. Their accounts of the self as multiple are historically based, material ones. The fractured or split self they posit is not ahistorical and inevitable, as in Lacan, but one resulting from class, racial or ethnic, sexual, and gender divides. Wholeness and self-knowledge are, therefore, not rejected as theoretical impossibilities or as a myth of humanism. In the play between essentialist and poststructuralist positions, these anthologies put forth a new model of the subject and of community: their practice of identity politics encompasses and holds in productive tension both identity and difference.[32]

If identity politics—along with continental poststructuralist theory—was "all the rage" in the late 1980s when I began conceptualizing this project, in the mid-1990s it seems fair to say that it is critiques such as Bourne's that have become "all the rage." In the 1990s, identity politics and the poststructuralism practiced by white European men and the "French feminists" Cixous, Irigaray, and Kristeva have given way to the overlapping discourses of queer theory, cultural studies, postcolonialism, and the new cultural politics of difference. Academics working in these new fields often take their vocabulary from, and/or trace their critical practices to, poststructuralist theorists such as Lacan, Derrida, and Foucault, and position their work against identity politics. Much as poststructuralists did in the 1980s, contemporary critics often equate identity politics with essentialism, with a naive belief in a singular and knowable self that ignores the lessons of poststructuralism. In addition, much contemporary criticism takes identity politics to task for being insufficiently revolutionary or transformative. Bourne's charges against identity politics—that it valorizes oppression, that its concept of identity is reductive and essentialist, that it is individualistic and inward-looking, that it mistakenly equates one's ethnic, racial, sexual, or gender identity with one's politics, that it views identity as an end rather than a means—now run throughout virtually any current academic book or journal that positions itself as politically progressive and concerns itself with issues of race, class, gender, sexuality, and culture. Critics in the 1990s level other related charges against identity politics: that it is separatist and that it often reproduces the problems that it attacks; that it is but a pluralist version of liberal humanism; that it has led to the hierarchizing of oppressions, and has obscured connections and similarities between different groups and subject positions, thus shutting down the possibility of a politics of alliances or solidarity; and that it can lead to a confessional politics "that all but forgets how the political is constituted in social and cultural forms outside of one's own experiences."[33] In "Difference, Diversity and Differentiation" (1992), Avtar Brah provides a particularly concise summary of the central problems critics have identified with identity politics, as her narrative effectively relegates the practice of such a politics to the past:

Instead of embarking on the complex but necessary task of sifting out the specificities of particular oppressions, identifying their similarities or connections with other oppressions, and building a politics of solidarity, some women [in the early 1980s] were beginning to differentiate these specificities into hierarchies of oppression. The mere act of naming oneself as a member of an oppressed group was assumed to vest one with moral authority. Multiple oppressions came to be regarded not in terms of their patterns of articulation/ interconnections but rather as separate elements that could be added in a linear fashion, so that the more oppressions a woman could list the greater her claims to occupy a higher moral ground. Assertions about authenticity of personal experience could be presented as if they were an unproblematic guide to an understanding of processes of subordination and domination. Declarations concerning self-righteous political correctness sometimes came to substitute for careful political analysis.[34]

What often accompanies such critiques is the heralding of a new kind of politics, what Cornel West has termed "the new cultural politics of difference." As conceived by West, "the new cultural politics of difference shuns narrow particularities, parochialisms and separatisms, just as it rejects false universalisms and homogeneous totalisms." Instead, as it deconstructs all binaries, it sets out "to construct new kinds of connections, affinities and communities across empire, nation, region, race, gender, age and sexual orientation."[35] A politics of difference, in other words, attempts to put postmodernism in the service of a radical politics.

West's call to challenge and destabilize accepted categories of identity, and to constitute new interrelations and alliances across these categories, is being echoed by theorists of all stripes, whether or not they specifically align themselves with "the new cultural politics of difference." Cultural studies, the current catch-all in the U.S. academy for politically progressive work, consistently takes up such a position. As the editors of the reader *Cultural Studies* claim, "An ongoing effect of cultural studies research has been to destabilize and de-essentialize standard categories of identity." This "deconstructive effect is not an end in itself," they explain; rather, "cultural studies undertakes the much more difficult project of holding identities in the foreground, acknowledging their necessity and potency, examining their articulation and rearticulation, and seeking a better understanding of their function."[36]

I agree with many of the criticisms of identity politics outlined above, and I find the movement towards a "new cultural politics of difference" a provocative way to push beyond some of the limitations of identity politics. Nevertheless, the academy's dismissal of identity politics strikes me as premature, as dismissive of the continuing reality that people experience oppression on the basis of their race, ethnicity, class, gender, and sexuality.[37] I believe that the (re)turn in the 1990s to "difference" (a keyword for queer theory as it obviously is for the new cultural politics of difference) can potentially obfuscate and perpetuate these forms of oppression. As Rosaura Sánchez incisively puts it, "Equally troubling is the exclusive focus on culture, micropolitics, and discourses of 'difference,' which have proliferated to the point that everything and nearly everyone is deemed potentially 'different' or 'marginal' in some measure. As difference is naturalized and made into a topical discourse, the more crucial and immediate issues of class and race are displaced from critical analyses in the name of cultural representation and inclusion. In effect, as 'difference' becomes a meaningless 'universal,' it also becomes a powerful ideological discourse masking social relations embodied within distinct spheres of difference."[38]

Furthermore, dismissals of identity politics in the name of difference, however politically progressive in intent, are often founded upon a poststructuralist perspective that obscures not only theorists' continuing reliance on the dismantlement of categories of identity, but also the complexity and multiplicity that can attend a practice of identity politics. Dismissing identity politics also obscures the ways in which current theoretical positions are anticipated by and continuous with identity politics, at least as theorized and practiced in multi-genre anthologies. Multi-genre identity-based anthologies of the early 1990s register with particular clarity the continuity between identity politics and a politics of difference; contributors' language in these anthologies often is indistinguishable from that of proponents of the new politics of difference, yet they base their formulations about identity on those of contributors to previous anthologies. Thus, *Our Feet Walk the Sky* contributor Suparna Bhaskara relies on Maria Lugones' essay in *Haciendo Caras* to argue for an identity politics that takes into account "multiple subjectivities, a cross section of different systems of meaning and a non-static positionality . . . in a transnational world."[39] Despite these anthologies' movement into the academy (a movement I will trace in the next chapter), they are largely ignored by the recognized producers of high theory. Norma Alarcón is one of the few theorists publishing in the academy's most prestigious books and journals to acknowledge the contributions of multi-genre anthologies in more than a cursory way. More commonly, critics issue wholesale critiques of identity politics without considering specific anthologies closely. At the same time, however, and as testimony to the way that they bridge identity and difference, these anthologies also serve as ready-made ways to insert difference into the classroom. A random review of syllabi in women's studies and feminist theory courses posted on the internet revealed to me that many of these courses rely on these anthologies, especially *This Bridge,* to provide a splash of color in an otherwise white syllabus.

This tokenism continues, and with it obscurity. While Bernice Johnson Reagon and Gloria Anzaldúa are tokenized (Anzaldúa has, in fact, attained shaman-like status in the academy, even receiving star billing on the announcements of the 1993 MLA Convention), the women alongside whom they write remain invisible.[40] And even when critics turn, as they occasionally do, to Reagon's essay in *Home Girls,* "Coalition Politics: Turning the Century," or, as they more often do, to Anzaldúa's essays in *Haciendo Caras* (and in *Bordelands/La Frontera*) on "the new mestiza," they usually wrench these women and their works out of their specific contexts within identity-based communities. Taking their writing out of context obscures the complexity of these women's positioning, as it does the consonance of identity politics as this is theorized and practiced in multi-genre anthologies, with theoretical models that profess a break from this politics. As I will be arguing throughout this study, the contradictions inherent in the heterogeneous multi-genre form and in an identity politics based upon exclusions enable these anthologies to stage, often unintentionally, the contradictions within the identities to which they give expression.

The Return of the Many-Headed Monster, with a *Différance*

If in the early 1980s members of the Dartmouth Collective were asserting women's commonalties in a way that excluded women different from themselves, by the late 1980s, as I have suggested, identity politics had been entertained and rejected for a poststructuralist embrace of difference (or *différance*). Published in 1989, Diana Fuss's *Essentially Speaking* marks a turning point in mainstream academic feminist responses to identity politics. It is also symptomatic of how, in the name of *différance*, theorists may not only make a false break from identity politics, but also may reinscribe the very hegemonic relations women in the multi-genre anthologies attempt to resist through identity politics. As *Essentially Speaking* critiques identity politics in the name of a *différance* that accounts only for differences within—and not between—subjects, it reproduces the exclusionary sameness that characterizes projects such as *YFS 62*. Thus, while my study traces the trajectory of identity politics from *This Bridge Called My Back* (1981) to its "sequel," *Making Face, Making Soul/Haciendo Caras* (1990), I might also have considered the trajectory from *YFS 62* to Diana Fuss's *Essentially Speaking*, for it, also, suggests the course of identity politics in the academy in the 1980s, and serves to contextualize the ongoing deployment of identity politics in the multi-genre anthologies.

One of Fuss's central insights in *Essentially Speaking* is that "anti-essentialism is always fundamentally dependent on essentialism in order to do its work" (40). Given that constructionist work relies on essentialism, Fuss urges, "The question we should be asking is not 'is this text essentialist (and therefore "bad")?' but rather, 'if this text is essentialist, *what motivates its deployment?*'" (xi). Fuss begins with the good constructionism/bad essentialism binary and proceeds to take this binary apart, showing that the two terms are interdependent and destabilizing the understanding of essentialism as always bad. What her otherwise rigorous deconstructive practice leaves intact, however, is the assumption that anti-essentialism is always "good." Fuss the poststructuralist assumes that a constructionist, or anti-essentialist, position does not need defense, that it is "always already" progressive. While she cautions against "efforts by hegemonic groups to use essentialism as a political tool waged against less powerful groups" (40), she does not pursue the ways anti-essentialism also may work against disempowered groups. *Essentially Speaking* itself, in fact, enacts this very process.

While Fuss's poststructuralist anti-essentialism in *Essentially Speaking* enables her to account brilliantly for the differences within single-subject identities, it leaves her resistant to theorizing those differences that exist *between* subjects. Fuss expresses concern regarding theories of "multiple identities," because such theories, "by locating difference outside identity, in the spaces *between* identities, . . . ignore the radicality of the poststructuralist view which locates differences *within* identity" (103). In short, Fuss's poststructuralism leaves her unwilling to analyze subject positions as interlocking and simultaneous.[41] And as Norma Alarcón notes, it is the spaces that Fuss discards between identities "which are paramount to cross-cultural exploration and analysis of 'women of color.'" Alarcón follows this observation up with a question, one that neatly reverses Fuss's regarding the motives of the essentialist position, to ask: "What is behind the anti-essentialist position?"[42] Alarcón's framing of this question suggests her answer to it: she links an anti-essentialist refusal to engage differences between identities to an unwillingness to address (the work of) women of color.

Fuss's refusal to focus on the differences between identities does indeed work to exclude women of color and their theorizings. In the chapter " 'Race' under Erasure? Poststructuralist Afro-American Literary Theory," gender functions as an analogy for race rather than as an interlocking term (see esp. pp. 90–91), with the result that it is black women and feminist analyses that are eclipsed. To echo Gloria Hull, Patricia Bell Scott, and Barbara Smith's all-too-familiar formulation, "All the women are white, [and] all the blacks are men."[43] In her defense of poststructuralist theory, Fuss aligns herself with Henry Louis Gates, Jr., and Houston Baker as she explores what she calls the "infamous" debate in *New Literary History* between Gates and Baker and Joyce A. Joyce. While the *New Literary History* debate is "infamous" primarily for the unpleasantness of its gender politics and the way it has contributed to the perceived split between African American male and female critics, Fuss, surprisingly, concludes that "Joyce's objections to poststructuralism are . . . really objections to literary criticism's recent in-roads into philosophy" (77). Fuss, writing philosophy from her location in an English department, at once reads the debate in terms central to her own position, and elides the gender politics that might complicate her defense of Gates's and Baker's poststructuralism and her own positionality. Fuss's cursory dismissal of Joyce is striking, given the complexity and nuance with which she approaches every other critic in her book, and it is not until the chapter's conclusion that she asks:

How are we to read the complicated and subtle sexual dynamics at play beneath the surface of the *New Literary History* debate? Do Joyce Joyce's and Barbara Christian's impassioned repudiations of "theory" necessarily warrant the counter-charge of "a new black conservatism" amongst black women critics . . . ? If such a conservatism can be convincingly established . . . , then is it possible that there might be an order of political necessity to these more essentialist arguments advanced by black women? These are difficult questions, for reasons not the least of which is the highly charged emotional and political climate in which they are posed, but they are also intractably insistent ones. (95)

In a book centrally concerned with the reasons for deploying essentialism, Fuss temporarily suspends these difficult questions, postponing them until the next chapter, "Lesbian and Gay Theory: The Question of Identity Politics"—where, perhaps not coincidentally, she can solidly and safely align herself with the marginalized identity of which she speaks.[44] While " 'Race' Under Erasure?" "rescues" "race" from erasure, this through a valorization of Gates's and Baker's theorizing, what is really under erasure, as bell hooks notes in her review of the book, are black feminist theorists and the reasons for insisting on the material reality of race.[45]

Fuss once again defends a poststructuralist anti-essentialism in her final chapter, "Essentialism in the Classroom," again in order to reinscribe her authority over and against an essentialism that might undermine it. Explaining her decision to conclude with this topic, she states, "This pedagogical issue may well be the most urgent (and the most frustrating to resolve) since it speaks to the very subject of who can speak" (xiii). Fuss's focus on the classroom in one sense suggests a turn from the realm of theory to the realm of practice. However, while in most of the previous chapters on theory she finds—however ambivalently—a place for essentialism, in this final chapter, on behalf of her students, she denounces a reliance on essence. She equates it with experience, and characterizes it as conservative and oppressive.[46] Fuss inverts the expected move, the one Gayatri Spivak has been so influential in promoting, of finding essentialism a problem in theory (albeit one not worth theorizing), but a necessary strategy in practice.[47] In her review of *Essentially Speaking*, bell hooks finds the anti-essentialism in Fuss's concluding chapter to be "profoundly disturbing" (174). She asks, "Why does Fuss's chapter ignore the subtle and overt ways essentialism is expressed from a location of privilege? Why does she primarily critique the misuses of essentialism by centering her analysis on marginalized groups? Doing so makes them the culprits for disrupting the classroom and making it an 'unsafe' place. Is this not a conventional way the colonizer speaks of the colonized, the oppressor of the oppressed?" (175).

While hooks's questions illuminate the way *Essentially Speaking* falls into the very trap it warns against—deploying an unacknowledged essentialism to bolster a position of privilege—the question that I would like to return to here is Norma Alarcón's, the question regarding the motivation for anti-essentialism. Through Fuss's book, and through the many charged responses to it, my own included, runs a concern with, as Fuss says, "the very subject of who can speak." And if, as Fuss rightly states, this is an urgent and frustrating pedagogical issue, so too is it an urgent—and often frustrating—issue in the production of academic feminist writing. As hooks points out, in Fuss's denouncement of essentialism (or identity politics) in the classroom, she imagines a classroom in which "essentialist exclusion" is a cultural practice exercised by marginalized groups (175). And as hooks further notes, rarely are classrooms so configured. It seems to me that the scenarios Fuss imagines reveal more about the anxieties white feminists experience as we engage in writing about identity and difference than they do about the operation of identity politics in the classroom.[48] In other words, I believe that Fuss's anti-essentialism in the final chapter might suggest a displaced anxiety about—and a reactionary response to—the ways in which identity politics can de-authorize white feminists.

As Fuss's final chapter argues against the utility of speaking from one's own experience, it demonstrates for me the importance of examining the position from which one speaks, of making explicit the positionality that underwrites and is used to authorize any given text. What I find most troubling in *Essentially Speaking* is the unself-consciousness with which Fuss's defenses of essentialism and anti-essentialism are linked to her own positionality and serve to consolidate her own authority. I do not believe that *Essentially Speaking* is singular in this respect, but rather that it is symptomatic of one response in the academy to the challenges women of color have posed to white feminists. Ultimately, I find that such feminist deployments of difference at the end of the 1980s have a discomforting amount in common with the exclusionary homogeneity of projects such as *YFS 62*. A book such as *Essentially Speaking* underlines, for me, the continuing need for a self-conscious and critical identity politics.[49]

Strategically Speaking

Not all theorizing, of course, dismisses the importance of identity politics—critics including Norma Alarcón, Inderpal Grewal, AnaLouise Keating, Teresa de Lauretis, Chela Sandoval, Marta Savigliano, and Gayatri Spivak all make crucial interventions on a poststructuralist terrain on behalf of the deployment of identity politics. Gayatri Spivak's advocacy of a "strategic use of a positivist essentialism in a scrupulously visible political interest" has been particularly influential.[50] Norma Alarcón and Chela Sandoval, who are among the few critics to consider seriously the work done by women in the multi-genre anthologies, also understand identity in terms of political strategy.[51] Sandoval describes the theory and practice of the politics of third world feminists including Moraga and Anzaldúa as evidence of what she calls a "differential consciousness," wherein "one experiences the violent shattering of the unitary sense of self, as the skill which allows a mobile identity to form. . . . Citizenship in this political realm is comprised of strategy and risk."[52] In "Conjugating Subjects: The Heteroglossia of Essence and Resistance," Alarcón finds this "differential consciousness" a revolutionary one, one that is crucial to a politics of liberation and resistance, and one that is first expressed in *This Bridge Called My Back*. Both Alarcón and Sandoval liken the deployments of identity politics by U.S. women of color to tactics of guerrilla warfare; as in Spivak's strategic essentialism, identity is provisional, and is constructed for political purposes.[53]

While I think such theorizing provides important models for activism, I also believe that many of the women in the anthologies, and the anthologies themselves, resist the above models in significant ways. To argue, as Spivak does explicitly, and as Alarcón does implicitly, that any articulation of identity or essentialism must be strategic to be politically effective is to be positioned on poststructuralist ground. Such a position does not exist *between* poststructuralism and essentialism; it makes identity politics and essentialism palatable by recasting them in poststructuralist terms. As I have argued, this is not the position of the anthologies. They, instead, hold in tension the two positions, allowing for the possibility of identities or experiences that contributors can claim and know, that are not merely strategic but have truth value—even though at the same time the multi-genre format, and the way that some of the same contributors highlight different subject positions in different anthologies, suggests a model of identity that is strategic. While categories such as "women of color" are strategically deployed, and are shown in the anthologies themselves to be constructions, the individual contributors who speak under the umbrella of such categories often simultaneously claim truth value for the identity or experiences they articulate.[54] The anthologies are therefore not fully assimilable to models of strategic essentialism.

Furthermore, I believe that such models set the individual in perpetual and atomistic motion in a way that leaves little room for community and its emphasis, however idealistic, on continuity, affectional ties, and emotional sustenance, all of which are central to the anthologies' transformational politics. To deploy an identity politics that is strictly strategic is to take up and cast off positions, to view alliances as provisional and shifting, to be willing to change positions, comrades, and allegiances at a moment's notice. In Spivak's terms, and more generally in the academy today, an investment in community is seen as idealistic, old-fashioned, and naive, and communities themselves are perceived to be stifling, inward-looking, and exclusionary. What strategic essentialism seems not to allow for, however, is the valid struggle to establish lasting communities, to imagine that a transformative politics can emerge from meaningful personal relationships as well as the other way around. In imaging alliances that are always shifting, provisional, efficacious, and intellectual, "strategic essentialism" discounts relationships that may be difficult but worth sustaining; it also can defer indefinitely the working through of difficulties that will erupt again and again, for to disband a group or identity when difficulties erupt in order to form new allegiances can serve to replicate, rather than circumvent, ongoing problems. Models of strategic essentialism also often discount the importance that political work be emotionally nurturing and pleasurable.[55]

For all these reasons I would resist the insistence on seeing all as strategic—even at the expense of falling into the idealism that an investment in community entails. I think the women in the anthologies strive for, and rely crucially on, such a conception of community. As Cherríe Moraga explains in the preface to *This Bridge*, "I fight the myriad voices that live inside me. The voices that stop my pen at every turn of the page. They are the voices that tell me here I should be talking more 'materialistically' about the oppression of women of color, that I should be plotting out a 'strategy' for Third World Revolution. But what I really want to write about is faith. That without faith, I'd dare not expose myself to the potential betrayal, rejection, and failure that lives throughout the first and last gesture of connection" (xviii).

Mediations, Meditations, and a Map

What makes Moraga's words so moving is the extent to which they render her so powerfully and entirely present in *This Bridge*. In *This Bridge* and the other anthologies under consideration here, the many genres they include seem not to mediate, but to express with clarity and immediacy the authentic and diverse selves of the writers. In my readings of these anthologies, I negotiate between respecting and questioning this equation of the literature with the true selves of the contributors. I view this equation sometimes as one editors and contributors strategically deploy, and sometimes as one they fully accept. At times, my reading method entails putting myself in a momentarily superior or knowing position to editors and contributors, as I expose their anthologies' blind spots (and often, in the process, my own as well).[56] Or, in some cases, it may involve teasing out strategies and negotiations editors and contributors have chosen not to highlight. This endeavor is a vexed one, particularly because, in coming to this study as a white, Jewish, middle-class feminist, I am exploring communities that, in most cases, do not offer me even an imaginary space of belonging. Yet I believe that it is time for white women, as well as women of color, to engage critically with these anthologies. And as someone socialized to avoid conflict and confrontation, and taught to strive for unity through similarities, I have received from these anthologies a model for renouncing the safety that comes with silence. These works have prompted me to begin refusing to respect the boundaries that they, in many ways, establish between women, particularly between white women and women of color, and, instead, to interrogate them. By questioning these boundaries— by locating, while trying not to exaggerate, the places they blur or break down—I hope to point to the places where productive dialogue between us is possible.

The chapters which follow depend heavily upon close readings of anthologies. Counter to the understanding that close readings are by definition old-fashioned and apolitical, or even retrograde, I am proceeding on the assumption that they can be of vital importance, especially for works and, in this case, genres, that have received minimal critical attention. I am interested in exploring the poetics of multi-genre anthologies, and also in engaging the anthologies as much as possible on their own terms, with attention to the stated concerns of their editors and contributors. Close readings of these anthologies, then, do not work to affirm traditional criteria for literature, or to valorize and depoliticize the aesthetic (charges often leveled against this practice). Instead, detailed textual analyses serve to complicate and reformulate such categories as they demand seeing the aesthetic and the political as inextricable, rather than divergent. In addition, close attention to these anthologies provides a way to challenge definitions and the privileging of "theory," and to critique contemporary theories about identity politics, including those found in this introductory chapter.

While this book surveys a range of multi-genre women's anthologies produced in the 1980s, it is not inclusive. For the most part, this book limits itself to anthologies produced in the United States, although the last two chapters, for reasons I will explain below, include readings of anthologies published in England and Canada. In each of the chapters that follow, I juxtapose anthologies organized under related and specific terms of identity. This structure enables me both to challenge the concept that any one community can adequately represent any one group, no matter how homogeneous that group may seem, and to locate the fissures within particular identities. Chapter 2 focuses on *This Bridge Called My Back* (1981) and its "sequel," *Making Face, Making Soul/Haciendo Caras* (1990). With publication dates framing the 1980s, these anthologies provide a way to chart the development of women's anthologizing practices, the movement into the academy on the part of women of color, and the contradictions, limitations, and possibilities this movement produces. In the third chapter, I turn to *Home Girls*, a black lesbian anthology, and to *Nice Jewish Girls*, a Jewish lesbian anthology, in order to explore the way in which any practice of identity politics necessarily ends up excluding, marginalizing, or strategically stabilizing some aspect of identity that it purports to represent. In chapter 4, I analyze the different ways in which two Asian American anthologies, *Making Waves* and *The Forbidden Stitch*, establish and make use of the otherness *within* Asian American identity to create communities that are not dependent upon exclusions. Chapter 5 considers an American working-class anthology, *Calling Home*, and two British working-class anthologies, *The Common Thread* and *Charting the Journey: Writings by Black and Third World Women*, in order to argue for the paradoxically liberating potential to constitute community within the relative rigidity of Britain's class structure, as compared to the less visible, but nevertheless confining, class structure in the United States.

A study of the British anthologies illuminates constructions of class and race in the American ones, and illustrates the ways that class, race, gender, and sexuality find their meanings in their particular historical contexts and locations; bringing them into relation with U.S. anthologies also enables me to explore the ways in which lines are being blurred within and between national identities.[57] Contributors' representations of their racial and ethnic identities—especially in these and other recent anthologies—unfix the national boundaries and identities ("American" and "British") that the anthologies demarcate and forge possibilities for new identities and alliances across nationalities.

In the sixth and final chapter, I foreground the diachronic movement of this study. Tracing the increasing insistence on transnational alliances and the disregard for geopolitical borders in multi-genre anthologies, my work has coincided with—and been energized and informed by— the movement in American literary studies and cultural studies for challenging national boundaries. This movement has been shaped in part by projects such as those undertaken in the anthologies I study here, and has come to seem especially crucial for me personally since my own relocation to Hawai'i, where I am confronted at every turn by the violence and instability of national boundaries. While chapters 1 and 2 establish one framework for understanding the movement of the anthologies into the academy, and their engagement with academic feminist theory, in the final chapter, I plot another, concurrent, movement, one by which to view the chronologically ordered case studies presented in chapters 3–5. The readings in chapter 6 of the 1994 anthologies *The Very Inside: An Anthology of Writing by Asian and Pacific Islander Lesbian and Bisexual Women* and *Returning the Gift: Poetry and Prose from the First North American Native Writers' Festival* enable me to put these two frameworks together, and to comment on the importance nation and location have come to assume in identity-based anthologies of the 1990s. As *The Very Inside* promotes a diasporic formulation of identity and *Returning the Gift* an indigenous one, both resist, often in opposing ways, dominant national identities. At the same time, along with anthologies produced by my students at the University of Hawai'i, they highlight the unstable and contextual nature, but also the power, not only of national identities, but of other categories of identity as well, including those upon which the previously considered anthologies depend.

Not only in the final chapter but throughout this study I engage the interrelations among anthologies in order to establish some ways in which different models of identity contradict, compete with, or reconfigure one another, and also to argue for this new genre's influence on academic anthologizing practices, feminist theory, and conceptualizations of identity and difference in the 1990s. Tracing the interrelations among anthologies opens up a way to utilize the exclusions, contradictions, and elisions that occur when individual anthologies deploy a politics of identity, and a way to find points of alliance or convergence among the identities they articulate. Just as these anthologies sometimes evidence surprising points of intersection between contributors along the axes of class, race, sexuality, and gender, at other times equally surprising points of connection cut across and render irrelevant these categories of identity. These latter moments, which exist in productive tension with the lessons of identity politics, result from the necessary, and often beautiful, excesses of literature and theory, and the movement between them. By locating such points of intersection and contradiction, we can use them not to override, deconstruct, or undermine the claims of specific groups, but to begin to theorize their interrelations, and address the possibilities they suggest for forming alliances or coalitions, or even for generating new identities that escape the exclusionary logic and divisiveness of existing ones.[58] Placing the anthologies in this study in dialogue provides a way to begin conceptualizing specific possibilities for alliances at our particular historical moment.

Anthology contributors and editors themselves, in their movements between anthologies, map out some overlapping points of identification that suggest possibilities for coalition. Anthology editors advocate for and express their feelings of connection to other anthology projects in book reviews, and also participate in various identity-based anthologies.[59] To cite a few examples, Cherríe Moraga edits both *This Bridge* and *Third Woman: The Sexuality of Latinas,* and she also participates in *Calling Home* and *Chicana Lesbians;* Mayumi Tsutakawa edits both *The Forbidden Stitch* and *Gathering Ground,* an anthology by women of color from the Northwest; Barbara Smith contributes to *This Bridge* and *Calling Home,* in addition to editing *Home Girls.* Beth Brant edits *A Gathering of Spirit* and has work published in *Returning the Gift* and *Haciendo Caras.* If the multiple locations of these editors suggest that the range of participants in these anthologies is somewhat narrowly circumscribed, they also show those participants engaging in identity politics and constructing communities, both of which are dynamic and coalitional, and allow for multiple points of overlap and entry.[60]

Paradoxically, further alliances can be constructed through the very challenges that the anthologies pose to one another, as well as through the common territory that they claim. Those qualities Barbara Smith designates as black in *Home Girls*—such as an emphasis on community rather than the individual—Janet Zandy designates as working-class in *Calling Home.* The working-class identity Zandy establishes in *Calling Home* challenges *This Bridge's* presentation of white women as middle-class, and points to the possibility for alliance between white working-class women and women of color. *Nice Jewish Girls* also complicates the divisions in *This Bridge* and *Haciendo Caras* between white women and women of color, and the interrelations between racism and anti-Semitism in these anthologies produce points of intersection between white Jewish women and women of color. A lesbian identity, consistently characterized as invisible, cuts across and prompts the articulation of many of the otherwise disparate identities established in *Charting the Journey, Home Girls, This Bridge,* and *Nice Jewish Girls.* In dialogue with many of the U.S. anthologies (particularly *Home Girls, This Bridge* and *Calling Home*), *The Common Thread* and *Charting the Journey* establish intricate alliances and points of convergence among working-class British women, black British women and U.S. women of color, and African American women in particular.

In suggesting the contextual nature, the instability, and the constructedness of categories of identity, I in no way mean to undermine their importance. In fact, I argue that their resistance to any generalizing theories on the one hand and to essence on the other makes these categories all the more powerful, both as a means for imposing hegemony and for mobilizing communal forms of resistance to it. In developing an exploration of the interrelations among these anthologies and mapping their movement over the course of the 1980s, I hope to suggest ways to build upon, rather than forgo, a politics of identity and the communities based on such a politics—ways to utilize not only the strengths and the insights of identity politics, but its blind spots and exclusions as well.

Around 1991 (Back to the Mirror)

Since I started working on this book, Jane Gallop has published *Around 1981: Academic Feminist Literary Theory*, the first full-length study of feminist anthologies. Gallop, writing *Around 1981* around 1991, fails to mention *This Bridge, Haciendo Caras,* or any other of the multi-genre anthologies considered here.[61] Gallop's exclusion of these anthologies suggests that the boundaries they transgress have not facilitated their entry into the mainstream of academic feminist literary theory. In fact, it is arguably their transgressive quality—the ways in which these works are not containable within the realm of academic theoretical writing—that results in their exclusion during a period when issues of race and identity politics occupy a position of centrality in academic feminist literary theory. For white feminist theorists and critics who are addressing race, the multi-genre format presents particular problems and discomforts. While fictional forms by definition assert distance between a writer and her work, and while academic theory usually maintains a level of abstraction that creates a sense of distance between it and its practitioners, these identity-based anthologies refuse critics the comfort and safety, however illusory, that such boundaries provide.[62] It is precisely because these anthologies continually unsettle distinctions between a writer and her work that their textual communities offer their editors and contributors a basis for establishing actual communities. On the other hand, this is also how they are able so powerfully to confront white academic feminists who study these communities with the danger of appropriating or objectifying the voices and lives of women marginalized in or excluded from the academy.

My scholarship addressing the writings of marginalized groups of women emerges out of a desire to struggle against forms of oppression through my work as an academic, and out of a commitment to connect myself to women whose oppression is more immediate than my own, and in whose oppression I am implicated. I suspect the same is true for many other white academic feminists as well. Using identity-based anthologies in such an enterprise makes the problems involved particularly inescapable and evident, but engaging the anthologies also provides myself and other academic feminists in positions of privilege with a way to decenter ourselves, if only to be confronted simultaneously with our own "otherness" in the eyes of "other" women. The double position of such a vantage point affords, if nothing else, a place to begin working against the divisions, while at the same time respecting the differences, that exist between us.

2

Another 1981

From *This Bridge Called My Back* to *Making Face, Making Soul/Haciendo Caras*

Quite frankly, *This Bridge* needs no Foreword. It is the Afterward that'll count.
　　—Toni Cade Bambara, foreword to *This Bridge Called My Back*, p. viii

Barbara says last night: "A bridge gets walked over." Yes, over and over again.
　　—Cherríe Moraga, preface to *This Bridge Called My Back*, p. xv

The Birth of *This Bridge*: A Collective Labor

In their introduction to *This Bridge Called My Back*, editors Cherríe Moraga and Gloria Anzaldúa claim, "This anthology was created with a sense of urgency. From the moment of its conception, it was already long overdue" (xxv). The anthology, a labor both of love and anger, emerges out of the contributors' frustration with the racism of the white women's movement and the sexism of civil rights movements of the 1950s, 1960s, and 1970s. The hunger for a work like *This Bridge* is obvious not only from its sales (as of the ninth and most recent printing of the second edition, 86,000 copies had been sold), but also from the number of other such projects that have cited its influence. *This Bridge*, the best known of the multi-genre anthologies, is commonly perceived by contributors to later anthologies, as well as by academic feminists, to have been the catalyst for the explosion of multi-genre women's anthologies of the past decade, and to be of central importance in establishing and articulating a third world feminism.[1]

However, to promote *This Bridge* as *the* work responsible for creating an academic movement on the part of women of color and other marginalized groups of women is to risk dehistoricizing it. While *This Bridge*

31

was indeed "long overdue," even more overdue is recognition of the small presses and works that made possible its publication. Although largely ignored, the contexts and traditions out of which *This Bridge* emerges have profoundly influenced—and continue to influence—the cultural politics of late twentieth-century writings on race, class, sexuality, and gender. Resituating *This Bridge* in relation to these historical contexts is essential to understanding the book's particular contributions, and suggests the broader influence of its predecessors, and of feminist publishing practices and politics of the 1960s and 1970s.

Before the publication of *This Bridge,* lesbian and feminist journals provided a publishing forum for marginalized groups of women, and many of the anthologies in this study were initially created as special editions of such journals. *The Forbidden Stitch: An Asian American Women's Anthology* initially was published as a double issue of the journal *Calyx.* Both *Tribe of Dina: A Jewish Women's Anthology* and *A Gathering of Spirit* constituted special issues of *Sinister Wisdom* before being published as books. *Home Girls: A Black Feminist Anthology* derives from the journal *Conditions,* as does *Third Woman: The Sexuality of Latinas* from the journal *Third Woman.* Some of these journals—*Calyx, Third Woman, Sinister Wisdom*—have also been responsible for publishing the book versions of these anthologies. These journals, and other lesbian or feminist ones, also have supported the anthologies by consistently publishing appreciative book reviews of them.

In addition to these journals, small presses developed in the 1970s and 1980s that were explicitly devoted to publishing books by lesbians, feminists, and women of color. These presses, which stated their immediate agendas as political rather than economic, dedicated themselves not only to publishing works such as *This Bridge,* but to soliciting or developing other such projects.[2] For example, Aunt Lute, a San Francisco-based press, has committed itself to diversifying and challenging representations of women and people of color not only through the books it publishes, but through manuscript tutorials, publishing workshops, and publishing internships. In a 1993 newsletter, as editor Joan Pinkvoss inspires women to write, she quotes Anzaldúa in *This Bridge* and recommends the anthology for its insight into how and why women seem absent in writing. Small-press newsletters and catalogues promote anthology editors and their work through interviews and articles that evidence their personal interactions.

The prefaces, introductions, and acknowledgments to the anthologies in this study further testify to the close relationship between the anthology editors and their publishers. In their acknowledgments to the recently published *Our Feet Walk the Sky: Women of South Asian Descent*, the editors give their last words to Pinkvoss: "Finally, a special thanks to Joan Pinkvoss for believing in us. Her continual patience, support and commitment to this book were invaluable."[3] Their introduction details weekly meetings with Aunt Lute Press in the four months before finishing their manuscript, and pays tribute to the press's cultural sensitivity. Anzaldúa dedicates *Haciendo Caras* to Joan Pinkvoss, her publisher and editor, and to the staff at Spinsters Press, among others. In the third edition to *Nice Jewish Girls*, editor Evelyn Torton Beck states that the idea for the anthology was first suggested to her by Gloria Z. Greenfield, publisher of Persephone Press. Such acknowledgments illustrate the vital role small publishers have played in making women's anthologies possible in the 1980s.

In some cases the writers, publishers, and editors of these anthologies overlap. The presses, in many cases, were founded by writers unable to find publishers for their work or that of their friends—for example, lesbian feminist writers Judith McDaniel and Maureen Brady initially founded the lesbian feminist press Spinsters Ink in 1978 as a way to publish their own books. In the second edition to *This Bridge*, its editors express pride that the anthology is now being published by Kitchen Table, a press owned by women of color. The anthology and the press are intimately related to one another: the press was co-founded by Barbara Smith, a contributor to *This Bridge*. Smith also published her black feminist anthology *Home Girls* through Kitchen Table.[4]

These presses are run not to make a profit, but to provide an avenue for women otherwise silenced by mainstream presses. Most subsist on volunteer labor and are driven by feminist ethics, not economics. As Joan Pinkvoss states in an Aunt Lute newsletter: "We intend to be accountable to the best possible definition of feminist publishing: we will publish books reflecting the wide range of differences in women's lives, books focusing on women's lives exclusively, and books echoing our feminist politics regarding the linking of and need to fight all oppressions."[5]

Of course, these presses are also business ventures dependent upon capital for their survival, and on marketing their books, along with feminist ideals. Thus, Spinsters Press's 1993 newsletter includes an account by founding editor Maureen Brady that highlights not its current good health but its beginnings. Using a birthing metaphor that runs throughout small-press literature, as well as throughout introductions to the anthologies themselves, Brady compares the first shipment of books to delivering a baby, then explains, "We never figured

out how to salary ourselves. Our labor was all volunteer. We worked
out of our farmhouse kitchen. The books were in a corner cabinet, the
packaging was done on top of the clothes dryer."[6] The homey women-
centered appeal of this narrative and its stereotypically feminine disregard—even ignorance—for the economics of running a business, an ignorance and disregard that the survival of the press belies, keep alive
for Spinsters customers (who are constituted as a community of readers) an alternative to the cold, impersonal world of mainstream publishing. In addition, the editors of these presses present themselves not
as operating on a model of competitive individualism or capitalism, but
as surviving through communal commitments and networking. In her
discussion of buying Spinsters in 1993, Joan Pinkvoss proclaims, "The
'old girls network' works!"[7] In this same catalogue, Maureen Brady acknowledges the networks with other lesbian and feminist publishers
that keep Spinsters alive, giving thanks to Aunt Lute, Pinkvoss, Ama-
zon Bookstore, Eighth Mountain Press, and "the women at Seal Press
for answering questions and sharing mailing lists in a truly unselfish
and feminist spirit."[8] The emergence and production of anthologies
like *This Bridge* are thus closely connected to the development of a network of small presses and journals founded upon and creating a market for women's communities and identity politics.[9]

In addition to the groundwork laid by small presses and journals of
the 1970s and 1980s, the foundations for *This Bridge* were also laid by its
literary predecessors. *This Bridge*, like the other anthologies I consider
in this study, builds on the models of anthologies produced by various
ethnic movements of the 1960s and 1970s, even as it points to the exclusions of these movements.[10] The Black Arts Movement of the mid-sixties,
led by Amiri Baraka and Larry Neal, linked the production of literature, particularly poetry, to the black power revolution. In 1968 Baraka
and Neal produced the multi-genre anthology *Black Fire*—"the blackest
canon of all," according to Henry Louis Gates, Jr.[11] Like *This Bridge*,
Black Fire yokes a literary movement with an identity-based struggle for
civil rights, thematically directs itself towards the liberation of the people it represents, and calls for and attempts to define an aesthetics
based upon a racial identity that expresses itself through shared culture. Its focus is relentlessly masculinist, however; black women have a
place in the anthology only insofar as they can uplift black men. The
first Chicano anthology by Chicanos, *El Espejo—The Mirror: Selected
Chicano Literature*, edited by Octavio Ignacio Romano-V. and Hermino
Rios C. (1969), stresses the need to create a Chicano identity, and presents itself as part of a struggle for self-determination. Its emphasis on

identity relates it to the other anthologies in this study, especially to *Making Face, Making Soul/Haciendo Caras* and *Third Woman: The Sexuality of Latinas*. However, like *Black Fire,* it leaves little place for women.[12] The three most important multi-genre Asian American anthologies of the 1970s, *Aiiieeeee!, Roots,* and *Counterpoint,* which I discuss in some detail in chapter 4, similarly focus on men as they struggle to assert an Asian American identity. One of the most direct predecessors to *This Bridge* is *Time to Greez! Incantations from the Third World* (1975). The editors, each of whom are identified on the title page by race, announce in their prologue, "Third World Communications, formed in 1971, is a coalition of Black, Raza, Asian, American Indian, and Native Island people. What we all had in common was our involvement in writing, art, and our communities." They state, "This book is a many-sided mirror of our lives."[13]

This Bridge also finds its predecessors in anthologies and other publications focused specifically on women of color, or on African American women. As Chela Sandoval notes, "By 1971 a grass roots movement of U.S. third world feminists began to form, bringing together women of color. . . . A great number of newsletters, pamphlets and books were produced by underground publishers during the 1971 to 1974 period, including separate works by Janice Mirikitani and Francis Beal, both entitled *Third World Women,* which were meant to affirm and develop the new kind of shared sisterhood/citizenship insistently emerging in the corridors and back rooms where women of color congregated."[14] African American women's anthologies published in the early 1970s, such as Mary Helen Washington's *Black-Eyed Susans* and Toni Cade's *The Black Woman,* which bring together and make known a community of black women writers, can also be seen as precursors to *This Bridge* and other anthologies of the 1980s.[15] In *The Black Woman,* Cade looks to writing as the means of establishing a black women's community; she dedicates the book to "the uptown mamas who nudged me to 'just set it down in print so it gets to be a habit to write letters to each other, so maybe that way we don't keep treadmilling the same ole ground.'"[16] Therefore, it is appropriate that Cade (now Cade Bambara), who provided a bridge to *This Bridge,* writes its foreword. *This Bridge* also builds on and revises the black women's literary anthology *Sturdy Black Bridges* (1979); while employing its title metaphor, *This Bridge* extends the earlier anthology to include other women of color. In doing so, it resists the prevalent black-white dichotomy in the United States that renders non-black women and men of color invisible.

This Bridge finds perhaps its most direct predecessor in the 1970 anthology *Sisterhood Is Powerful: An Anthology of Writings from the Women's Liberation Movement,* edited by Robin Morgan. Although unmentioned by *This Bridge,* it at once shares much with *This Bridge* and represents that which *This Bridge* defines itself against. It shares with *This Bridge* a mixture of revolutionary optimism and rage, as well as a connection between a multi-genre form and activism. Morgan opens her introduction with the announcement "This book is action,"[17] and links the collection's multi-genre form and its rejection of traditional ideas of literary quality to its feminist political agenda: "There is also a blessedly uneven quality noticeable in the book, which I, for one, delight in. There is a certain kind of linear, tight, dry, boring, male super-consistency that we are beginning to reject. That's why this collection combines all sorts of articles, poems, graphics, and sundry papers" (xvii). Morgan reworks traditional literary forms to reflect her politics; she concludes her introduction with an extended poem/letter to a woman worker who went "underground." This "poem" calls into question and begins to redefine the purpose and definition of poetry, repudiating the privilege and pure aestheticism associated with poetry:

Well, it's a poem, or non-poem, because
I don't write what I once called poems anymore—
the well-wrought kind that you and I
might once have critically discussed over a gentle lunch

. . . .
Instead I write, or try to, between actions
(which hardly leaves much time but that's okay)
things about my sisters and myself. (xxxvii)

Sisterhood presents itself as a place for women to find their own reflections—the poem concluding Morgan's introduction ends, "Watch for me when you look in the mirror; / I see you all the time" (xl)—and to raise their consciousnesses: like *This Bridge, Sisterhood Is Powerful* progresses from pieces about contributors' oppression to their changing consciousnesses to their calls for protest and revolt.

However, *Sisterhood* establishes its connectedness to historical predecessors that contributors to *This Bridge* have been marginalized by and consequently repudiate. Morgan's sources, listed both in appendices and a bibliography, include primarily groups of white women, and these groups—and implicitly most of the women in *Sisterhood* itself—are rejected by *This Bridge* for their exclusion of women of color. Though *Sisterhood* demonstrates some sensitivity to women's racial, class, and sexual diversity, its emphasis is on women's sameness. For example, in her introduction Morgan states, "It also seems obvious that half of all oppressed peoples, black, brown, and otherwise, are *women*, and that I, as a not-starving white American woman living in the very belly of the beast, must fight for those sisters to *survive* before we can ever talk together as oppressed women" (xxxv). But while she acknowledges and strives to resist the specific oppression of women of color, she does not address the ways in which her own location implicates her in this oppression. Instead, her impetus in the introduction is to subordinate differences of race and class to those of gender. For example, in claiming the potential for women's liberation cells to form "what would be a perfectly organic alliance with welfare rights organizations, which are made up of women most of whom are black and brown," Morgan states, "We share a common root as *women*, much more natural to both groups than the very *machismo* style of male-dominated organizations, black, brown, *and* white" (xxvi).[18] Morgan's attention to the position of women of color and—through opposing welfare organizations to women's liberation cells—to the class and race biases of the women's liberation movement, exists in tension with her elision of the hierarchized differences among women.

Parts of Morgan's introduction, as well as the cumulative effect of the individual pieces the anthology includes, reveal an insensitivity to or erasure of women who are not white, middle-class, or heterosexual. Morgan and other contributors constantly erase black women's specificity and, perhaps even more dramatically, that of non-black women of color, in their analogies between women and blacks. Although Morgan is concerned to represent a diversity of women in *Sisterhood*, her idea of adequate inclusiveness positions women of color, lesbians, and young women on the margins of the book. She states, "There are three articles by black sisters in this book written specifically about the oppression of black women; it was important to have more than one or two voices speak for so many sisters, and in differing ways" (xxvi); she gives the same rationale for the inclusion of pieces by two (white) lesbians and three pieces by teenagers. Three of the four entries by black women and the contributions by teenagers occur in a section, "Go Tell It In the Valley: Changing Consciousness," making a troubling link between racial minorities and "under age" minorities, and Morgan places the lesbian contributions in a section entitled "The Invisible Woman: Psychological and Sexual Repression." The two contributions by Chicanas are grouped in a section with an article on China, suggesting that Chicanas occupy the status of foreigners in *Sisterhood*.[19] Those pieces by white, middle-class, and heterosexual contributors generally assume all women to share their traits, belying the rhetoric of inclusiveness stressed in Morgan's introduction. Perhaps it is for these reasons that *Sisterhood* goes unmentioned in *This Bridge* or any other of the multi-genre women's anthologies of the 1980s, despite its striking similarities to and shared interests with them.[20]

Although women in other anthologies and other academics usually cite *This Bridge* as the first, groundbreaking, multi-genre anthology, the book also exists as part of a larger literary movement in the early 1980s on the part of marginalized groups of women. Dexter Fisher's *The Third Woman: Minority Women Writers of the United States* (1980), while not directed towards establishing community or challenging definitions of literature and theory through genre experimentation, has been very influential in determining curricula focusing on women of color in women's studies and ethnic studies programs.[21] Furthermore, *This Bridge* was published in 1981, the same year as *All the Women Are White, All the Blacks Are Men, But Some Of Us Are Brave*, and just one year before *Nice Jewish Girls*. And Smith's *Home Girls* anthology, although published two years later, had grown directly out of *Conditions: Five, The Black Women's Issue*, which was published in 1979.

One reason for *This Bridge*'s representative status might be the striking degree to which it reflects on and articulates its own status and its purposes. By giving evidence of a movement on the part of women of color, *This Bridge* involves itself in actively creating and expanding this movement, not merely in reflecting it. Contributors, particularly the editors, present and interpret the anthology in terms of its historical significance. *This Bridge*'s current printing contains twenty-six pages of prefatory material—three forewords, a preface, and an introduction—all devoted to explaining the anthology's history, significance, and motives. In this prefatory material, Moraga and Anzaldúa chronicle their experiences with publishers and include a portion of their solicitation letter to potential contributors. *This Bridge* presents itself not as a timeless piece of literature but as the result of a process and of a particular moment in history. It positions itself on the cusp of a new movement on the part of women of color, and as a precursor of changes this movement will bring. In highlighting its own location in this way, *This Bridge* attempts to dictate the terms of its reception, and combines writing with activism.

Contributors to *This Bridge* present their model of community as a revolutionary force for fighting racism, sexism, classism, and homophobia. The editors' choice of subtitle, "Writings by radical women of color," transforms the term "radical," which in white academic feminist circles describes a feminism, usually lesbian in orientation, that views gender as society's central organizing category. By associating the term "radical" with "women *of color*," and therefore with race as well as gender, "radical" in its feminist context is redefined while still retaining its associations with a revolutionary lesbian feminism. Many, though not all, of the contributors identify themselves as lesbians, and the anthology itself demonstrates the richness of the contributors' connections to one another: they publish letters and dedicate their writings to one another, refer to each other as friends or sisters in both their writing and their biographies, and quote each other's unpublished words. The women of color in the anthology also base their community on their differences, presenting them as sources of strength, or as sources of conflict that, because faced head on, can be overcome. Audre Lorde explains, "As women, we have been taught to either ignore our differences or to view them as causes for separation and suspicion rather than as forces for change. Without community, there is no liberation, only the most vulnerable and temporary armistice between an individual and her oppression. But community must not mean a shedding of our differences, nor the pathetic pretense that these differences do not exist" (99). According to the women in *This Bridge*, the radicalness of the community depends on its refusal to deny differences among women.

Bridging Identity and Difference

At the same time that it constructs a community of women of color, *This Bridge* also makes evident the contradictions and arbitrariness of such a grouping. The editors call attention to the fact that this alliance of women of color is strategic, not essential. In the foreword to the second edition, Moraga explains: "We are not so much a 'natural' affinity group, as women who have come together out of political necessity" (n.p.). Also, the oscillation in the anthology between the terms "women of color" and "Third World women" suggests the inadequacy of both terms. As Mirtha Quintanales observes, "Not all Third World women are 'women of color'—if by this concept we mean exclusively 'non-white.' I am only one example" (151). Conversely, the example of Japanese women shows that "not all women of color are really Third World" (151), and that many third world women/women of color "have grown up as or are fast becoming 'middle-class' and highly educated, and therefore [are] more privileged than many of our white, poor and working-class sisters" (151).[22] Thus, at the same time that the women in *This Bridge* strategically employ the category "women of color," they also denaturalize and destabilize it as a category.

Despite the fact that some contributors show the distinctions between white women and women of color to be far from absolute, however, the community in *This Bridge* is held together, and is dependent
upon, the "othering" of white women. The coherence of the community
depends upon keeping the racial division intact, even though the contributors take a variety of stances towards white women, from doris
davenport's assertion that "white wimmin" are repulsive to women of
color, and "have a strange body odor" (89) to Cheryl Clarke's statement, "All of us have to accept or reject allies on the basis of politics not
on the specious basis of skin color" (135). When Anzaldúa confesses, "I
have been terrified of writing this essay ["La Prieta"] because I will
have to own up to the fact that I do not exclude whites from the list of
people I love" (206), her terror is a register of the danger posed to this
community when white people cease to be the other. Another sign of
this shaky division and the need to keep it intact can be read through
Moraga's name. The dedication to *This Bridge* names Moraga's mother
as Elvira Moraga Lawrence. In claiming her mother's family name,
Moraga reconnects herself to her mother and to her Chicana heritage;
she also erases the traces of her father and her white heritage from her
name, making more absolute her position in the women of color/white
women binary, and making this binary itself more absolute.[23] In *This
Bridge* (and also in *Loving in the War Years*), Moraga writes about her
white father, deconstructing her identity as a woman of color as she
affirms it. And yet, silence surrounds Moraga's claiming of her mother's
name; as the editor of *This Bridge*, Moraga unequivocally names herself
as Chicana. How, I wonder, would the boundaries of *This Bridge*'s community shift if the names of its editors were Anzaldúa and Lawrence,
and if the anthology carried a picture of Moraga, who can "pass" as
white? Her position illustrates the radical indeterminacy and constructedness of racial categories, even as it points to *This Bridge*'s need to
maintain, and even reinforce, these categories.

Furthermore, perhaps because the identity "woman of color" is not
stable enough, *This Bridge* does not itself directly present divisive (rather
than enriching) differences among women of color. While Moraga does
contend that "the *idea* of Third World Feminism has proven to be much
easier between the covers of a book than between real live women"
(n.p.), and while contributors sometimes refer to painful differences
they have experienced with other women of color, *This Bridge* does not
inscribe conflicts between the contributors themselves. For example,
Aurora Levins Morales writes of her anger toward, distrust of, and feelings of betrayal by other Latina women in ". . . And Even Fidel Can't

Change That!": "And not to betray you [Latinas] in the face of their [white women's] racism, I betray myself, and in the end, you, by not saying: it's not the men who exile me . . . it's the women. I don't trust the women" (54). She does not direct this distrust at other contributors, however, despite Moraga's urging that "if it takes head-on collisions, let's do it: this polite timidity is killing us" (34). Are there no "head-on collisions" in *This Bridge* because Anzaldúa and Moraga were in concert—with each other and with the other contributors—throughout its production? In the anthology's thematizing of its own production, it presents strictly harmonious relations among contributors. Thus, while the editors organize *This Bridge* to present a range of views, and while the women in *This Bridge* acknowledge their conflicts with other women of color, these conflicts occur outside the book.

The Matter of Theory

In addition to its goal of building a community based on differences, *This Bridge* is also engaged in forging an alternative to academic theory, a "theory in the flesh," as Moraga and Anzaldúa phrase it in the title of the second section to *This Bridge*. Anzaldúa encourages women of color to "throw away abstraction and the academic learning, the rules, the map and compass. Feel your way without blinders. To touch more people, the personal realities and the social must be evoked—not through rhetoric but through blood and pus and sweat" (173). "Theory in the Flesh" is Anzaldúa's and Moraga's attempt to find a language for this "blood and pus and sweat." In the introduction to this section, Moraga explains, "A theory in the flesh means one where the physical realities of our lives—our skin color, the land or concrete we grew up on, our sexual longings—all fuse to create a politic born out of necessity" (23). Moraga underlines this emphasis on physical realities in the conclusion to her preface: "For the women in this book, I will lay my body down for that vision. *This Bridge Called My Back*" (xix). Here, Moraga puts forth her body and the anthology as one and the same. Similarly, when she and Anzaldúa employ birth imagery to describe their work on *This Bridge* (xxv), they emphasize their investment in embodying language, in connecting *This Bridge* to their own bodies.

They urge other women to do the same. Anzaldúa instructs women, "While you wash the floor or clothes listen to the words chanting in your body" (170). Both she and Moraga inspire women of color to transform their lives and bodies into language, a language that will in turn live inside the bodies of other women of color. Their project, in some ways, constitutes a revision of Cixous's cry to women (i.e., privileged white women) to write their bodies; however, unlike Cixous, Anzaldúa and Moraga are specific about which women they address, and these are the very women Cixous leaves out. Also unlike Cixous, they foreground and thematize the material conditions for writing, and, in employing the collective format of an anthology, they give women the space and place to try out this writing of their bodies.[24]

Despite their oppositional stance toward the academy, the women in the anthology nevertheless address themselves, indirectly, to white academic feminists, and the anthology has been widely read and taught—and sometimes appropriated—by us.[25] One of the problems *This Bridge* faces in the academy is that because it is not in recognizable theoretical form, its theoretical concerns can be dismissed. *This Bridge* generally does not appear on the syllabi of graduate classes in feminist theory, nor is it often included on the feminist theory lists of graduate students taking oral examinations. In standard academic feminist essays, critics rarely cite the work for its theoretical insights, but rather for its status as an object signifying the entry of U.S. women of color into feminism. Furthermore, for white feminists *This Bridge* often becomes representative of the work of U.S. women of color, and a hierarchical dichotomy is established in the academy wherein white women who "do" theory are considered superior to women of color, who "do" this "other" kind of writing.[26] In the last several years, the class as well as racial dynamics of this dichotomy have become increasingly complex as, especially in the field of postcolonial studies, third world intellectuals have attained prominence as theorists. Nevertheless, a hierarchized distinction continues between writing that is considered to be academic theory and writing that challenges the class as well as racial privilege of such writing.

I believe it is the threat that *This Bridge* poses to the governing assumptions of mainstream feminist academics that has caused it to be so quickly dismissed or contained. In a contribution to *Conflicts in Feminism*, Katie King reflects on the increasingly narrow definition of theory in the academy: "As mixed genres emerging from and theorizing mixed complex identities are produced in the feminist press, genres of academic feminist writing are increasingly compartmentalized in production, distribution, consumption in the academic and commercial presses. Political meanings are assigned to all these activities, redrawing political communities. 'Theory' here has shifted from an activity possibly (though not without exception) embodied in many written genres to a genre of writing itself."[27] Though King's formulations occur in the context of her exploration of the gay/straight splits in feminism, they also illuminate the divide between *This Bridge* and more strictly academic feminist texts. As highly specialized theoretical discourses develop alongside mixed genres of writing by marginalized groups of women, these discourses in effect help ensure the continuing status and privilege of its still predominantly white, middle-class practitioners in the academy.[28] Therefore, although *This Bridge* might be read in the academy, as Norma Alarcón notes, ten years after its publication, "the impact [of *This Bridge* and other writings by women of color] among most Anglo-American theorists appears to be more cosmetic than not."[29]

Anzaldúa remarks, "There is an enormous contradiction in being a bridge" (206). There is also an enormous contradiction in editing and writing *This Bridge*. While the anthology is read by many of the academic feminists it opposes, one of its most difficult tasks is to reach a range of women of color. In the foreword to the second edition, Moraga includes an excerpt from 19-year-old Alma Ayala's letter to Anzaldúa, in which she speaks of the book's impact on her. But is Ayala's response the exception or the rule? In this foreword, Moraga says third world women writers "know full well our writings seldom *directly* reach the people we grew up with" (n.p.). In the introduction, in discussing the intended uses for the anthology, the editors express the expectation that the book will be used as a required text in women's studies and ethnic studies classes, as well as off campus by white women in efforts of consciousness raising. They also hope it will be translated (it has since been translated into Spanish by Norma Alarcón). After covering a range of intended uses for the anthology, they conclude, "Finally *tenemos la esperanza que This Bridge Called My Back* will find its way back into our families' lives," because, "the revolution begins at home" (xxvi). The "finally" seems to indicate not only "most important," but also, "lastly." That the book will "find its way" there is a hope rather than an expectation, suggesting that Anzaldúa and Moraga believe reaching their own families may be more difficult than reaching women in other countries.

It seems that, finally, *This Bridge* runs up against the limits of an activism that takes place in writing, though it does much to undo the dichotomy often set up between activism and writing. As hattie gossett asks, what can one do when "a major portion of your audience not only cant read but seems to think reading is a waste of time? plus books like this arent sold in the ghetto bookshops or even in airports?" (175). Women who do not have access to *This Bridge,* either because they do not read or because it will not reach their bookstores, are perhaps the women the contributors to *This Bridge* most want and need to reach. As Norma Alarcón concludes in her essay on *This Bridge* in *Haciendo Caras,*

"It must be noted . . . that each woman of color cited here, even in her positing of a 'plurality of self,' is already privileged enough to reach the moment of cognition of a situation for herself. This should suggest that to privilege the subject, even if multiple-voiced, is not enough" (366). *This Bridge* itself contains acknowledgments of the limitations of an intellectualized, textually based form of activism; at the same time, its contributors refuse to be paralyzed by these limitations, and use the multi-genre form to push against them.

Facing Forward: From *This Bridge* to *Haciendo Caras*

Ten years after *This Bridge,* its "sequel," *Making Face, Making Soul/Haciendo Caras,* comes from and addresses itself more clearly to those women "already privileged enough to reach the moment of cognition." "For years," Anzaldúa announces in the introduction to *Haciendo Caras,* "I waited for someone to compile a book that would continue where *This Bridge Called My Back* left off" (xvi). Having tired of waiting, Anzaldúa put together *Haciendo Caras* as a reader for a course on third world women she was teaching at the University of California at Santa Cruz in 1988. Published in 1990, *Haciendo Caras* departs in some striking ways from its predecessor, mainly in that it reflects and responds to a different moment in feminism. In 1990, women of color had become more established—both inside and outside the university—as a political force and as a community; however, despite the wide readership of works such as *This Bridge,* they still experienced the persistence of white racism and classism in feminist movements, and sexism from men of color. Therefore, contributors to *Haciendo Caras* are at once stronger and surer, yet also more cynical and less optimistic, about their abilities to effect change. The anthology's very title illustrates some of its differences from *This Bridge Called My Back.* Though both draw on bodily metaphors, the title *Making Face, Making Soul/Haciendo Caras* presents the contributors as active, in charge, and confrontational, whereas *This Bridge* presents them as victims, as conduits for the actions of others. As Anzaldúa explains in her introduction, "For me, *haciendo caras* has the added connotation of making *gestos subversivos,* political subversive gestures, the piercing look that questions or challenges, the look that says, 'Don't walk all over me,' the one that says, 'Get out of my face'" (xv). The subject in *Haciendo Caras,* no longer willing to serve as bridge to be walked upon, looks the world defiantly in the face, proclaiming herself in charge of her own making. "'*Making Face,*'" Anzaldúa asserts, "is my metaphor for constructing one's identity" (xvi). While *This Bridge* offers itself as a means to raise women's consciousness, the subjects in *Haciendo Caras* and the audience they address are already highly conscious and politicized.

At the same time, contributors to *Haciendo Caras* form a less closely knit community than the women in *This Bridge,* partly because many more contributors are involved, and partly because Anzaldúa constructs it largely from previously published pieces of writing. Whereas in *This Bridge* many of the contributors clearly know each other, and even address each other in their writings, in *Haciendo Caras* this occurs only infrequently. Some of the women in *This Bridge* appear again in *Haciendo Caras* (Chrystos, Barbara Smith, Audre Lorde, Pat Parker, Norma Alarcón, and Mitysuye Yamada), but *Haciendo Caras* includes the work of over fifty additional women, producing a more diffuse community than the earlier one in *This Bridge.* Also, 50 of the 72 entries in *Haciendo Caras* have been previously published, as compared to 9 of 46 in *This Bridge. Haciendo Caras* thus conveys less of that sense of direct personal ties among contributors that makes *This Bridge* so compelling.

In gathering together and arranging previously published material, Anzaldúa in *Haciendo Caras textually* constructs community, whereas in *This Bridge* the contributors responded directly to Anzaldúa and Moraga's call, presented by way of a soliciting letter, and work together to produce the anthology. The contributors' biographies demonstrate this difference: while in *This Bridge* they are playful and familiar, mentioning contributors' zodiac signs and their personal lives, in *Haciendo Caras* they are more straightforwardly professional, describing contributors' jobs and publications. The single editorship of *Haciendo Caras* further contributes to its less communal feel, as does the slightness of Moraga's presence in *Haciendo Caras:* the anthology contains only a previously published poem of hers, and she is not included in Anzaldúa's acknowledgments of the many people who have supported and inspired her work. While the *Haciendo Caras* community is, in many ways, more established, it is also less intimate, and shows traces (through Moraga's absence) of shifting allegiances within the community of women of color.

Other(ing) Women

Under Anzaldúa's editorship, the anthology reflects a stronger Chicana emphasis than does *This Bridge.* The title, a combination of English and Spanish, and the artwork from Judy Baca's mural, "The World Wall," featuring pictures of brown-skinned women, establish this emphasis, as does Anzaldúa's introduction, in which she alternates between the En-

glish term "women-of-color" and the Spanish term "mujeres-de-color."
Employing this bilingualism in the introduction allows Anzaldúa to
mark the identity "woman of color" with her inflection as a Chicana;
while preserving the category of women of color, Anzaldúa simultaneously introduces into it the notion of difference, and calls it into question as a uniform or unifying category. The Spanish form also works to
complicate issues of racial difference, which too often are presented in
the United States in the bi-polar framework of black versus white. However, while I believe Anzaldúa's shifts between Spanish and English are
strategically brilliant in *Borderlands/La Frontera,* and in her essays in the
body of *Haciendo Caras,* in the introduction to *Haciendo Caras,* when she
is speaking less clearly for herself alone, I find the term "mujeres-de-
color" troubling as well as enabling, since the term risks alienating non-
Chicana/Latina women of color who might not identify themselves as
"mujeres." Moving between her particular identities and those general
to women of color sometimes allows Anzaldúa a "both/and" perspective, but also sometimes verges on making her viewpoint an ethnocen-
tric one. In the anthology's title, artwork, and introduction, Anzaldúa's
particularity as a Chicana bumps up against the anthology as one belonging more generally to women of color.

The greater emphasis on Anzaldúa's Chicana identity reflects the anthology's/Anzaldúa's greater engagement in the differences and divisions among women of color, and their struggles to avoid oppressing or
judging each other. The section of *Haciendo Caras* entitled "Denial and
Betrayal" testifies to contributors' increased consciousness, since *This
Bridge,* of the difficulties of being part of a community of women of
color. In fact, the community advanced in *Haciendo Caras,* given its stress
on its internal divisions, might best be termed a coalitional community.[30] The section contains works such as Audre Lorde's poem "Between Ourselves," which begins, "Once it was easy to know / who
were my people" (139). And in their essay devoted to developing unity
among women of color, Virginia R. Harris and Trinity A. Ordoña ask,
"How many times have you felt that women of color are the enemy?
Too many times for comfort" (308). In "En rapport, In Opposition: Co-
brando cuentas a las nuestras," Anzaldúa herself expresses concern
over divisions among women of color, noting, "One of the changes that
I've seen since *This Bridge* was published is that we no longer allow
white women to efface us or suppress us. Now we do it to each other"
(142). *Haciendo Caras* plays out ways in which this can happen; indeed,
Anzaldúa herself is at times implicated in making women "pass the
ethnic legitimacy test we have devised" (143). When she asserts that,

"To speak English is to think in that language, to adopt the ideology of the people whose language it is and to be 'inhabited' by their discourses" (xxii), she emphasizes the importance of resisting the dominant culture through expressing oneself bilingually (or multilingually). Anzaldúa's argument throughout *Haciendo Caras* linking linguistic identity to ethnic identity suggests a standard of authenticity for women of color, implying that women of color who might not have grown up with a language other than standard English are, perhaps, less "authentic" than those fluent in their ethnic languages. At moments like this, *Haciendo Caras* reestablishes some of the hierarchies and standards for authenticity its contributors protest.

As in *This Bridge*, what holds the women of color community together in *Haciendo Caras* amidst all their differences is an "othering" of white women and white culture in general. However, in *Haciendo Caras*, the contributors seem both angrier with and more resigned to white women's racism as an ongoing condition. The title to the first section of *Haciendo Caras* announces, "Still Trembles Our Rage in the Face of Racism." This section, as well as the rest of *Haciendo Caras*, employs a sophisticated and precise definition and analysis of racism and its relation to dominance. While in *This Bridge* a contributor such as Barbara Cameron refers to her "racism toward other people of color" (49), in *Haciendo Caras* not a single contributor uses the word "racism" to describe hostilities among women of color; instead, they develop language to distinguish between their own antagonisms and the racism of whites, thus increasing the divide between themselves and white women. At moments, *Haciendo Caras* seems to essentialize whiteness as evil in a metaphysical sense rather than in its historical context in the United States. In the "Denial and Betrayal" section, contributors time and again find "whiteness"—either external or internalized—ultimately to blame for divisions among women of color. When Anzaldúa argues that "it is exactly our internalized whiteness that desperately wants boundary lines (this part of me is Mexican, this Indian) marked out" (143), she ignores the ways women of color also have histories which create boundaries (or divisions) between them; Korean Americans, for example, may meet Japanese Americans on American ground with their own ethnically imposed boundaries. Similarly, when Virginia R. Harris and Trinity A. Ordoña claim, "We know racism from whites" (308), they view all racism through the lens of white supremacy in the United States. In doing so, and in order to make a clear division between whites and women of color, Harris and Ordoña must ignore the histories of women of color experienced before entering this country.

The position Anzaldúa takes towards white Jewish women in her introduction also shows the difficulty of and need for maintaining a women of color/white women dichotomy, and for denying differences among white women. Detailing the dynamics of a class on women of color that she taught at Santa Cruz, Anzaldúa explains, "Because they [the white Jewish women] felt isolated and excluded, they felt that their oppressions were the same or similar to those of women-of-color. Some *mujeres-de-color* questioned the concept of 'same' oppressions and claimed that all oppressions were being collapsed into one. The problem was that whitewomen and white Jewishwomen [*sic*], while seeming to listen, were not really 'hearing' women-of-color and *could not get it into their heads* that this was a space and class on and about women-of-color" (xx, emphasis added). Anzaldúa found that "the inability to listen and hear . . . almost tore our class apart" (xx). Although she attributes impatience and anger towards the white Jewish women in her class to her students of color, Anzaldúa clearly aligns herself with those students—the phrase "could not get it into their heads" seems to communicate Anzaldúa's exasperation as well as her students', and the listening she advocates seems to be one-sided. By letting this exchange represent white Jewish women's relationship to women of color, Anzaldúa chooses to ignore a broader range of relations that exist among white Jews and women of color, and the complexity of the interrelations between anti-Semitism and racism, both of which complicate the dichotomy between white women and women of color.

Anzaldúa adopts a similar strategy in "Bridge, Drawbridge, Sandbar or Island: Lesbians-of-Color *Hacienda Alianzas*," her contribution to *Bridges of Power: Women's Multicultural Alliances* (1990). In this essay, which addresses the possibilities for alliances between white women and women of color, Anzaldúa includes the following comment as her first note: "Rather than discussing anti-Semitism, a dialogue I choose not to take on in this paper for reasons of length, boundaries of topic, and ignorance on my part of all its subtleties (though I am aware that there is a connection between racism and anti-Semitism I am not sure what it is), I've decided not to take it on nor even make a token mention of it. I realize that this is a form of 'If you don't deal with my racism I won't deal with yours,' and that pleading ignorance is no excuse."[31] Anzaldúa explicitly dismisses considerations of anti-Semitism here because it unsettles boundaries, and because she claims not to know much about it. Given the Jewish women she acknowledges and cites in this essay (Helene Moglen, Joan Pinkvoss, Audrey Berlowitz, Judit Moschkovich, and Elana Dykewomon), as well as the evidence in her own and other writings of her friendships and coalitional work with Jewish activists such as Melanie Kaye/Kantrowitz and Irena Klepfisz (whom she does poetry readings with, and dedicates a poem to in *Borderlands*), I find her remark that her lack of attention to anti-Semitism "is a form of 'If you don't deal with my racism I won't deal with yours'" especially unsatisfying.[32]

Anzaldúa's position in *Haciendo Caras* depends upon overlooking her own alliances with Jewish women, as well as the work by both white Jews and women of color exploring the relationship between anti-Semitism and racism. For example, the 1986 anthology *The Tribe of Dina*, edited by Irena Klepfisz and Melanie Kaye/Kantrowitz, includes essays that work to negotiate responsibly the relationship between white Jews and women of color; these essays insist both upon white contributors' complicity in the oppression of women of color, and also upon the ways in which, as Jews, their histories have sometimes converged with those of women of color.[33] Women of color have also asserted connections between racism and anti-Semitism. In particular, black feminists have analyzed the shared and divergent histories of Jews and African Americans because, as bell hooks contends, "White supremacy relies on the maintenance of anti-black racism and anti-Semitism, hence there will never be a time when these two struggles will not be connected."[34]

While it is not the project of *Haciendo Caras* to explore the interrelations among white Jewish women and women of color, I would like to resist the way in which it seems to foreclose such an exploration by others. In their reviews of *Haciendo Caras* in *Bridges: A Journal for Jewish Feminists and Our Friends,* neither Cheryl Clarke nor Bernice Mennis addresses Anzaldúa's stand towards white Jewish women[35]—a significant omission given the context in which the reviews are written (particularly on the part of Mennis, a white Jew).[36] In part, perhaps, this omission may be attributable to the way the anthology positions its white Jewish readers: to question *Haciendo Caras*'s position towards white Jewish women is to become indistinguishable from the women in Anzaldúa's class. However, my impetus to call Anzaldúa on this position comes not because I feel hurt or angry (although I do), but because I believe that this moment in *Haciendo Caras* marks one of the blind spots upon which a clear division between white women and women of color depends. And I believe it is necessary to question this boundary if we are to begin building alliances which can, in admitting both our commonalities and our differences, move us beyond the strictly temporary and strategic.[37]

To some extent, the anthology and the racial and ethnic identities of the contributors do challenge distinctions between women of color and white women. Following the section "Still Trembles Our Rage in the Face of Racism," which focuses on white racism, is one entitled "Denial and Betrayal." This section includes contributors' discussions of their complex identities, ones that often do not fall neatly into established categories, and which are often partly white. "Denial and Betrayal" includes essays about being a light-skinned black, and about having a white as well as a Japanese or Chicana identity or background, and the writers often use their culturally or racially mixed identities to act as bridges between communities. Siu Wai Anderson, who was raised by an Anglo minister's family, proclaims, "Not white, certainly, but not really Asian, I straddle the two worlds and try to blaze your trails for you" (157). Thus the essays in this section destabilize the boundaries which the previous section, "Still Trembles Our Rage," asserts. In "La conciencia de la mestiza: Towards a New Consciousness," Anzaldúa herself, looking to "the mestiza" and "the queer" as proof "that all blood is intricately woven together and that we are spawned out of similar souls" (383), insists that the future depends on breaking down dualities, including the one separating people of color and whites.

The anthology also allows white women some entry, however limited, into *Haciendo Caras*. Lynn Weber Cannon, a white working-class woman, co-authors "The Costs of Exclusionary Practices in Women's Studies" along with three women of color, Maxine Baca Zinn, Bonnie Thorton Dill, and Elizabeth Higginbotham. And in her essay "La conciencia de la mestiza," Anzaldúa expresses the belief that "we need to allow whites to be our allies. . . . They will come to see that they are not helping us but following our lead" (384). Although whites remain a "they" in opposition to women of color's "we," and are followers rather than equal allies, Anzaldúa does here indirectly reach out to the whites who constitute a portion of her audience. The heterogeneity of the multi-genre form thus enables Anzaldúa to adopt two contradictory positions towards white women—one that establishes connections, and one that casts white women as irrevocably other. Each of these positions serves as a necessary corrective to the other's limitations, especially given the academic context in which Anzaldúa puts together her anthology, one in which she must negotiate her relationship to white academic feminists.

Making Face: In and Against the Academy

Though *Haciendo Caras* maintains *This Bridge*'s oppositional stance toward the academy, it is more firmly rooted in it, and more concerned with its relationship to it. When she put *Haciendo Caras* together as a reader, Anzaldúa herself was positioned within the academy (though somewhat provisionally, as a graduate student). The unpublished work Anzaldúa began to include when compiling *Haciendo Caras* draws on her UC Santa Cruz community, and reinforces its academic focus. Anzaldúa explains that she began including pieces that "give fresh, immediate voice to the issues facing women who, in their university surroundings, are often thrown into confusion about their ethnic and/or racial identity" (xvii). The academy is the crisis ground for many of the writers of *Haciendo Caras:* while they have been permitted entry into the academy, they are cut loose from, and must strive to assert, their ethnic and racial (and often their working-class) identities.[38]

Because so many of the writers of *Haciendo Caras* speak from and are positioned in the university, they address themselves more specifically to an academic audience than do the women in *This Bridge*. (In *Haciendo Caras,* 36 of the 62 contributors mention teaching at the college or university level in their biographies, while in *This Bridge* only two women explicitly note their academic positions.) At times, however, contributors are evasive about the narrowness of their audience. In her introduction, Anzaldúa declares, "This book aims to make accessible to others our struggle with all our identities, our linkage-making strategies and our healing of broken limbs" (xvi). Just who these "others" are, however, remains indeterminate, though they seem not to be those whose limbs are still broken. Paradoxically, becoming accessible to "others"—people, possibly academics, who are not women of color—might mean adopting a more academic language, thus becoming less accessible to women untrained in such a language.

In *Haciendo Caras,* Anzaldúa's relation to the academy is an uneasy one, more vexed and ambivalent than in *This Bridge*. In her introduction she expresses the two opposed positions almost simultaneously:

Some feminist theorists-of-color write jargonistically and abstractly, in a hard-to-access language that blocks communication, makes the general listener/reader feel bewildered and stupid. These theorists often mistakenly divide theory and lived experience and are more off-putting than many of the masters they ape. Operating here may be defense mechanisms that an intellectually colonized person adopts. I too am seduced by academic language, its theoretical babble insinuates itself into my speech and is hard to weed out. At the same time I feel that there is a place for us to use specialized language addressed to a select, professional, vocational or scholarly group. . . . We should not give up these 'languages' just because they are not accessible to the general public. (xxiii–xxiv)

In a single passage, Anzaldúa moves from an indictment of academic language to an admission of her own implication in it to a qualified de-

fense of it. In using the term "general public," Anzaldúa is able to glide
over just whom she and her "we" exclude—non-academic women of
color. In *Haciendo Caras*, the site and language of address have shifted
and become more specialized, either at the expense of reaching a wide
audience, or perhaps with a clearer sense of just whom anthologies
such as *This Bridge* and *Haciendo Caras* actually reach.

With its emphasis on academia comes a corresponding emphasis on
publishing as well as writing. When Anzaldúa explains in *Haciendo
Caras*, "We begin to displace the white and colored male typographers
and become, ourselves, typographers, printing our own words on the
surfaces, the plates, of our bodies. We begin to acquire the agency of
making our own *caras*" (xvi), her metaphoric language connects the act
of self-making to the *publication* of writing, rather than to writing itself.
Even more insistently than *This Bridge*, *Haciendo Caras* links writing and
publishing to self-making and identity, and attempts to collapse any
distinctions between them. Thus, while in *This Bridge* Anzaldúa discloses, "The voice recurs in me: *Who am I, a poor Chicanita from the sticks,
to think I could write?*" (166), in *Haciendo Caras* she presents writing and
identity not as being at odds, but as inseparable. And while in *This
Bridge* one of the primary goals seems to be to rouse every woman of
color, no matter how materially impoverished, to write as a means of
spiritual survival and empowerment, in *Haciendo Caras* the reflections
on writing are by, and more directed towards, women who are already
writing and publishing, and who are already conscious of the importance and power of doing so.

For the contributors to *Haciendo Caras*, writing has become a primary
means of activism. "These pieces are not only *about* survival strategies,
they *are* survival strategies," announces Anzaldúa (xviii). In *Haciendo
Caras*, the section entitled "In Silence, Giving Tongue: The Transformation of Silence Into (An)other Alphabet" presents writing as a primary
means of resisting dominant cultural norms. In doing so, the anthology
loses its focus on the privilege—educational, if not class-based—associated with an activism that takes place through writing in an academic
context. In *Haciendo Caras* the women speak as an established community of writers, as, and largely to, academic/intellectual activists.

Correspondingly, engaging in theory—or as Anzaldúa puts it in the
title of the final section, " 'Doing' Theory in Other Modes of Consciousness"—has become a privileged mode of activism. In placing the theory section last, Anzaldúa gives it the prominence of seeming to be "the
last word," unlike in *This Bridge*, where it occurs midway through, and
so appears to prepare the way for the final, all-encompassing section,

"*El Mundo Zurdo:* The Vision." In spite of the colloquialism of "Doing" and the quotes that surround it, which perhaps undercut this "high" enterprise and suggest that it must not be taken too seriously, its intellectualized abstraction nevertheless marks *Haciendo Caras*'s departure from *This Bridge* and its "Theory in the Flesh." Anzaldúa devotes part of her introduction, "Haciendo teorías," to explaining the need to engage in, and thus transform, what the academy defines as theory: "Because we are not allowed to enter discourse, because we are often disqualified and excluded from it, because what passes for theory these days is forbidden territory for us, it is *vital* that we occupy theorizing space, that we not allow whitemen and women solely to occupy it. By bringing in our own approaches and methodologies, we transform that theorizing space" (xxv). She further claims: "If we have been gagged and disempowered by theories, we can also be loosened and empowered by theories" (xxv–xxvi). Many of the essays in the " 'Doing' Theory" section work to transform an academic theorizing space by introducing into it concerns particular to women of color. Essays by Norma Alarcón and Trinh T. Minh-ha, with their academic/theoretical language, prevent readers from being able to line up white feminists with theoretical/intellectual/academic concerns and feminists of color with exclusively material ones which they express "naively," or without explicit theoretical underpinnings.

The anthology does not, however, unequivocally privilege theoretical language, even in transformed terms, nor does it (re)impose traditional academic definitions of what constitutes theory. The first two essays in " 'Doing' Theory"—Barbara Christian's "The Race for Theory" and Tey Diana Rebolledo's "The Politics of Poetics: Or, What Am I, A Critic, Doing in This Text Anyhow?"—argue against or question the language of academic theory. Also, Anzaldúa keeps the boundaries of what constitutes theory fluid by including in this section Alice Walker's "Definition of Womanist" and Pat Mora's poem "Legal Alien," which, in its themes and form, could be traded with any number of poems from other sections. Anzaldúa's own essays, along with many others in *Haciendo Caras*, convey theory in a variety of genres, including poetry, personal narrative and fiction. Thus, *Haciendo Caras* demonstrates a way of participating in a theoretical discourse that is relevant to women of color, while also embedding theory in other forms and genres.[39]

Haciendo Caras pushes simultaneously against two fronts: it attempts to enter into and thus challenge and transform the elitist academic realm of theory, and it also attempts to make theory accessible to communities for whom academic discourse is alien. Transforming theory in the academic realm does not necessarily make it accessible to non-academic communities, but, as Anzaldúa says, "We need to de-academize theory and to connect the community to the academy. 'High' theory does not translate well when one's intention is to communicate to masses of people made up of different audiences" (xxvi). How to reach and communicate "to masses of people" becomes, in *Haciendo Caras*, increasingly difficult and urgent. Anzaldúa voices one of *Haciendo Caras*'s central preoccupations when she asks, "What does being a thinking subject, an intellectual, mean for women-of-color from working-class origins?" (xxv). She provides one response to this question: "It means not fulfilling our parents' expectations, it means often going against their expectations *by exceeding them*. . . . It means continually challenging institutional discourses. . . . It means being what Judy Baca terms 'internal exiles'" (xxv). This condition of being "internal exiles," in relation to both one's home community and academic institutions, is what *Haciendo Caras* struggles with and delineates. The anthology attempts to bring these sites of identity together, and testifies to the difficulties and contradictions of doing so. In mapping out the power and possibilities of a women of color intellectual community, *Haciendo Caras* also manifests the limitations of an activism that takes place through writing predominantly in and for university communities.

Academic Currency

Since I began writing this chapter—the first I undertook for this project—much seems to have changed in the academy. When in 1991 I submitted a version of this chapter to a feminist journal, the two anonymous readers questioned—albeit from diverging theoretical perspectives—my right to engage these anthologies and their editors. What the reports shared in common was their anger. Receiving these reports was painful; rather than help initiate dialogue, my work seemed to be reinforcing the very divides that I had hoped to work against. The reports suggested once again that for a white person addressing racism, good intentions are far from enough. I thought then about retreating to some safer, less fraught line of inquiry, and it was some time before I could reconfirm my belief in the work that I was doing, and my conviction that critical separatism does not constitute a solution to racism in the academy. I sent out the article again in 1993 (having reinserted the parts that had angered the previous readers), and received the readers' reports early in 1995. This time, the article was dismissed by one reader on the grounds of the predictability of its findings about identity politics. In the space of a few years, the work had gone from being explosive to ho-hum.[40] I found myself in at least partial agreement with this reader's point; in significant ways, the "discoveries" this chapter makes about the difficulties and problems with identity politics have been made eloquently, widely, and intelligently. If, however, academics can find the topic of identity politics passé in professional journals, we are afforded no such luxury in the halls and classrooms of our workplaces, where the issues these anthologies raise about identity politics, specifically as they pertain to relations among white women and women of color, are still very much alive, and continue to be difficult and painful. Furthermore, much remains to be said—from a variety of perspectives—about these particular anthologies, and their specific contributions to practices and critiques of identity politics. For me, a close reading of these anthologies constitutes a means for respectfully learning from them, for working through both my points of agreement and of dissent. I have found the points of dissent to be particularly productive. In thinking through my resistance to Anzaldúa's hesitation in *Haciendo Caras* to consider white Jewish women's position, and the way in which the latter position destabilizes the white women/women of color divide, I have come to see that this point of friction also serves, for me at least, as a point of entry, a place where dialogue—about our differences as well as our similarities—becomes both possible and necessary. And if the climate in the academy is now such that calling for such dialogue no longer proves inflammatory, and if we refuse to consign identity politics to already-spent academic currency, perhaps a space opens where some work can get done.

3

Coming Out and Staying Home

Nice Jewish Girls and Home Girls

> The general public does not want to know that it is possible to be a lesbian of whatever color and not merely survive but thrive. And neither does the heterosexual publishing industry want to provide them with the information.
> —Barbara Smith, "The Truth That Never Hurts," pp. 116–117

> I want a button that says Pushy Jew. Loud Pushy Jew. Loud Pushy Jew Dyke.
> —Melanie Kaye/Kantrowitz, "Some Notes on Jewish Lesbian Identity," p. 48

While *This Bridge* and *Haciendo Caras* illustrate some of the possibilities and limitations of establishing a community based upon difference and diversity, *Nice Jewish Girls: A Lesbian Anthology* (1982) and *Home Girls: A Black Feminist Anthology* (1983), in basing their communities on the relatively homogeneous identities of their contributors, illuminate another set of possibilities and limitations. *Home Girls* authors are mostly African-American working-class lesbian feminists; *Nice Jewish Girls* authors, Jewish lesbian feminists. Unlike contributors to *This Bridge* and *Haciendo Caras*, contributors to *Nice Jewish Girls* and *Home Girls* do not define themselves against the communities, institutions, or movements that have excluded them. They instead respond to their exclusion from already marginalized communities by attempting to (re)connect themselves to those communities, or even to claim a place of centrality in them. The women in both anthologies challenge their exclusion from white, gentile lesbian communities, and also from their racial or ethnic communities: in *Home Girls*, from their African American communities, and in *Nice Jewish Girls*, from their Jewish communities. At the same time, the contributors to both anthologies employ identity politics in the effort to establish textual homes that offer unconditional acceptance and support.

Both anthologies have served as powerful models for women from other marginalized groups, and have been greatly influential in various lesbian and feminist communities, particularly for the challenges they have offered to unified definitions of "woman," and to Monique Wittig's concept of a "Lesbian Nation"—an international community and culture shared by all lesbians—that was promoted by white middle-class lesbians in the 1970s. They provide a way to view both the possibilities anthologies based upon identity politics have for establishing and redefining communities and a way to understand the limitations of such a basis for community. An exploration of *Nice Jewish Girls* and *Home Girls* reveals the ways in which, no matter how narrowly defined, an identity-based community inevitably requires the exclusion or strategic stabilization of some aspects of identity that community purports to represent, and thus how such a community finally resists offering a place of unqualified belonging.

In *Nice Jewish Girls*, contributors come together both as Jews and lesbians. However, their lesbian identities consistently pose serious challenges to their identities as Jews. Through the course of the anthology, while lesbian identity remains stable, contributors question and complicate their Jewish identity, often in terms of how it relates to their lesbian identity. In their willingness to destabilize Jewish identity so that it may enrich rather than conflict with their lesbian identity, contributors articulate an identity politics that paradoxically depends upon the unfixing of identity. In doing so, they challenge the politics upon which the anthology is based, and also their exclusions from both Jewish and lesbian communities. At the same time, the anthology dramatizes the problems of a group that claims a position in the margins (in this case, as lesbians in Jewish communities and as Jews in lesbian communities) without exploring the ways in which its members might occupy positions of centrality or privilege.

Home Girls, like *Nice Jewish Girls*, makes evident the possibilities and drawbacks of claiming a specific identity and using it as the basis for community and political action. In contrast to *Nice Jewish Girls*, the contributors to *Home Girls* do not question any aspect of their "home girl" identity: they present blackness, lesbianism, and working-class status as fixed and knowable entities. They are enabled in doing so because they view the different strands of their identity not as contradictory, as in *Nice Jewish Girls*, but as unified and complementary. The cohesiveness of this identity, I argue, rests upon nostalgic versions of an African and an African American past. Smith and other contributors deploy forms of nostalgia, along with an idealization of present realities, to assert places of belonging for black lesbians. Smith presents lesbianism as central to, even indistinguishable from, black feminism, and as a natural extension of contributors' home communities. By claiming lesbianism's foundational importance to black feminist communities, Smith resists her own and other contributors' marginalization and invisibility as lesbians in these communities, and lays the groundwork for theorizing lesbianism in a way that makes it integral to black and feminist identities. Thus *Home Girls* demands a rethinking of nostalgia, and the recognition that nostalgia need not be reactionary and conservative, but can be part of a progressive, even radical, politics.

While contributors to both *Nice Jewish Girls* and *Home Girls* engage in acts of writing largely in order to establish homes as places of comfort, Barbara Johnson, in a talk delivered at UC Berkeley, addressed the comforts of leaving home through the activity of reading. Johnson addressed the ways that "cross-reading" (reading works written from and about a subject position different from one's own) offer a reader experiences of "transport without cost," "identification without responsibility."[1] As a Jewish, but neither black, lesbian, nor working-class reader, I am afforded the possibility of such experiences by *Nice Jewish Girls* and, to an even greater extent, *Home Girls*. However, I believe that critics engaged in cross-readings must resist an abdication of responsibility—must resist either assimilating the differences between our own set of identifications and the ones a text puts forth, or placing the text and its author(s) in the position of idealized Other. Instead, I believe that as we engage in such readings we must question the comforts of staying as well as leaving home, and that we must complicate the distinctions between that which is home and that which is not. This entails moving beyond, without forgoing, a politics of identity. Both *Nice Jewish Girls* and *Home Girls*—in ways I shall demonstrate—advocate precisely such a position.

Between the Ridiculous and the Threatening

In the introduction to *Nice Jewish Girls*, the editor Evelyn Torton Beck suggests "that it is a radical act to be willing to identify publicly as a Jew and a lesbian."[2] To claim both identities, according to Beck, is to "[exceed] the limits of what was permitted to the marginal. You were in danger of being perceived as ridiculous—and threatening" (xv). For Beck, the threat Jewish lesbians pose to the broader Jewish and lesbian groups has to do with their exposing the ways in which these groups may themselves act oppressively. Similarly, the threat that Jewish lesbians pose to mainstream society is their double marginalization, which places them so far outside of it. At the same time, Beck notes, Jewish lesbians are also often perceived as ridiculous, either for the very excessiveness of this double marginalization or because the anti-Semitism Jews experience is so often dismissed, by Jews and non-Jews alike.[3]

As a Jew, I myself have failed, and at times continue to fail, to acknowledge anti-Semitism. Whereas Anzaldúa's dismissal of white Jewish women in *Haciendo Caras* brought out for me the extent to which I identify myself as Jewish, in *Nice Jewish Girls* I paradoxically found myself disidentifying as a Jew, or at least with the Jewish identity asserted by Beck. In fact, I approached the anthology with a fair amount of skepticism and resistance to its claims of anti-Semitism, and frequently found myself annoyed with Beck's insistent focus on the ways in which Jews are oppressed. The anthology has made me think about the reasons for my resistance, and, more generally, about why we Jewish women, though figuring prominently in both academic and lesbian feminist movements, seldom highlight our identity as Jews. Jewish women's leadership roles within predominantly white academic and lesbian feminist communities enable our Jewishness to go curiously unmarked. We often disclaim Jewishness both as a dominant identity (which might make credible the anti-Semitic perception that the Jews are taking over) and as a minority identity. In a time when people of color are articulating and resisting their oppression, one experienced inside academic and feminist communities as well as outside of them, it seems difficult (perhaps even ridiculous?) for Jewish academics to position themselves as marginal. Our ability to pass, and our general economic well-being and privileged class status in relation to other minority groups, adds to this difficulty, as does the difficulty of arriving at a definition of just what it means to be Jewish. (As Daniel and Jonathan Boyarin remark, "Jewishness disrupts the very categories of identity because it is not national, not genealogical, not religious, but all of these in dialectical tension with one another."[4]) And yet, anti-Semitism continues to thrive in this country in a variety of guises, and to speak out against this anti-Semitism, to make it visible, is to pose a threat. Therefore, to claim a minority identity as Jewish, even without also claiming a lesbian identity, does, as Beck puts it, place Jewish women between the ridiculous and the threatening.

Many of the contributors to *Nice Jewish Girls* seem to have shared my ambivalence and discomfort about their Jewish identities at one time, and to have come to discover and assert their Jewishness only by way of coming out as lesbians. Many of them, Beck included, were previously married and assimilated Jews; furthermore, in contributing to

Nice Jewish Girls, they were engaged in creating the first entire work given over to Jewish lesbians. Therefore, throughout the anthology, they employ the language of coming out to describe the process of identifying as Jews as well as lesbians. They argue that arriving at one's Jewish identity entails a process of discovery, and, as is the case for lesbianism, that this identity is not immediately evident to one's self or to others. In making their coming out as Jews contingent upon their coming out as lesbians, contributors suggest that confrontation with and acceptance of one form of marginalized identity leads to an awareness and an embrace of other, more hidden forms of marginalization.

Nice Jewish Girls allows contributors both to theorize the effects of their invisibility as Jews and lesbians and to render themselves visible in language. Contributors fight the argument, commonly used in the early 1980s to dismiss the existence of anti-Semitism, that invisibility (or being able to pass) is enabling. Beck asks, "Why is the possibility of 'passing' so insistently viewed as a great privilege open to Jews, and not understood as a terrible degradation and denial?" (xxvi). As she and other contributors foreground ways in which their ability to pass damages them, they use the anthology to mark themselves, to announce an identity that does not announce itself.[5] Thus, JEB puts together a photo essay of Jewish lesbians and entitles it "That's Funny, You Don't Look Like a Jewish Lesbian," and contributors throughout the anthology emphasize the role that naming themselves plays in the process of rendering themselves visible. Melanie Kaye/Kantrowitz concludes "Some Notes on Jewish Lesbian Identity" with the statement, "I want a button that says *Pushy Jew. Loud Pushy Jew. Loud Pushy Jew Dyke*" (48). For Kaye/Kantrowitz, language rather than skin color or hair or clothing style becomes the means of identifying herself, of manifesting and claiming Jewish and lesbian stereotypes. She appends the name "Kantrowitz" to her parents' name "Kaye" to disclose her family's history of assimilation and to record her resistance to this assimilation: "Kaye is both history and closet. history of a kind of closet. Kaye is Kantrowitz Kaminisky Keminetsky Kowalsky Klutz Korelowich Ka . . ." (39). Other contributors such as Elana Dykewomon and Chaya Shoshana also re-name themselves to make visible their Jewish and/or lesbian identity.

Nice Jewish Girls contributors also use the multi-genre form and the anthology's overall structure to reflect their engagement with and attempt to transform Jewish traditions. Beck links the multi-genre form of *Nice Jewish Girls* to the Jewish tradition of asking a variety of questions, and evokes the Passover Seder's tradition of question-asking in her introductory essay, "Why Is This Book Different from All Other

Books?" She opens this essay, "Why? I'll tell you why. According to Jewish Law, this book is written by people who do not exist" (xv). As she employs the traditional question-answer form of the Seder, she critiques and challenges the Jewish tradition it emerges from, acknowledging Judaism's erasure and denial of Jewish lesbians as she asserts their presence and place in this history. Other contributors engage with Jewish forms and language to establish their ties to Jewish culture, as well as to challenge this culture. The poems "Bashert" and "Kaddish" by Irena Klepfisz and Kaye/Kantrowitz draw on Jewish forms, and use Yiddish and Hebrew to argue for tolerance and acceptance of *all* people: "Let no faction keep me / from those who suffer," writes Klepfisz (110). The anthology takes part of its organizational structure from Rabbi Hillel, containing sections entitled "If I am not for myself who will be?" and "If I am only for myself what am I?" In reinscribing Jewish traditions and forms, Beck and the other contributors attempt to transform them by asserting and making a place for their lesbianism within them.

The anthology also serves Beck and the other contributors with a locus to evidence and further establish a Jewish lesbian community. Throughout the anthology, the twenty-three contributors emphasize the networks of friendships and the Jewish lesbian communities that sustain them and the anthology. Beck's extensive acknowledgments make clear her and the anthology's indebtedness to various Jewish lesbian groups and individuals, particularly the support/study group Di Vilde Chayes, which contributes significantly to the anthology. Chayes members Kaye/Kantrowitz, Klepfisz, Bernice Mennis, and Adrienne Rich include pieces in it, and Nancy K. Bereano is the editor who saw *Nice Jewish Girls* back into print. When Klepfisz discloses, "One reason I am willing now to write about the mixture of feelings that I have [towards Jewish people] is that I trust you [Beck] and trust the anthology" (114), she endows the anthology with a sense of intimacy and trust. Contributors describe the friendships they have developed through *Nice Jewish Girls,* and they also use the anthology as a means to extend and garner support for their Jewish lesbian community. Dovida Ishatova begins her piece in *Nice Jewish Girls* by asking, "So what's a nice Jewish girl like me doing in a book like this? Why, flaunting it, of course, and hoping maybe to meet some other nice Jewish girls" (202). The familiarity of her (Jewish) humor and idiom here underline her appeal to other Jewish lesbians.

Later editions of the anthology attest to its success in reaching other Jewish lesbians, recording the way in which it has served as an occasion for readings and other cultural events, and noting its favorable reviews in both Jewish and lesbian publications. Women in subsequent anthologies make clear its influence in inspiring like projects, and comment on the importance it holds for other Jewish lesbians. Klepfisz and Kaye/Kantrowitz, who go on to edit the 1986 Jewish women's anthology *The Tribe of Dina*, state in that book that their starting point was "an event that marked a starting point for many Jewish feminists, the publication . . . of . . . *Nice Jewish Girls: A Lesbian Anthology*" (9).

Tensions in *Nice Jewish Girls* do develop, however, between the anthology as an individual expression on the part of Beck and her friends and the anthology as representative of Jewish lesbians as a whole: the smallness and selectiveness of the community represented in the book raises questions about how well it speaks to the entire range of Jewish lesbians and how this might consequently limit its success in extending its community to them.[6] Because pieces by just four of the contributors (Beck, Klepfisz, Kaye/Kantrowitz, and Dykewomon) comprise eighteen of the anthology's thirty-nine pieces, the anthology establishes an "inside" group of contributors, and conveys a sense of hierarchy among contributors. The anthology's first section, "From One Generation to Another," consists solely of work by Beck and her daughter Nina Rachel, despite the various other essays in the anthology which address and enact relations between generations. Its opening essay, "Daughters and Mothers: Three Generations," details Beck's relationship to her mother and to her daughter. Beck professes this essay and the anthology's introductory essay to constitute "the very core of my autobiography" (12). Both the essay and the section as a whole oscillate between the presentation of Beck's own family history and a more general commentary on mothers and daughters. Furthermore, the anthology's focus on Yiddish and Eastern European Jewish experience (only two contributions are by Sephardic women) further narrows *Nice Jewish Girls*'s scope. For an anthology which Dykewomon predicts will be *"the 'source book' on judaism* [sic] *within the lesbian community for some time"* (176), the small pool of contributors in some ways serves to falsely anchor and unify Jewish lesbian experience.

Even given its selective and close community, however, *Nice Jewish Girls* contains within it divisions and exclusions that reveal the ways in which no community—no matter how small and specifically defined— can provide absolute belonging and support. In particular, the section entitled "Jewish Identity: A Coat of Many Colors" poses a challenge to the relative unity and homogeneity of the anthology's Jewish lesbian community. This section includes essays by Josylyn Segal, a Jewish woman of color; Rachel Wahba and Savina Teubal, Sephardic Jews; convert Chaya Shoshana; and Adrienne Rich, who has a Jewish father and a Southern gentile mother. The women in this section stand apart from the rest of the anthology's contributors, all of whom are white, Ashkenazi, and born to Judaism, and they call attention to their experiences of being excluded by other Jewish lesbians. Shoshana likens the experience of being a convert in Jewish lesbian circles to that of being a lesbian in Jewish circles. Other contributors' commentaries on conversion confirm Shoshana's outsider status, even within the *Nice Jewish Girls* community. For example, in "The Fourth Daughter's Four Hundred Questions," Dykewomon responds to a friend's conversion by asking, "What right have you to think you know, Wendy? What a jewish womon is? What right have you to voluntarily join the ranks of slaves when I have spent my whole life rolling in specific jewish anger and pain? What right have you, woman who has worked beside me, to choose to bind yourself to some prick and leave me here alone again? Using a memory that doesn't even belong to you, using my past to do it?" (182). Though Dykewomon directs some of her anger at the impetus for her friend's conversion (a man), she also clearly feels converts are wrongly appropriating her history, and thus indirectly excludes Shoshana from her community. In grouping Shoshana and the other contributors in this section together, Beck effectively marks, and even reinforces, their status as outsiders. However, in placing this section in the middle of the anthology, she asserts the centrality of the questions its contributors pose: the section thus destabilizes any assumption about what it means to be (or become) a Jew, and makes evident the exclusions and precariousness of even the most seemingly homogeneous identity-based communities.

As the anthology stages the difficulties of establishing a Jewish lesbian identity and community, it also struggles to make a place for lesbians in Jewish communities, to negotiate the tensions and contradictions lesbianism poses to these communities. Despite the fact that contributors explicitly address and reach out to the Jewish communities in which they grew up, these efforts exist alongside their admissions of a lack of communication with their families, particularly their mothers, or other members of the older generations. Many of the contributors concede that they are not yet "out" as lesbians to their families; Beck herself admits of her essay "Daughters and Mothers: Three Generations," "I have never shown it to my mother" (13). She and other contributors, including her daughter, Nina Rachel, express anxiety about their Jewishness, a distance from it, or a defensiveness concerning their right to be Jewish.

Their insecurities about their place in Judaism seem inevitable given the fact that, as Beck explains in the anthology's opening pages, in Jewish law, Jewish lesbians are "not proscribed because we don't exist. If we existed, believe me, they'd [the *rabbonim*] be against us" (xv). And as Marcia Freedman points out in "A Lesbian in the Promised Land," no Hebrew words even exist for "lesbian" and "feminist." If invisibility characterizes anti-Semitism in lesbian feminist circles, it likewise characterizes homophobia in Jewish religion and culture.

One strategy contributors adopt to assert their belonging to their Jewish communities is to present lesbianism as an extension of Jewish culture and a Jewish personality. The women in the anthology call themselves "nice Jewish girls" not simply out of irony, but also to appeal to and insist upon their place in their Jewish communities. Several contributors express the belief that Jewish women have a propensity towards lesbianism. In "What May Be *Tsores* to You Is *Naches* to Me," Dovida Ishatova begins a letter to parents: "Besides, Jewish girls make such nice lesbians. We're loud, we're boisterous, we know how to cuddle, we know how to squeeze" (202). Through statements such as this one, contributors evoke for their non-lesbian Jewish audience the similarities between the stereotypes for nice Jewish girls and Jewish lesbians. The use of Jewish humor, the emphasis on Yiddish as a specifically mother tongue and the frequency with which it is employed, as well as the many sections in *Nice Jewish Girls* focusing on family, all become the means by which contributors (re)assert their ties to and address their Jewish community. Contributors also take traditional definitions of Jewish women and claim them as particularly lesbian. In "Resisting and Surviving America," for example, Klepfisz reappropriates the traditional role ascribed to Jewish women—ensuring Jewish survival—by broadening it to include activities other than motherhood: "It is lesbians like the ones I've just named who are actively helping guarantee Jewish survival, just as much as the Jewish women who bear Jewish children—perhaps even more" (123).

As the vehemence of Klepfisz's remark might suggest, contributors' difficulties integrating Judaism and lesbianism also surface in conjunction with the topic of motherhood. Despite the fact that many women in *Nice Jewish Girls* actually *are* mothers, they seem unable to portray their motherhood and their lesbianism as coextensive. In part, this may be because the mothers in *Nice Jewish Girls* defined themselves as lesbians after having their children; thus their motherhood emerges out of their previous, heterosexual, existence. As lesbians, they portray themselves almost exclusively as daughters (hence the *Girls* of the title). The language Beck and Adrienne Rich (both mothers) use to describe their coming out as lesbians is striking. Rich claims, "The suppressed lesbian I had been carrying in me since adolescence began to stretch her limbs and her first full-fledged act was to fall in love with a Jewish woman" (89). Beck also speaks of her lesbian self as a daughter she gives birth to: "As for me, in coming out I finally gave birth to the woman I had been carrying for decades. She has learned to love herself as she has allowed herself to love and be loved by another woman" (11). Both Rich and Beck portray their lesbian selves as rebellious daughters oddly separate from the (maternal) "I." Especially for Beck, who literally has given birth to a lesbian daughter, her language aligns her self with her daughter, who had to do battle with her mother, Beck, to assert her lesbianism (at the time, Beck was married and identified herself as heterosexual). Contributors' feelings of separateness, as lesbians, from motherhood, gives evidence to the tensions and rifts they experience in maintaining their identities as lesbian and Jewish.

While at times the anthology explicitly thematizes the uneasiness of contributors' relationship to Judaism, in many ways it reveals or explores this relationship only obliquely. Contributors frequently evade the question of how fully Jewish religion and culture can accommodate lesbians, and fail to take on ways in which their two allegiances pose contradictions. While insisting on their own inclusion into and revision of Judaism, contributors do not engage with many of the theoretical and theological problems they face. What, for example, is their relationship to Jewish men? Where does God fit into their Judaism? Is there a God? If so, what/who is this God? If not, where do they draw the line between Judaism as a culture and Judaism as a religion?[7]

In *Nice Jewish Girls*, the subject of Israel also presents crucial contradictions between contributors' lesbianism and their Judaism, contradictions they sometimes evade. Israel functions in the anthology alternatively as a promised land or a homeland (as it does for Shelley Horwitz), and as what Beck calls "a patriarchy and theocracy hostile to women and lesbians" (222). Israeli law prohibits male homosexuality, for example, and it fails even to recognize the existence of lesbianism. How Jewish lesbians negotiate between the two versions of Israel remains unclear in this anthology, even as its contributors address many other questions and problems regarding Jewish identity. Marcia Freedman, in "A Lesbian in a Promised Land," does address some of the contradictions Israel poses, but for the most part Israel poses irreconcilable contradictions that are left unarticulated.

The anthology also either avoids controversial issues Jewish lesbians face in their relationships with other oppressed groups, or else presents careful positions on them. Throughout *Nice Jewish Girls,* the relationship between anti-Semitism and racism is at once repeatedly asserted and gingerly sidestepped. "Oppression is never less oppressive simply because it takes a different form. Success has never protected Jews from anti-Semitism" (xxiv), states Beck, maintaining a simple equation between oppressions despite her acknowledgment that these may take different forms. The anthology focuses on establishing the truth of Beck's equation without considering ways in which different forms of anti-Semitism and racism complicate it. Contributors repeatedly position Jewishness against whiteness. Kaye/Kantrowitz, in "Some Notes on Jewish Lesbian Identity," says she's always aware of her lesbian identity. "But the rise of Klan activity, Reagan and his white-on-white cabinet, synagogues bombed in France, have me in a sweat" (34). Dykewoman, in "The Fourth Daughter's Four Hundred Questions," asserts, "It is a dangerous business in a dangerous time, working for lesbians and affirming any racial heritage in white america" (176). And Rachel, in her poem "On Passing: From One Generation to Another," equates passing with whiteness and defines herself against it: "Living in anger I would never try to pass, / never learn all the ways of / white" (14). In equating racism and anti-Semitism, contributors counter the dismissal of anti-Semitism by both women of color and white women—gentile and Jewish—and they accept and turn to their own advantage the anti-Semitic belief that Jews constitute a race, and one that is threatening to whites.[8] Yet to adopt this position so unequivocally avoids the complexities of the relationships among anti-Semitism and racism, not to mention those raised by racism in general.

Contributors' general avoidance of these complexities allows them to maintain a clear and stable position as oppressed, anchoring both their Jewish and lesbian identities. Indeed, in the third edition, when Klepfisz does take on the oppressive roles played by Israelis and American Jews in regard to Palestinians, her very identity as a Jew comes unmoored: "Israel's invasion of Lebanon changed everything. . . . How were Jewish lesbians to express pride in their Jewishness when Israel was invading another country, killing another people?" (263). A few days later, when she heard that the Glens Falls synagogue's walls were painted over with swastikas, she found that her "Jewishness felt familiar again" (264). As lesbians and as feminists unwilling to endorse the patriarchal elements and underpinnings of Jewish religion and culture, the women in *Nice Jewish Girls* become particularly dependent upon Jews' oppressed status for their own definition as Jews and for their unity with other Jews.

Essays by *Nice Jewish Girls* contributors in the 1986 *The Tribe of Dina* and the 1989 additions to *Nice Jewish Girls* reflect a different moment in the Jewish lesbian movement (and in feminist movements in general). In these later pieces, the same contributors are much more willing to probe the differences between anti-Semitism and racism, and have shifted their focus from assertions of sameness to alliance-building.[9] This shift follows increased foregrounding of anti-Semitism by other writers as well as those included in *Nice Jewish Girls,* in their reactions to the revival in Klan and other anti-Semitic activity and to changes in Israeli policy and actions (in particular, the invasion of Lebanon and the Intifada). These occurrences dictated a more considered working out of the relationship between Jewish women and women of color.

In fact, the carefulness and "correctness" of the two additions to the Israel section in the 1989 edition of *Nice Jewish Girls,* both by Klepfisz, suggest the anxiety and sensitivity on the part of Beck/the anthology when it comes to relations between Jewish women and women of color. By 1989, the subject of Israel had become particularly explosive and threatening. It was as the issue over which alliances between women of color and Jewish women were most likely to break down, the issue over which the two groups did not come together as oppressed, but, often, in opposition. In the first edition of *Nice Jewish Girls* contributors are perhaps too quick to equate racism and anti-Semitism. In the third edition, in her care to establish alliances between white Jewish women and women of color, Beck—in including only Klepfisz's position—misses the chance to take on more fully an issue that provides the greatest difficulties, but also the greatest possibility for constructive work between the two groups.

While the women in *Nice Jewish Girls* go only so far in questioning their position and definition as "Jewish," they do not question their lesbian identity at all. Put forth by contributors as the untroubled half of the "Jewish lesbian" equation, lesbian identity in *Nice Jewish Girls* is not probed or questioned as much as it is asserted. The lesbian identities of the contributors remain fairly homogeneous. As Rachel says of Beck in their 1989 mother-daughter dialogue, "I used to get annoyed when you said, 'A lesbian wouldn't do *that,'* to whatever was not in your experience." (26). Rachel sees lesbians as being a more diverse group, but this narrowness of definition she calls attention to holds true for Beck's anthology. For the women in *Nice Jewish Girls,* their lesbianism appears to be more of a theoretical concern than a sexual or material one: it emerges out of, and is irrevocably connected to, their feminism, so much so that, through the course of the anthology, lesbianism and feminism appear to be interchangeable, and lesbianism unequivocally signifies resistance to patriarchal structures. Thus Beck says of Rachel, "That she is a lesbian comforts me. Whatever her struggles, I don't worry she will give her power away to the patriarchy" (9).

Contributors' silence around issues of sexuality helps to maintain the anthology's ideologically rooted and unified presentation of lesbianism. Their silence also contributes to their status as "nice Jewish girls": if nice Jewish girls have sex, they certainly do not talk about it, and the women in the anthology provide no exception. In *Nice Jewish Girls,* lesbian sexuality is largely occluded, present only insofar as contributors refer to relationships which are invariably represented as stable and long-standing ones. The anthology contains no mention of aspects of lesbian sexuality, such as S/M or butch-femme role-playing, that might cause controversy.

Contributors to *Nice Jewish Girls* leave issues of lesbian definition unquestioned; to open up such questioning in conjunction with their probing of Jewish identity and the questions their lesbianism poses to their Judaism might prove too destabilizing to the identity upon which they constitute themselves, their community, and their politics. In combining its strong lesbian base with its willingness to open up questions about Jewish identity, *Nice Jewish Girls* is able to provide Jewish lesbians with a community from which they may find support and from which they may struggle against anti-Semitism and homophobia. It also sets the stage for interrogating and recognizing the limits of the bases upon which such a community founds itself.

When There's No Place Like Home

Barbara Smith concludes her 1977 essay "Towards a Black Feminist Criticism" with: "I want most of all for Black women and Black lesbians somehow not to be so alone. . . . I finally want to express how much easier both my waking and my sleeping hours would be if there were one book in existence that would tell me something specific about my life. One book based in Black feminist and Black lesbian experience, fiction or non-fiction."[10] Two years later, Smith began to realize these desires for herself and other black women when she and Lorraine Bethel edited a special edition of the lesbian feminist journal *Conditions.* In *Conditions: Five, The Black Women's Issue,* she and Bethel explain that in putting together the edition they "tried to maintain a consciousness of the way that traditional white/male literary standards have been used oppressively against Black/female writers, and worked to set these standards aside as much as possible. We realize that Black women's writing is generally grounded in a tradition of oral expression, and tried to establish artistic guidelines appropriate to the aesthetic criteria intrinsic to Afro-American culture."[11] In editing *Home Girls*, an anthology which emerges out of, and takes nearly half its pieces from the *Conditions* volume, Smith continues with this project and makes the work of black lesbian feminists available in more durable form. *Home Girls* can also be seen as a companion piece for *All the Women Are White, All the Men Are Black, But Some of Us Are Brave: Black Women's Studies*, edited in 1983 by Smith, Gloria T. Hull, and Patricia Bell Scott. This collection addresses the lack of attention "given to the distinct experiences of Black women in the education provided in our colleges and universities"[12] and calls for and suggests ways to implement the study of "ordinary Black women." In editing *Home Girls*, Smith provides teachers of black women's studies with a valuable tool, and also provides black working-class lesbian feminists outside the university with a book meant to speak to their experiences.

Like *Conditions: Five*, *Home Girls* uses a multi-genre format to work against what Smith and Bethel call "traditional white/male literary standards." By including transcribed conversations, journal entries, song lyrics, letters, and prose poems, genres which are relatively accessible to women with limited time, money, or formal education, Smith clearly intends to make writing and publishing more accessible to other "home girls." Other contributors share Smith's aim. In detailing how she came to publish "The Wedding," a collection of journal entries, Beverly Smith expresses the hope that "after reading this other women, especially Black women, will be enspirited to tell their own essential stories."[13] In addition to inspiring other (black) women to write, the anthology works to define and represent an African American lesbian/feminist literary tradition, both through its large number of short stories and poems, and also through the section entitled "Artists without Art Form," which consists of essays about black lesbians in literature (and which, through its title, puts Toni Morrison's *Sula* at the center of this tradition). At the same time that *Home Girls* reaches out to other "home girls," it challenges and provides an alternative to white/male literary standards.

Home Girls also challenges the boundaries of what constitutes literary criticism by mixing the creative and the critical, the non-academic and the academic. In her introduction, Smith issues the challenge "for women of color to take themselves seriously as writers" (1), and in the anthology, she includes pieces which reflect black women's engagement and experimentation with traditional literary forms. Michelle Cliff's "If I Could Write This in Fire I Would Write This in Fire," an essay consisting of fragments, notes, and memories, resists classification, as does Smith's own introduction, which mixes together song lyrics, myth, autobiography, history, theory, and personal narrative. She places Patricia Jones's prose poem "I've Been Thinking of Diana Sands" in "Artists without Art Form," a section otherwise consisting of fairly standard literary criticism.[14] Essays by Hull frame this section and adopt white/male literary standards but apply them to African American lesbian writing. Hull, for example, celebrates Angelina Weld Grimké's "precision and subtlety," though she critiques most of Grimké's poetry for being "fragmentary and unpolished" (79), attributing Grimké's failures to the oppression she experienced as black, female, and lesbian. Thus, although the anthology in many ways works against white/male literary standards and traditions, in other ways it evaluates black lesbian writing in accordance with them.

Presenting an oral tradition in a written form presents similar contradictions in *Home Girls*. Even more than she and Bethel did in *Conditions: Five*, Smith in *Home Girls* incorporates works that emphasize and continue the oral traditions of African American culture. Donna Kate Rushin's poem, "The Black Back-Ups" not only pays tribute to black women singers, but also depends for its effects upon verbal play. Other contributors incorporate blues and other song lyrics into their essays to support their points. Smith includes two speeches and two transcribed conversations between herself and other contributors, and the anthology's epigraph consists of an excerpt from a conversation between herself and Beverly Smith.[15] Thus, an oral tradition pervades the anthology and is integrated into its variety of written forms.

However, to convey an oral tradition in written form presents Smith and the anthology's contributors with certain difficulties. In a preface to "The Blood—Yes, the Blood: A Conversation," Smith acknowledges the inadequacies of conveying her dialogue with Cenen in written form, saying of laughter in particular, "this is undoubtedly the non-verbal element I most wish it were possible to recreate. It seemed like such an integral part of what we were saying, because so often it was the laughter of recognition" (31). Smith attempts partially to redress this loss by parenthetically indicating places punctuated by laughter, but the written form clearly flattens the dynamics of their conversation. In her introduction to "Women's Spirituality: A Household Act," Luisah Teish, informing her readers that she initially delivered her article orally, announces that "spontaneous explanations and anecdotes which helped the flow of it are unavailable to you" (333). Both in pointing to the limitations of written forms, and in attempting to convey the richness of oral expression, *Home Girls* privileges an African American oral tradition over what Smith (and Bethel) call a "traditional white/male" one. At the same time, constricted by its written form, *Home Girls* cannot invest itself fully in this tradition and thus records the loss of this tradition as well as its presence in African American writing. In this way, *Home Girls* is infused with a sense of longing and nostalgia.

In *Home Girls,* contributors also look to the past, to an African American/female folk tradition, in their efforts to promote other ways of knowing that counter traditional white/male ways of knowing. In "Women's Spirituality," Teish informs the reader, "In this paper you will find information that is contrary to the opinions of 'scholarly authorities,'" and she explains that she received help with her work on voodoo from "a spirit who identified herself as Mary Anne" (333). Alice Walker's "Only Justice Can Stop a Curse" follows Teish's essay. Like Teish, Walker looks to the power of African American female ancestors for help, invoking an ancient curse collected by Zora Neale Hurston to combat contemporary evils. By way of these concluding essays, the anthology challenges "scholarly authorities" with alternative (African female) sciences and history, and attempts to show their ongoing vitality. However, although these essays achieve prominence because of their positioning, their folk vision does not inform the majority of essays in the anthology, which come mainly from women living in New York City or other large East Coast cities. As do the oral elements in *Home Girls,* these folk elements provide glimpses into a past that remains largely inaccessible to most of the contributors.

Many of the pieces in *Home Girls* focus not on a folk past, but on the contemporary material realities and physical as well as emotional struggles of working-class African American women's lives. What these pieces do share with essays by Teish and Walker is the attempt to embody what traditional white/male literature and scholarship so often omit. The first section, entitled "The Blood—Yes, the Blood," and the section "Who Will Fight for Our Lives But Us?" evoke not only the ways in which contributors' skin color defines them, but also the fact that their struggles are visceral and life-threatening. Pieces in these sections describe black women's struggles against male violence, black and white, and their economic and material hardships as well. The anthology also contains several pieces of writing that are richly erotic and detail sexual relations between black lesbians. Audre Lorde's "Tar Beach," for example, is full of passages such as, *"There were ripe red finger ba-*

nanas, stubby and sweet, with which I parted your lips gently, to insert the peeled fruit into your grape-purple flower" (154). In contrast to *Nice Jewish Girls, Home Girls* contributors, from their positions outside the academy, construct for their readers aspects of their lives that the academy leaves out. Rather than denying stereotypes of black women, so often represented in white, middle-class scholarship as objectified bodies existing solely in the realm of the physical, contributors, in presenting the emotional and spiritual richness of black women's physical lives with one another, claim and celebrate their bodies and their sexuality.

As this erotically charged black lesbian literature in *Home Girls* defies traditional white/males standards for writing, it also challenges the sexism and homophobia of writing that emerged out of the Black Power movement of the 1960s and 1970s. The nationalist leaders during this period, as Joyce Hope Scott notes, "uniformly espoused a rhetoric of female subordination and role assignment based on traditional biological function."[16] As Stokely Carmichael so infamously but aptly summarized the prevailing ideology. "The only position for the woman in the revolution is prone,"[17] and this prone position was a relentlessly heterosexual one; homosexuality was viewed as an act of cultural betrayal, decadence, perversion, and weakness. The Black Arts movement, led by artists including Larry Neal and Amiri Baraka, clearly articulated the sexism and homophobia of the Black Power movement, along with a sense of the militancy and violence, and the excitement and energy, that more generally characterize the Civil Rights era. As a women-centered anthology charged with a lesbian erotics, *Home Girls* puts forth an aesthetics and politics that counter those of the Black Arts movement, as it offers a haven to its contributors and black lesbian readers.

In *Home Girls,* contributors reveal their openness and the trust that they place in each other and in their audience. The relations the anthology enacts between contributors emphasize a close community of friends who are also writers and activists. Unlike in *Conditions: Five,* which she and Bethel gathered through a wide call for submissions, in gathering the twenty-two new pieces for *Home Girls* Smith solicited specific articles or asked specific writers to submit work. As Beck does in *Nice Jewish Girls,* Smith draws on her circle of friends to put together *Home Girls,* and the anthology also highlights contributors' interactions. Contributors continually refer to each other, and "talk" to each other in their biographies. The transcribed conversations are marked by patterns of constant reinforcement, affirmation, and encouragement. Smith also creates community in *Home Girls* by arranging the pieces in such a way as to create conversations intertextually. For example, Deidre McCalla's lyrics "Billy de Lye" respond to and provide a solution for Shirley O. Steele's story "Shoes Are Made for Walking": in the first piece, a woman is killed by her husband; in the second, the woman fights back against the man who will otherwise kill her. Because *Home Girls* contains so many more contributors, and because it includes no more than a few pieces by any one contributor, its community appears to be more wide-ranging than that of *Nice Jewish Girls*.

Whereas the writers in *Nice Jewish Girls* often must negotiate between their Judaism and their lesbianism, contributors to *Home Girls* present their black working-class feminist/lesbian identity as a seamless whole. In establishing the continuity between lesbian feminism and black working-class existence, Smith and the contributors point to their fore-mothers who worked and fought for their freedom, and to the contemporary prevalence of female-headed households. Throughout, *Home Girls* welds together definitions of feminism and lesbianism. The anthology's full title reads "Home Girls: A Black *Feminist* Anthology," yet nearly all of the contributors write from an explicitly *lesbian* perspective and/or identify themselves as lesbian in their biographies. Thus, despite Smith's claim in the introduction that "Black feminism and Black Lesbianism are not interchangeable" (xxx), in the course of the anthology, as in Smith's 1977 essay, "Towards a Black Feminist Criticism," black lesbianism and black feminism are presented as synonymous. Thus Smith places lesbianism at the very center of feminism, and in so doing makes a home for black lesbians within black feminist communities—and, at the same time, moves heterosexual feminists to the margins. The strategy here is in part a response to the ways in which black feminist communities and earlier black women's anthologies such as Toni Cade's *The Black Woman* (1970) and Mary Helen Washington's *Black-Eyed Susans* (1975) and *Midnight Birds* (1980) have marginalized lesbians.

Smith also puts lesbian feminism at the center of black families and communities. As Beck does with the term "nice Jewish girls," Smith, by calling herself and other contributors "home girls," (re)claims the connection to the home communities, and (re)establishes a belonging to these communities. The epigraph to *Home Girls*, from "A Sister to Sister Dialogue" between Beverly and Barbara Smith, establishes a continuum between the contributors' lesbian feminist community and their home communities at the outset of *Home Girls*. The section entitled "A Home Girls' Album" consists of pictures of various contributors with their (biological) family members. By presenting these various pictures as part of one family album, *Home Girls* makes black home life constitutive of black lesbian feminist community, thus reinforcing Smith's claim in the introduction "that Black feminism is, on every level, organic to Black experience" (xxiii). Smith uses *The Color Purple* to "corroborate the rootedness of Black lesbianism in 'core' Black experience" (1), and contributors dramatize this rootedness in their poems and stories. The title of Alexis De Veaux's "The Sisters" refers to the lovers Selina and Ntabuu. And in Toi Derricotte's poem to her godchild Regina, though their relationship is not sexual, it is richly erotic and physical as well as spiritual: "we smear blood over our thick / red lips / we smear blood under our heavy breasts / it is our baptism, our commitment / to each other's souls" (3). Sexual relations between women are portrayed as a natural extension of their family ties. Contributors claim not the margins but the center for lesbians in black families, and they celebrate this centrality.[18]

In contrast to the *Nice Jewish Girls* contributors, many of whom exhibit feelings of separateness from older (female) relatives, the women in *Home Girls* look to their older female relatives, especially to their mothers, to establish their connectedness to their home communities and families. Their constant references to their mothers—biological and literary—support Smith's claim in the introduction that "the origins of contemporary Black feminism [are] in the lives of our mothers" (1). Smith herself counters contemporary myths that work to oppress black women, contending, "History verifies that Black women have rejected doormat status, whether racially or sexually imposed, for centuries" (xxiii), and she draws upon African American women's resistance to slavery and their organizing around women's issues in the nineteenth century to evidence this history. Other contributors, too, find sources of strength in women from previous eras. Hull claims Angelina Weld Grimké as a literary foremother. Teish calls the book she is writing "a tribute to my foremothers" (331). Eleanor Johnson concludes "Reflections on Black Feminist Therapy" with, "We seek our grandmothers' strengths, our great-grandmothers' strategies—We find our sources. We discover/recover ourselves" (324). In turning to the past, to their foremothers, contributors at once establish role models and find their own reflections.

Smith and other contributors' recreation of an African American history and the connections they claim to this history work to refute the tenets of the black nationalism of the past two decades, and to dismiss homophobia and sexism as aberrations from a women-centered African American history. In "The Failure to Transform: Homophobia in the Black Community," Cheryl Clarke links the sexism and homophobia of black nationalist leaders to the prevalence of these views in

American culture, giving as an example the 1965 Moynihan report, *The Negro Family: A Case for National Action*. She opposes such views to those traditionaliy found in the poor and working-class black community, which she believes is "historically more radical and realistic than the reformist and conservative black middle class and the atavistic, 'blacker-than-thou' (bourgeois) nationalists" (206), and more accepting of homosexuality,[19] and her short story in *Home Girls* serves to support these claims. In "Women of Summer," a revolutionary lesbian couple receives protection from an 80-year-old rural woman who puts away her shotgun as she admits them into her house. Other stories further establish a line of connection between young black lesbian feminists and women from older generations. As Smith explains, "Unlike some white feminists who have questioned, and at times rightfully rejected, the white patriarchal family, we want very much to retain our blood connections without sacrificing ourselves to rigid and demeaning sex roles. Home has always meant a lot to people who are ostracized as racial outsiders in the public sphere. It is above all a place to be ourselves. Being ourselves, being home girls, is, of course, what *Home Girls* is about" (li).

And yet, these portrayals of home as a place where black lesbians can "be themselves" run counter to contributors' accounts of homophobia and misogyny in their home communities, and depend upon a denial or repression of these accounts. Throughout *Home Girls*, narratives and poems contain moments of violence that women experience in relation to men in their working-class communities. In her introduction, Smith herself details the violence done to her in her neighborhood by black men and boys. In "Before I Dress and Soar Again," Donna Allegra asks lesbian mothers with sons, "Why have you shown him the way / to pull at the wings / and stop the wide stroke / of your lesbian angel / courage?" (167). Raymina Y. Mays's story, "LeRoy's Birthday," which follows the poem and dramatizes a son turning away from his lesbian mother, in effect responds to Allegra's poem by suggesting that the father and a homophobic community, not the mother herself, are responsible for this antagonism. Time and again, the older men in the families are represented as exhibiting and inculcating in their children a hatred of women/lesbians. Because these male family members so often have left home, women-centered households can be portrayed as safe and nurturing, and contributors can maintain a continuum between their lesbianism and/or feminism and their home communities. Yet to focus on the safety and nurture of home is to idealize and falsely insulate the home space, and to deny or repress its vulnerability, as well as men's place in and access to it.

Black women, too, pose real problems to this idealized view. In attributing homophobia almost exclusively to the black community's male members, contributors often deny the homophobia that exists among women. In addition, at times the perfect relations between women family members are predicated on loss or absence, as is the case in Barbara Smith's essay "Home," in which Smith expresses a longing for the older female members of her family and details her former closeness to them. Yet they died before Smith came out as a lesbian, and thus her closeness to them is in part, as Smith herself acknowledges, a product of nostalgia. Only rarely in *Home Girls* are black women held accountable for homophobia.[20] When contributors do confront differences between black women, they primarily focus on issues of colorism rather than homophobia. (e.g., Michelle Cliff's "If I Could Write This in Fire" details colorism in Jamaica, and Cenen, in "The Blood—Yes the Blood: A Conversation," talks about colorism in Puerto Rico.) Not only are the divisions among black women resulting from colorism attributed specifically to white imperialism, but they are represented as taking place elsewhere, outside the continental United States. Only Spring Redd, in "Something Latino Was Up with Us," discusses feeling at home in neither her African American nor her Puerto Rican community.

The anthology particularly idealizes relations between black lesbians: any divisions that occur between black women occur between black women in general, rather than between lesbians or feminists. Differences between lesbians, when they are represented, are ultimately rendered in a positive light. Though Michelle Clinton's poem "Debra" begins with an assertion of differences between the speaker and her lover, the speaker comes to celebrate these differences, saying, "And what ever explosions come between us are *of* us" (14). Both the fiction in *Home Girls* and the essays which analyze representations of black lesbians in literature present such consistently positive representations.[21] Finally, it seems, to explore differences or rifts between black lesbians poses too great a threat to the *Home Girls* community. Threatened from every direction possible, the anthology's contributors need, unsurprisingly, to assert a home, a safe space. And yet, as Lorde says in *Sister Outsider*, "Often we give lip service to the idea of mutual support and connection between Black women because we have not yet crossed the boundaries to these possibilities, nor fully explored the angers and fears that keep us from realizing the power of a real Black sisterhood. . . . We cannot continue to evade each other on the deepest levels because we fear each other's angers, nor continue to believe that respect means never looking directly nor with openness into another Black woman's eyes."[22]

In addition to idealizing relationships among black lesbians, another way in which contributors in *Home Girls* avoid looking directly into each other's eyes is by leaving definitions of what constitutes blackness, lesbianism, or feminism unquestioned. Contributors essentialize these terms, and present them as unambiguous and knowable. Whereas in *Nice Jewish Girls* contributors question and complicate definitions of Judaism (even as they unify around a stable definition of lesbianism), the *Home Girls* contributors fix, and connect, all the terms of their identity. Throughout the anthology they adopt the capitalized forms of "Black" and "Lesbian" and make absolutes of them. As for their working-class identity, contributors scarcely discuss it at all. Because it is present as an unspoken base they share, they can avoid the slipperiness and complexities of defining their working-class identities.[23] Leaving the terms of a "home girl" identity unquestioned gives the contributors a clear and specific identity to rally around, but it also prevents them from probing their differences, and from acknowledging and exploring the fluidity of these identities. The seeming fixity and clarity of these categories of identity may also alienate women who feel less certain or differently about how to categorize themselves in terms of race, sexual orientation, or class. And the untroubled definition of "home girl" in the anthology as a woman who is black, working-class, and lesbian creates a chasm between the women in the anthology and those women who may share, say, two out of three of these identities.

While *Home Girls* does not interrogate the politics of identity upon which it is constructed, it does assert the inadequacy of identity politics as a stopping point, and the need to move beyond the sense of home the anthology concentrates on establishing. In the introduction, Smith, stating the need for autonomy rather than separatism, expresses the necessity of, and her commitment to, forging coalitions with an international black population, women of color, and Jewish feminists. *Conditions: Five* also evidences Smith's concern with coalitional work, as it suggests the dangers that can attend it. This issue includes Judy Simmons' "Minority," a poem in which Simmons states, "mine is not a People of the Book / taxed / but acknowledged; their distinctiveness is / not yet a dignity; their Holocaust is lower case" (93). An "Editor's note" by Smith and Bethel is appended to the poem that attests to "a difficult process in deciding to publish 'Minority' because of the way in which it raises issues about political and personal relationships between Black and Jewish people" (94). Smith and Bethel explain their decision to publish the poem, made in consultation with the ongoing editors of *Conditions: Five*, who include Klepfisz and Elly Bulkin, by expressing their hope that the poem will "encourage dialogue between Black and Jewish women" (94). This poem, however, provoked not a dialogue, but rather a response of anger and charges of *Conditions: Five*'s anti-Semitism from Beck in *Nice Jewish Girls*. Noticeably omitted from *Home Girls*, its absence reflects both Smith's concern not to alienate Jewish women, and her decision to keep her focus in this anthology more strictly on "home girls" and their relations.

The last essay in *Home Girls* challenges the narrowness of its focus. In "Coalition Politics: Turning the Century," Bernice Johnson Reagon argues the need to go beyond the home the anthology provides its contributors and other home girls. Stating, "There is nowhere you can go and only be with people who are like you. It's over. Give it up" (357), Reagon urges the necessity of coalition work, despite the fact that "it is some of the most dangerous work you can do. And you shouldn't look for comfort" (359). As a survival strategy, she encourages women to move back and forth between coalitions, which are crucial to effecting change, and their home communities, which provide sustenance. Initially a speech delivered at a 1981 women's music festival, Reagon's essay in its *Home Girls* context is applied to black lesbian feminists in particular. In its conclusion, then, *Home Girls* offers the readers no closure, no resting point, but instead challenges the very premises upon which the anthology rests.

Home Girls builds for its contributors (and other black lesbians) such a firm base and strong sense of identity that coalition work becomes less threatening, as contributors both have a home to retreat to, and a sense that work with other groups will not threaten the boundaries of their identities. In predicating this home upon an unquestioned definition of black lesbianism that is in some ways reductive and essentializing, and upon a nostalgic version of the past and an idealization of present realities, *Home Girls* shows not only the limits, but also the political possibilities, of essentialism and nostalgia.[24]

Between Home and Coalition

Feminists' concern with home continues through the 1980s and into the present decade. However, rather than celebrating home, many feminists have come to insist on the need to resist home, to work from multiple sites of displacement. Going further than those women in *Nice Jewish Girls* who challenge the sturdiness of the identity politics upon which the anthology is predicated, feminists today more commonly refute the concept of home altogether. Teresa de Lauretis, to cite one example, works from a position of "displacement—that dis-identification with a group, a family, a self, a 'home,' even a feminism," stating, "I believe that such an eccentric point of view or discursive position is necessary for feminist theory at this time."[25] Though she labels this eccentric position lesbian, this lesbian position provides no sense of refuge or home with other lesbians. In "Identity: Skin Blood Heart," Minnie Bruce Pratt's lesbianism propels her into an awareness of the way in which no community or home offers complete acceptance or belonging, and she comes to insist upon a continual interrogation of how one's home is always contingent, never complete. In these essays, by exposing and resisting the blindness, the illusions, and the exclusions that attend concepts of home, de Lauretis and Pratt seem to have moved beyond the binary that Reagon and other *Home Girls* contributors establish between home and coalition.

While I, too, think that home and coalition form a false dichotomy, I believe that exclusively emphasizing the impossibility and reactionary attributes of home, if done from a position of privilege, can be akin to white educated European males claiming the death of the author at a moment when white women and people of color are coming into their own as authors. When de Lauretis advocates the abdication of home, and maps it as a primarily psychic, conceptual, or discursive site, she elides the costs of homelessness, or the privilege of being in a position to choose this option. I am interested instead in unsettling the distinctions between a home and a coalition. This interests me not only because I believe that no home offers complete safety and belonging, but also because positing such a distinction makes too absolute the boundaries between self and other, between one set of identifications and another. I would like to hold out the hope that from the multiple strands that constitute our identities, just as there is no home that is absolute, there are few coalitions that do not, with enough work, offer some of the possibilities and comforts of home.[26]

In her essay "Home," Barbara Smith leaves the race/ethnicity of Leila, the lover with whom she shares her home, indeterminate. This indeterminacy opens the door to the possibility that a home may admit (racial) difference, that it may (in *Home Girls*'s terms) share elements with a coalition. As it stands, the essay "Home" has found a home in multiple locations: in addition to *Home Girls*, it has been published in the lesbian journal *Conditions: Eight*, and in *Calling Home*, a multi-genre anthology of working-class women of all races and sexual orientations. In these various publications, "Home" both does coalition work—bringing Smith into alliances with women from various groups—and makes a home, a place of belonging, for Smith within these groups.

Other contributors to *Nice Jewish Girls* as well as to *Home Girls* do similar work in unfixing the boundaries between home and coalition (as well as those between white Jewish and black lesbians). For example, Klepfisz, a key contributor to *Nice Jewish Girls* who goes on to edit the Jewish feminist anthology *Tribe of Dina*, also edits *Conditions*, the journal in which Smith's "Home" initially appeared. And, as she discusses in *The Tribe of Dina*, in her readings with *This Bridge Called My Back* and *Making Face, Making Soul/Haciendo Caras* editor Gloria Anzaldúa, she and Anzaldúa affirm their shared lesbianism and explore their respective forms of bilingualism. The interrelations among anthologies and their contributors thus offer models for challenging the concepts of home and coalition from which they derive their political purpose.

4

The Making and Unmaking of Asian American Identity

Making Waves and The Forbidden Stitch

The term [Asian American] is inherently elastic and of fairly recent currency. . . . It carries within it layers of historical sedimentation. Not merely a denotative label with a fixed, extralinguistic referent, it is a sign, a site of contestation for a multitude of political and cultural forces. It is the semiotic status of the term Asian American that shapes our understanding of what kind of discourse Asian American literature is, and in turn, what kind of practice Asian American criticism is.

—Sau-ling Cynthia Wong, Reading Asian American Literature, p. 5

In 1989, three landmark publications in Asian American studies made their appearance: Making Waves: An Anthology of Writing by and about Asian American Women, edited by Asian Women United of California (AWU), The Forbidden Stitch: An Asian American Women's Anthology, edited by Shirley Geok-lin Lim, Mayumi Tsutakawa, and the Calyx Collective, and Ronald Takaki's Strangers from a Different Shore.[1] Compared to the accolades—and controversy—that have attended the publication of Takaki's history, Making Waves and The Forbidden Stitch have met with considerably less attention. This relative lack of attention strikes me as symptomatic not only of the privileging in the academy of single-authored works over communally produced ones, but also of the marginalization of feminist issues in Asian American studies, despite the quality and amount of women-centered work.[2] In this chapter, I give sustained attention to Making Waves and The Forbidden Stitch not only to advance my argument for the important work anthologies do in shaping communal histories and identities, but also because these anthologies—

marked as they are by pronounced differences from one another—provide insights into the range of Asian American women's deployments of identity politics at the close of the 1980s. As these anthologies challenge and provide alternatives to some of the exclusions that attend "one-man" histories such as Takaki's, they also speak to the difficulty of encompassing the full range of Asian American (women's) voices, and of establishing a women-centered history that goes beyond the compensatory.

Published within six months of each other (*The Forbidden Stitch* appeared first), but without reference to each other, both *Making Waves* and *The Forbidden Stitch* claim to be the first anthologies by and about Asian American women since the early 1970s.[3] They are also the first anthologies to negotiate the recent challenges to conceptualizations of "Asian American" as either a political or descriptive identity.[4] The 1965 change in immigration law and the wars in Southeast Asia resulted in the radical growth and shift in population among peoples of Asian origin in the United States.[5] In "Denationalization Reconsidered," Sau-ling Cynthia Wong usefully employs the term "denationalization" to describe the dramatic changes that those in the field of Asian American studies confront due in large part to these demographic shifts.[6] The most important transformations for which she uses this term include the easing of cultural nationalist concerns, the increasing permeability in boundaries between Asian Americans and "Asian Asians," and the turn from a domestic to a diasporic perspective. In often opposing ways, both *Making Waves* and *The Forbidden Stitch* are centrally concerned with these developments, and provide often opposing responses to them.

As these anthologies respond to the movement towards denationalization and also address concerns particular to women, they participate in the reconfiguration of Asian American identity, and Asian American studies. In particular, they help shape debates concerning gender, feminism, nationalism, class, and sexuality. Furthermore, in their concern to attend to the diversity among Asian American women, these anthologies demonstrate the possibility of creating identity-based communities not dependent upon exclusions. While *The Forbidden Stitch* uses the growth, diversification, and denationalization of the Asian American population to call Asian American identity into question, and to celebrate an unassimilable sense of the heterogeneity of Asian American women and their literature, *Making Waves*, with its historical and sociological emphasis, instead gives background on, and works to overcome this heterogeneity, by unifying and introducing various groups of Asian Americans to one another.

Making Waves on Firm Ground

Although both *Strangers from a Different Shore* and *Making Waves* construct sweeping histories of Asian Americans that encompass people of Japanese, Chinese, Korean, Filipino, Indian, Vietnamese, Cambodian, and Laotian origins, and although both works rely upon a combination of narrative history, personal recollections, and oral testimony, *Strangers* espouses gendered viewpoints that *Making Waves* works against. Indeed, in a 1990 *Amerasia* forum on Takaki's book, *Making Waves* contributor Sucheng Chan and editor Elaine Kim identify problems with *Strangers* that *Making Waves* seems designed to counter. In this forum—which stages debates about the role of the individual scholar doing community history, the ethics of compiling and using knowledge, and whether or not there are separate gendered histories—both Kim and Chan charge Takaki with appropriating the work and words of Asian American scholars and community members. Kim states, "Although Takaki contends that he will establish the self and subjecthood of Asian Americans by retrieving their voices . . . , his strategy in fact takes away the voices of those Asian Americans who spoke, disempowering their constructions while giving voice only to himself as master storyteller and orchestrator of elements into a kind of Asian American metahistory. Thus in the end, there is only one voice."[7] Kim and Chan also claim that Takaki's history marginalizes the history and lives of Asian American women. *Making Waves*, as a collective and communal effort, and as a women-centered project, provides an alternative to, and implicitly positions itself against, master narratives such as Takaki's. At the same time, in constructing history communally, *Making Waves* does not escape the problems Kim and Chan find with Takaki's text. Indeed, the correspondences between these texts illuminate some of the problems of speaking for or about Asian Americans as a collectivity, and suggest the difficulties of overturning paradigms that limit conceptualizations of Asian American women and their histories.

Making Waves, funded in large part by the U.S. Department of Education Women's Educational Equity Act Program, is one of AWU's many projects of outreach to Asian American women since the group's founding in 1975.[8] Organized thematically with brief introductions at the start of each of its seven sections, the 481-page anthology includes a wealth of historical and sociological studies, as well as fiction and poetry. With contributions predominantly by Asian American women, but also by one white woman, and three Asian American men, much of this literature works to acquaint readers with specific populations of Asian American women.

Because the anthology does not assume Asian American women to be familiar with, let alone to share, one another's histories or cultures, it locates otherness within the "Asian American" classification, and also addresses itself to a non-exclusive community of readers. With its emphasis on overcoming differences among Asian American women, the anthology provides a model for community that bases itself on identity politics without depending on the exclusions that so often attend the practice of such a politics. The book's non-divisive style and non-confrontational strategies—which make it vulnerable to charges of reinforcing Asian American stereotypes—do not lead it to erase or make irrelevant any of the subject positions it explores. Nor does its accessibility and openness to non-Asian American women necessarily entail its assimilation to the mainstream or to other groups outside the mainstream. Instead, what *Making Waves* offers is a useful way for Asian American women to manipulate their perceived role as a "middle minority." The anthology utilizes its access to whites and other people of color, but without promoting assimilation. It also works to correct any assumptions these readers might hold regarding Asian Americans' homogeneity—including the assumption that all Asian Americans can be said to occupy a "middle minority" position.

Navigating Diversity

The anthology's openness to both Asian and non-Asian American women results in part from the editors' self-presentation. In contrast to the other anthologies, *Making Waves* presents neither personality nor politics as the basis for establishing, or becoming part of, a community of Asian American women. *Making Waves* is produced by a collective, and the anthology itself is carefully crafted, but AWU members Elaine Kim, Janice Mirikitani, Diane Yen-Mei Wong, Emily Cachapero, Chung Hoang Chuong, Sucheta Mazumdar, Jane Singh, Judy Yung, and Nancy Hom do not remark upon their interactions or their process of putting together the anthology, nor do they put forth a unified political agenda. This self-positioning serves as an effective strategy for stressing AWU's collective identity, and for empowering the other women in the anthology.

This does not mean that the many voices of *Making Waves*'s contributors come through without mediation: as the women of AWU foreground the voices of the anthology's other contributors, they also—as does Takaki—create a narrative, selecting and ordering the pieces that make up *Making Waves* to bring out and underline connections among Asian American women. As the *Making Waves* editors evidence the multiple histories, ethnicities, and cultures of Asian American women, they insist upon their interconnections, making no mention of the racial differences, inter-ethnic divides, and competing loyalties that exist among Asian American women. Subtitled "An Anthology of Writings By and About Asian American Women," *Making Waves* does not introduce the complexities a Pacific Islander identity poses to an Asian American one, as do other collections of the late 1980s and early 1990s which— sometimes without even including Pacific Islander contributors—announce themselves as "Pacific/Asian," or "Asian American/Pacific Islander."[9] Although *Making Waves* does not have a Pacific focus (Nilda Rimonte is one of the few contributors to identify herself as a Pacific Asian), the editors' lack of discussion about the absence of Pacific Islander contributors, or about the relationship of Asian Americans and Pacific Islanders, works to elide the challenges this relationship poses to Asian American unity. Nor do the editors dwell on the significant differences and histories that often lead to a separation of these groups. Sucheta Mazumdar's general introduction, "A Woman-Centered Perspective on Asian American History," reflects AWU's strategy of unity: it proceeds chronologically and emphasizes a shared history for Asian Americans, rather than presenting their histories group by group, or highlighting the contradictions, questions, and incoherences which attend the definition "Asian American." Mazumdar's work in *Making Waves*, then, strikingly contrasts with her work in *Frontiers*, where she details how, in the United States, "South Asians' perception of themselves as white prevented the immigrants from making common cause with other Asians who were barred from citizenship on grounds of race."[10] Like Mazumdar, Elaine Kim also thematizes interethnic tensions in her *Asian American Literature: An Introduction to the Writings and Their Social Context*. However, in these texts, Mazumdar and Kim primarily address Asian American scholars; in *Making Waves*, their audience is a more general one, and this dictates their strategy of unifying Asian Americans.

In stressing the unity of Asian Americans, AWU must weave together their cultural, generational, and regional differences, and their various patterns of settlement.[11] And while *Making Waves* participates in the new movement to unsettle boundaries between Asian and Asian American identity, it does so in a way that ultimately maintains rather than disrupts a cultural nationalist Asian American identity. The book's first section, "Immigration," sets the tone by smoothing over the differences between refugees and other immigrants. Rather than set the experiences of recently arrived refugees or immigrants apart from those of native-born Americans or long-established immigrants, this section destabilizes in a more uniform way the geographical and psychological boundaries between the United States and the specific countries the contributors were sometimes forced to leave. The first piece, Meena Alexander's "Poem by the Wellside," details Alexander's feelings of belonging to neither the United States, the speaker's present "home," nor to India, her place of birth. Sakae S. Roberson's poem "Okasan/Mother" follows Alexander's, and similarly complicates issues of national belonging, this time for a woman who moved from Japan to the United States twenty-five years earlier. In "The Hopeland," K. Kam, a Chinese American, expresses feelings of kinship with Southeast Asian refugees. Throughout *Making Waves,* the editors select and organize literature to unify the experiences of Asian Americans' various histories.

They extend this strategy to unify the experiences of Asian Americans across classes. Many more people from the post-1965 groups of Southeast Asian refugees enter the United States as professionals rather than, as was previously true of many Asian immigrants, as industrial or agricultural workers. Class differences exist within as well as between specific ethnic groups. For example, the class backgrounds of post-1965 immigrants from China and the Philippines, who tend to be from urban, upwardly mobile middle classes with strong professional backgrounds, dramatically diverge from those of first-wave immigrants, who mostly came from rural backgrounds and were without formal educations. Furthermore, while some groups have been able to work their way to positions of relative privilege, others face oppressive conditions that virtually insure their poverty.[12] While Mazumdar alludes to the resulting class tensions in the introduction, stating, "Working-class Asians view the professionals' tendency to be spokespersons for the community with suspicion" (14), neither she nor the other contributors engage these tensions, which have become particularly complex and pronounced in the past few decades. Unlike in other identity-based anthologies, where editors and contributors stress their working-class backgrounds (c.f. *Home Girls* and *This Bridge Called My Back*), in *Making Waves* the contributors are for the most part professionals, even though they often present themselves as part of the working-class communities they study. The editors also stress commonalities across the class disparities the anthology represents, especially in the section entitled "Work." They dismantle the "success myth" of Asian American workers by portraying women in a wide range of jobs, from broadcasting to factory and domestic work. And, from the outset of this section, they emphasize the inequities faced by all Asian American women, "whether immigrant or American-born, in professional or more traditional occupations" (130). The "Work" section closes with Deborah Woo's "The Gap between Striving and Achieving: The Case of Asian American Women," an article which further stresses the obstacles Asian American women workers encounter regardless of class.

Such unity, however, is achieved at the expense of exploring the differences class creates among Asian American women. In fact, the unremarked-upon presence of poor or working-class women as objects of study rather than as authors in *Making Waves* testifies to the significance of class-based power differentials even as the anthology attempts to unify women across them.

Anthologizing Activism/Activist Anthologizing

In editing *Making Waves,* the scholars and writers in AWU participate in a tradition of bringing together literary, academic, and activist concerns. From its inception in the late 1960s, Asian American studies has maintained close ties to community-based forms of activism. As Gary Y. Okihiro asserts, "Asian American studies was built with the stones hurled through closed windows at San Francisco State in 1968. The hands that threw them were the same hands that laid railroad tracks, planted vineyards, and sewed garments."[13] While Asian American scholars find themselves questioning the extent to which this connection remains vital, they unequivocally assert, and the work of earlier anthologies and journals confirm, a history of this integral relationship.[14]

In *Making Waves,* contributors suggest no disparity between their roles as scholars/writers and their roles as activists. The way in which *Making Waves* does differ from these earlier anthologies, however, is in its more measured tone. *Roots* and *Counterpoint,* despite their generic similarity to *Making Waves,* communicate a greater sense of revolutionary fervor. In part, this tonal shift might reflect the split Asian American critics currently perceive and are heatedly debating between academic and non-academic Asian American communities. Michael Omi, for example, is just one of the contributors to *Reflections* who finds "a steady 'depoliticization' of Asian American Studies."[15] The "60s spirit" Omi finds absent from Asian American Studies is largely absent from *Making Waves* as well, as is the 1980s-style revolutionary spirit fueling anthologies by women of color such as *This Bridge. Making Waves*'s lack of passion and urgency also may be attributed to its emphasis on soci-

ological and historical studies as a means for educating readers. Because such studies are governed by their own styles and languages,
conforming to them often requires a writer to suppress her own opinions, and to communicate her investment in her subject indirectly.

Making Waves's measured tone cannot, however, be attributed simply
to the dictates of genre; the editors also adopt a form of address that
places them at a remove from other Asian American women, and that
depersonalizes racial oppression. For example, the editors include descriptions such as the following, in the introduction to the section entitled "Crashing Waves: War": "Panic-striken and racially motivated
forces erroneously equated Japanese Americans with the Japanese
enemy, even though there was no evidence of wrongdoing by the
American residents" (75). While the injustice done to Japanese Americans comes across clearly here, the description does not focus on, and
in fact disembodies, the agents of this injustice—white government
officials, media, and citizens. The editors also at times distance themselves from the Asian American women on whose behalf they speak.
They alternate throughout the section introductions between a first-
and third-person address. For example, in the final section, "Making
Waves: Activism," they state, "In the end, though, no one else can
speak for them [Asian American women]. They, *like all of us,* must speak
for themselves. We can expect no one else to fight our battles; we must
fight them ourselves. We must make our own waves" (348, emphasis
added). In addressing Asian American women in this manner, AWU
members avoid presuming that they can speak for all Asian American
women, but the effect is to remove themselves from that community to
which they set out to give voice.

The editors' form of address is consonant with their other strategies,
which seem designed to avoid alienating any potential audience members, including white women and men. In contrast to the directly confrontational style (and title) of *Making Face, Making Waves* disrupts the
status quo by stirring up the surrounding environment. Such a strategy,
which is perhaps dictated by AWU's institutional location and dependence upon federal funding, opens the anthology to interpretations of
being stereotypically Asian American, of being passive or assimilationist, of *not* making waves. I have considered such interpretations
while reading *Making Waves*, but always with a strong sense of uneasiness, and not only because *Making Waves*, with its emphasis on Asian
American women's agency, and its insistent focus on refuting and resisting stereotypes, works to counter such interpretations. My discomfort also results from the way the anthology brings me up against the

cultural biases that inform my assumptions about what constitutes activism. The overall effect of *Making Waves* is to challenge the assumption that activism need be characterized by explicitly voiced anger or opposition to mainstream acceptance and institutions.

Silencing Stereotypes

As *Making Waves* refutes stereotypes of Asian American women as silent, passive, submissive, and assimilationist, it also challenges the definition of silence as a state of passivity or submission.[16] The anthology's various positions towards silence intersect with, support, and undo one another. The editors assert Asian American women's activism as they refute "the erroneous stereotype that Asian American women are passive and submissive" (xi). Individual contributors present this stereotype as a condition imposed by Asian culture, one that Asian women in America are overcoming, or as an American-imposed stereotype that Asian Americans have internalized or felt pressure to conform to.

On the other hand, some contributors claim Asian American silence as a source of resistance or a form of activism, as a strategy women and men adopt to survive the forms of racism and sexism that they experience in the United States. The speaker in Janice Mirikitani's poem "In Remembrance" shows her uncle's silence not to be cultural, but brought on by historical forces in the United States: "When did you vow silence, Minoru? / After the camps, / after you buried a daughter?" (350). Yet other contributors see silence and submissiveness as states imposed upon women by Asian cultures and traditions, and show the ways in which women use this silence either to act or to resist oppression. The effect of *Making Waves*'s different positions regarding silence is to unsettle and complicate, if not overturn, Asian American women's associations with silence. What unites these various and often contradictory responses is contributors' resistance to being stereotyped, and their struggles for self-definition. Their multiplicity of responses to this stereotype undermines any clear sense of what defines activism; in *Making Waves*, silence becomes a quality that can characterize as well as prevent "making waves."

Contributors respond to the "model minority" stereotype in a similar manner, and to similar effect; they either deny Asian Americans' mainstream "assimilation" and success as racist stereotypes or myths, or accept the "model minority" myth with qualification and deploy it to their own advantage. In "The Gap between Striving and Achieving," for example, Woo critiques this myth, exposing its contradictions and racist purposes, even as she also cautions against dismissing it and advocates that Asian American women use it to their advantage. In "Asian Pacific American Women in Mainstream Politics," Judy Chu focuses not on the truth of "positive" stereotypes about Asian American women (an issue she does not address), but on ways women may use them to obtain mainstream success and influence.

Making Waves spends less energy challenging the model minority myth than do collections such as *Roots* and *Counterpoint*. Although many of its pieces clearly refute or critique Asian Americans' "model minority" status, its contributors tend to utilize the mainstream influence and acceptance this status affords some Asian American women, including many of the contributors themselves (about 20 percent of whom mention being recipients of mainstream academic or literary awards and honors).[17] In fact, Chu's essay on mainstream politics concludes both the section on activism and the anthology as a whole, thus giving weight to its model for "making waves." While this model might be the most effective one available to the editors, given AWU's institutional location, dependence on it undercuts the anthology's oppositional edge, its ability to make waves that will transform rather than unsettle the status quo.[18]

Unmaking Man-Made Authenticity

Making Waves makes no mention of the debates on authenticity (and its relationship to feminism) that have resounded through the late 1970s and 1980s in the wake of Maxine Hong Kingston's phenomenally successful *Woman Warrior* (1974). This may be so because the focus here is not literary; but it is also consonant with the book's strategy of non-divisiveness. Kingston and Frank Chin, one of the editors of the groundbreaking Asian American anthology *Aiiieeeee!* (1974) and Kingston's most vociferous critic, are the figures through whom Asian American literature has come most commonly to be polarized in the 1980s, and through whom its central debates have been staged.

Since the publication of *The Woman Warrior*, the *Aiiieeeee!* editors—Chin, Jeffery Paul Chan, Lawson Fusao Inada, and Shawn Wong—have directed the full force of their machismo against Kingston, and have come to define their vision of Asian America through opposition to her work. In *Aiiieeeee!* they respond to a history wherein Asian men have been emasculated by defending and defining their manhood at the expense of—indeed in opposition to—Asian American women and Asian cultures. Thus, for the *Aiiieeeee!* editors, the commercial success of some Asian American women writers results from their catering to white racist stereotypes that degrade Asian American men, and thus constitutes a sell-out to Asian American literature and men (and, by the time of *The Big Aiiieeeee!*, to Asian history and civilization as well). Attributing the success of Kingston's work, along with Amy Tan's and David Henry Hwang's, to its related qualities of being feminist, assimilationist, inauthentic or fake, racist, and white-Christian, they oppose her work to their own and that of the other writers they anthologize.

If Chin et al. are the most widely known and flamboyant proponents of this masculinist model, they are certainly not the only ones. This model, with its sexism and attendant homophobia, has dominated much writing about Asian Americans and their literature. The anthologies *Roots* and *Counterpoint*, despite being edited by women, at times adopt a position similar to that of *Aiiieeeee!* For example, in *Counterpoint*'s literature section, editor Bruce Iwasaki focuses on male authors. In a sexist and homophobic spirit evocative of Chin's, Iwasaki calls David Rafael Wang an "aging literary eunuch," and says of David Hsin-Fu Wand's anthology, "Here the dual personality number goes beyond goofiness [a favorite word of Chin's] almost to the level of transvestism." He continues, invoking the very stereotype of the emasculated Asian male that he rails against elsewhere, "Wan() is a withered example of false historical consciousness."[19] While work in the 1980s has been inherently less masculinist in its structure, it has maintained an insistence on differentiating between real (activist, historically accurate) and fake (assimilationist, ahistorical, or inaccurately historical) Asian American literature.[20]

Making Waves, with its focus on women and its diversity of political vision, serves as a corrective to the macho, male-centered perspectives of previous Asian American anthologies without placing itself in opposition to Asian American men, and without referencing or calling attention to the exclusions of these anthologies. In *Making Waves*, AWU upholds Kim's contention elsewhere that "although sexism has been an issue in Asian American communities, racism has usually been pinpointed as the more important barrier to social and economic equality for Asian American women."[21]

Making Waves, which provides more space than most other identity-based women's anthologies for men's voices and concerns, portrays Asian American men in alliance with, as well as in opposition to, Asian American women. The anthology includes three articles co-authored by men and women, and several contributors describe themselves working in partnership with their husbands on community projects. A significant 20 percent of the contributors refer to husbands in their contributors' biographies. The "Work" section emphasizes the hard work of Asian American men as well as women, and the editors organize the anthology so that pieces critical of Asian or Asian American men, or ones exclusively about women, are balanced by ones centering on and sympathetic to men. The book's empathy for men and its focus on men and women's united struggles against racism can be attributed in part to the history of Asian Americans in the United States. Various related factors in this history—immigration (and anti-miscegenation) laws, white stereotypes gendering the entire Asian American population as feminine, Asian Americans' dependence on family businesses for economic survival in a discriminatory labor market—all have served to unite Asian American men and women, and to make the family a site for survival and resistance in a white racist society.[22] For Asian American women, therefore, marriage and the family constitute important structures both for countering the dominant society's racism and for experiencing oppression as women. In *Making Waves*, many contributors consequently negotiate between the need to critique and the need to defend their specific Asian/Asian American culture. Furthermore, their defenses arise not only out of their need for solidarity with Asian American men, but also serve as a means of challenging stereotypes of Asian (American) women as passive and subservient. Thus, while Rashmi Luthra's "Matchmaking in the Classifieds of the Immigrant Indian Press" concludes the section "Injustices," Luthra nevertheless shows possibilities for women's agency in such matchmaking, and gives a limited endorsement of marriage ads. The oscillations and unresolved contradictions that run through this article and many others in the anthology testify to the complexity of negotiating between maintaining loyalty to one's ethnic community and opposing its patriarchal structures.

In her critique of *Strangers from a Different Shore,* Kim finds that Takaki's book reveals the need for new categories for women's history. She states, "I am not calling for another compensatory history that tucks in and tacks on Asian American women. What we need instead is to rupture and break free from that script, not to correct and add to it."[23] Although women constitute *Making Waves*'s central subjects, in negotiating their allegiances to their particular ethnic communities, its contributors, both individually and collectively, revise rather than rupture Asian American history. Indeed, what such a rupture would look like, and how it would be made, remain unclear in *Making Waves,* although in its structure and focus the anthology moves towards the kind of history Kim calls for.

(Re)Making Feminism?

The cultural and historical contexts which contribute to *Making Waves*'s position towards men, marriage, and family also complicate its relationship to white middle-class understandings of feminism, which insist upon women's resistance to or independence from men and/or patriarchal structures. *Making Waves* contains few explicit mentions of feminism: in the contributors' biographies, only four of the fifty-three contributors identify themselves as feminists, and women who reference feminism in their writing generally code it white or black, in tension with Asian American identity. In the only article in the anthology focused on feminism, "The Feminist Movement: Where Are All the Asian American Women?" Esther Ngan-Ling Chow views feminism as a white movement that "pits ethnic identity against gender identity" (367).

While the few pieces in *Making Waves* that explicitly mention feminism either cede it to white or black women or show a conflicted relationship to it, others express, if they do not name, forms of feminism both particular to Asian American women's concerns and consonant with more broadly defined Anglo-European understandings of it. Particularly in its selections of fiction and poetry (and thus presumably reflecting the influence and interests of Janice Mirikitani, the Creative Editor), the anthology includes many tributes to women that focus on previous generations and involve a celebration of their resistance, and/or the strength inherent in their silence. In R. A. Sasaki's story "The Loom," the daughters come to understand, in much the same way as in Walker's "In Search of Our Mothers' Gardens," the expressivity and engagement their mother's knitting reveals, despite her silence and apparent passivity.

The majority of pieces in *Making Waves*, while women-centered, resist any easy classification as feminist or non-feminist. Indeed, the anthology's range of literature renders the term "feminist" inadequate. For me, the anthology defamiliarizes any easy understandings of what feminism means or includes, as it points to the cultural biases of the term. By leaving open whether or not the anthology is "feminist," and by including a range of sometimes conflicting positions towards and expressions of feminism, the editors are able to include and address both women who identify as feminists and those who believe feminism undermines the concerns of Asian Americans. This means, however, that the collection falls short of a distinctively Asian American feminism.

Lesbianism and the Exclusions of Non-Exclusivity

The intent not to alienate its Asian American audience results in *Making Waves's* dismissal of lesbianism, and the ways in which lesbianism potentially disrupts patriarchal elements of both mainstream and Asian American communities. In *Making Waves*, AWU does limited battle against the lack of acceptance of lesbianism within Asian American communities. They do not problematize the sparse attention in the anthology to lesbianism, and their only allusion to lesbianism, in the introduction to the "Identity" section, is a troubling one. Their comments on Pam H.'s article on lesbianism are preceded by the statement, "Sexual preference and physical disabilities are other factors that shape the identities of some Asian American women" (239). The editors here both avoid direct mention of lesbianism and present it as a form of disability. And Pamela H.'s article, "Asian American Lesbians: An Emerging Voice in the Asian American Community"—the anthology's only piece about lesbianism—appears more as an impartial, informational essay than it does as one giving voice to a lesbian point of view. Pamela H. does not herself come out in the article (though she does in her biographical note), and her language is careful and distanced. In the context of the article, Pamela H.'s withholding of her last name seems more illustrative of the difficulty Asian American lesbians have in coming out than indicative of a feminist undermining of patronyms. Besides Pamela H., the only contributors to give lesbianism a name are Jyotsna Vaid, Nellie Wong, and Chea Villanueva. Villanueva, although she does not thematize lesbianism in her poem, is the only contributor besides Pamela H. to identify herself as lesbian in the biographies.

In part, the invisibility of lesbianism can be attributed to the cultural biases focused in the term and the relatively few Asian American women speaking out as lesbians. The term "lesbian" and the rhetoric of "coming out" have in fact been pinpointed by lesbian activists including Cristy Chung, Aly Kim, Zoon Nguyen, and Trinity Ordoña as part of a distinctively white model of sexuality,[24] and Kitty Tsui's poem in *Making Waves* supports this critique. The speaker in that poem states, "my grandmother, / a woman with three daughters, / left her husband / to survive on her own. / she lived with another actress, / a companion and a friend" (134). These lines suggest both that love between women is neither new nor a "white" phenomenon, and that to term all love relationships between women as "lesbian" might entail wrenching these relationships out of their particular cultural contexts.

Nevertheless, rather than highlight or address such issues—to raise crucial questions about the relationship of sexual and racial identity—and/or include writings from an explicitly lesbian viewpoint, AWU reinscribes the silence (in this case, I would argue, an oppressive one) surrounding questions of sexuality for Asian American women, and the invisibility of those women who resist heterosexual institutions.[25] Of the three women Pamela H. cites when discussing "the best known writers and voices for the Asian American lesbian community" (290), only Tsui is included in *Making Waves*. And while Villanueva and Tsui may have chosen not to include explicitly lesbian writings, the lack of such writing, especially in the "Activism" section, reflects the editors' decision not to present lesbianism as a way that Asian American women "make waves."

In its care not to exclude any of its broad audience, *Making Waves* in fact places Asian American lesbians on the very margins, if not outside, of the community of readers it creates.[26] In the introduction to *Between the Lines: An Anthology by Pacific/Asian Lesbians*, the editors Connie Chung, Alison Kim, and A. K. Lemeshewsky state, "Our writings are our visibility and our community. They are our survival."[27] *Making Waves's* failure to give Asian American lesbians greater voice, including its failure to reference *Between the Lines* when claiming itself as the first "major" Asian American women's anthology since the 1970s, thus contributes to its act of erasure. The book demonstrates how even a strategy of nonexclusiveness produces exclusions. Kim's response to Takaki's *Strangers from a Different Shore*, then, constitutes my response to *Making Waves*: "What we need now is to disrupt, dehierarchize, and subvert, if our aim is to be more, much more than claiming the Master's house for some of us."[28]

Unraveling *The Forbidden Stitch*

The Forbidden Stitch in many ways stands as a complement to *Making Waves*. While *Making Waves* emphasizes the sociological, the emphasis in *The Forbidden Stitch* is literary. Consisting of poetry, prose, artwork, and literary reviews, *The Forbidden Stitch* stands at the forefront of a new literary movement on the part of Asian American writers and critics, and is indicative of the shifting currents in Asian American literary and cultural studies.

While Asian American activists and scholars have been recovering and promoting ignored works of Asian American literature since the 1970s, only in the last several years has Asian American literature begun to receive widespread recognition and come into its own as a field of study. Elaine Kim attributes what she calls "the start [in the 1980s] of a golden age of Asian American cultural production"[29] to groups such as the Combined Asian Resources Project (CARP), as well as to the changing political relationships between the United States and China, Japan, Korea, and the Philippines, and changes in immigration policy. Kim is but one of the many critics to remark upon this cultural production in the outpouring of Asian American literary studies, journals, and anthologies.[30]

Part of what is truly "new" about this literary movement is the changing definition of what constitutes Asian American literature, and who writes it. With the movement away from the nationalist cultural concerns and explicit activism that characterize much Asian American literature and criticism of the 1970s and 1980s, current literature and criticism maintain a more global, diasporic perspective and a more diverse one ideologically.[31] As new population groups have blurred the boundaries between Asian and Asian American literature, they have also raised questions about how newer and/or lesser-known and studied Asian American literatures complicate assumptions about Asian American literature that are based primarily upon studies of Chinese and Japanese American literature (with often cursory attention to Korean and/or Filipino literature as well). Critics such as Oscar V. Campomanes are calling attention to "a pronounced but unacknowledged focus on Chinese and Japanese American writings and their telos of immigration and settlement, to the unintended exclusion of other Asian American writings and their concomitant logics."[32] Furthermore, the emergence of full-length studies on specific, already established groups of writers are opening up of the field of Asian American literature, as are studies of writers formerly ignored because they did not conform to prevailing definitions of Asian American literature.[33]

The Forbidden Stitch exemplifies and reflects upon these new directions in Asian American literature and its increasing diversification. As editor Mayumi Tsutakawa notes in her introduction, "There is no single definition of Asian/Pacific American literature, no uniformly homogenized theme as may have been the case ten or fifteen years ago" (13). Rather than explicate or draw out the similarities inherent in this diversity, as *Making Waves* does, *The Forbidden Stitch* chooses not to work to make this literature unified or accessible. Instead, as it participates in the creation of the category of Asian American women's literature, *The Forbidden Stitch* also insists upon this literature's unassimilable alterity, and challenges its coherence as a unified body of literature.

The editors' introductions call the very category "Asian American"

into question. *The Forbidden Stitch* was conceived not by guest editors
Shirley Geok-lin Lim and Mayumi Tsutakawa, but by the Calyx collective, a collective dedicated to publishing writings by women of color in
their journal *Calyx*. In Calyx editor Margarita Donnelly's introduction,
she explains, "In our naiveté we initially chose '*Asian American Women's
Anthology*' as an acceptable and descriptive title for the anthology. During production and the ensuing editorial discussions we discovered
that title does not accurately describe the diverse cultural groups included in this anthology" (15). Both Lim and Tsutakawa subtly critique
and destabilize the designation "Asian American" by using it interchangeably with the term "Asian/Pacific American." Lim's introduction,
which precedes both Tsutakawa's and Donnelly's, brings to the forefront even more basic questions about using "Asian American women"
as descriptive category.

Lim's opening statement challenges the anthology's very premises:
"When I accepted the offer to help edit this anthology of Asian American women's writing, I knew I was in for some exciting experiences. As
a first-generation 'Asian American woman,' for one thing, I knew there
was no such thing as an 'Asian American woman'" (10). Refuting the
idea that any single common thread joins Asian American women writers, she instead images their relationship as "a multi-colored, many-
layered, complexly knotted stitch" (10). Lim announces, "This anthology takes its name from an embroidery knot which, while it resulted in
a luxurious beauty, was so difficult to sew that *it led to blindness* in many
of the Chinese artisans assigned to embroider the robes and altar hang-
ings so beloved in feudal China" (10, emphasis added). In explaining
the forbidden stitch, Lim then quotes from Maxine Hong Kingston's
Woman Warrior, where the narrator identifies herself with makers of the
forbidden stitch, whom she calls "outlaw knot-makers" (11). The title,
then, conveys not only the idea that, in engaging in artistic expression,
Asian American women participate in a form of expression forbidden
to them; this title also signifies the tremendous artifice, and even the
blindness that results from constituting the category "Asian American
women." As Lim glosses this title, it subverts the anthology's subtitle,
"An Asian American Women's Anthology," and challenges Calyx's very
premises for the anthology. At the same time, Lim also endorses the political efficacy of Calyx's project, calling it one "of community-healing
and of community-teaching" (12).[34]

If, in some measure, Lim sets out to undermine the category "Asian
American women" in *The Forbidden Stitch,* Mayumi Tsutakawa's introduction, which follows Lim's, works to define Asian American women

and make known their literature.[35] Tsutakawa announces, "Discover-
ing new voices and planning their escape from the fate of anonymity:
this was my dual goal in editing *The Forbidden Stitch*" (13). After emphasizing the anonymity of the artisan of the forbidden stitch, she posits
the anthology as the means to effect the demise of this anonymity and
thus of *The Forbidden Stitch* itself: "The forbidden stitch *is no longer with
us—it is replaced* with the art work which is both beautifully crafted and
no longer anonymous" (15, emphasis added). Tsutakawa's gloss to the
title thus counters Lim's: it bolsters the subtitle, "An Asian American
Women's Anthology," as it dismantles the "The Forbidden Stitch." And
while Tsutakawa does not contest the heterogeneity Lim insists upon,
she seems to proceed upon the assumption that Asian American women
comprise a definable and identifiable entity. In fact, she expresses regret
for having to bypass submissions "which did not carry a recognizable
Asian voice" (14), thus suggesting a standard for authenticity and a
commonality that Lim's introduction counters.

Taken together, the editors' introductions set forth the project's instability and multiple significances. They also establish the anthology
as a place wherein questions will not be answered definitively nor explanations offered: instead, they establish the anthology as a site to engage and negotiate—often in contradictory and competing ways—the
complexities of defining an "Asian American" identity and literature.

Shifting Terrains of Asian American Literature

As one of its strategies, *The Forbidden Stitch* lays claim to the Americanness of Asian American literature, and its conformity to canonical genres
of American literature. In accordance with the *Calyx* journal's format,
the literature in *The Forbidden Stitch* appears in the table of contents
under headings by genre. The anthology rotates sections of poetry,
prose, and art (there are three of each) and concludes with reviews. If
the editors of the other anthologies in my study resist such organization due to the elitism and ties to traditional definitions of literature
they believe it reflects, the structure of *The Forbidden Stitch* by contrast
seems more traditional and less politically motivated. However, *The
Forbidden Stitch*'s conformity to canonical literary categories must be
read against the exclusion of Asian American literature from the realm
of literature in the United States, and against a history in which Asian
Americans, unlike other immigrant groups, are treated as perpetual
house guests.[36]

Likewise, the presence in *The Forbidden Stitch* of literature that does not thematize specifically Asian American concerns asserts that Asian American writers need not be limited to exclusively "ethnic" subject matter. Sau-ling Cynthia Wong illuminates why such literature might be included in an anthology interested in promoting a "recognizable Asian voice." In a discussion of ludic discourse, Wong argues that in showing interest in "the 'playful' and seemingly gratuitous aspects of artistic creation, Asian American authors are not . . . promoting a rarefied aestheticism. Instead, they are formulating an 'interested disinterestedness' appropriate to their condition as minority artists with responsibility to their communities but also a need for room to exercise their creativity."[37] The editors of *The Forbidden Stitch*, in their choice of literature, thus give Asian American writers room—and license—to play.

Many of the literary reviews which conclude *The Forbidden Stitch* also focus on Asian American literature's universal or canonical American qualities rather than its ethnic Asian ones. Reviewers stress the universal qualities of poetry by Diana Chang, Fay Chiang, Mei-Mei Berssenbrugge, and Shirley Lim, and link their work to that of Allen Ginsberg, Georgia O'Keeffe, or William Wordsworth. They insist upon Asian American literature's relevance for readers of canonical American literature.

What keeps this strategy from being an assimilationist one (and thus from fulfilling the flipside of the stereotype of Asian Americans as perpetual and exotic foreigners) is the anthology's assertion, at other moments, of a specifically Asian American point of view, one resistant to universalist interpretations or a canonical Anglo-American framework. If, by claiming that the literature in the anthology is characterized by "a recognizable Asian voice," Tsutakawa risks erasing differences among Asian Americans (and Asians and Asian Americans), she also suggests that a knowledge of Asian American literature and culture might yield readings of the anthology unavailable to less knowledgeable readers. In this way, and in contrast to *Making Waves*, the anthology prevents non-Asian American readers from feeling a sense of mastery over it. The first grouping of artwork emphasizes a cohesive Asian American identity, particularly Roberta May Wong's "All Orientals Look Alike" and other pieces exposing and denouncing white American racism and imperialism. The anthology concludes with eleven-year-old Michelle Yokoyama's review of Helen Chetin's historical book *Angel Island Prisoner 1992*. By ending with a young Japanese American's engagement with Chinese American history, the anthology promotes a vision of solidarity among Asian Americans that is not essentialist, but based upon Asian Americans paying attention to and learning about each others' specific histories.

The claim *The Forbidden Stitch* makes for the Americanness of Asian American literature and the anthology's endorsement of a specifically Asian American voice and perspective are countered by its challenge to both of these positions. The diversity and deliberate inaccessibility that characterizes much of the literature in *The Forbidden Stitch* renders alien the otherwise familiar generic structure the anthology adopts, undermines its correspondences to canonical white literature, and challenges its unity as Asian American literature. The anthology opens with a section of poetry that deconstructs a nationalist Asian American framework by introducing a diasporic perspective. In the first poem, Marilyn Chin's "We Are Americans Now, We Live in the Tundra," the American identity avowed in the title is no cause for celebration, and, similarly, the narrator both identifies and dis-identifies with China. The poem opens:

Today in hazy San Francisco, I face seaward
Toward China, a giant begonia—

Pink, fragrant, bitten
By verdigris and insects. I sing her

A blues song; even a Chinese girl gets the blues,
Her reticence is black and blue. (17)

While the slippage in these lines between China, the speaker, and the Chinese girl suggests the speaker's identification with China, China remains distant and remote. The speaker also evokes, but eludes identification with, America and its literary traditions, both mainstream and minor. The phrase "even a Chinese girl gets the blues" references Tom Robbins's novel *Even Cowgirls Get the Blues* (an association which in turn may evoke Frank Chin as "Chinatown Cowboy") and the African American blues tradition, particularly Bessie Smith's "What Did I Do to Be So Black and Blue?" Unlike the situation described in the Smith song, however, the Chinese girl's "black and blue" connotes an internal bleeding caused by her failure to come to voice—"her reticence is black and blue." If these literary allusions serve to establish the speaker as belonging to America, they also suggest that what Americans share is their experience of alienation. Marilyn Chin's poem proceeds to depict a narrator estranged both from her American country and China. Although the representation of China in this poem remains confined largely to American stereotypes of "extinct Bengal tigers" and "giant Pandas," the speaker's irony deflates these stereotypes:

Farewell my ancestors:
Hirsute Taoists, failed scholars, farewell

My wetnurse who feared and loathed the Catholics,
Who called out:

Now that the half-men have occupied Canton
Hide your daughters, lock your doors! (17)

Chin doesn't merely mock American stereotypes here with her references to hairy Taoists and failed scholars; by ending the poem with the
wetnurse's words, which establish Westerners as "half-men" to be met
with fear and loathing, she provides the Chinese counterpart to these
stereotypes: Chinese people ("even" from the servant classes) regard
Westerners as alien and inferior. Thus, the poem that opens *The Forbidden Stitch* represents both America and China as simultaneously alien
and alienating to its Chinese American narrator. Nor does the poem
proffer an "Asian America" in which the narrator or other Chinese
Americans may find a home. Despite the title's collective pronoun ("We
Are Americans Now"), the narrator is depicted as isolated from Chinese Americans and other Asian Americans (and arguably from herself, given the language which makes interchangeable the speaker and
the China from which she is alienated). Thus the vision in this opening
poem unsettles a cultural nationalist model of Asian American literature and identity and resists absorption into a dominant American one.

The following two poems, by Myung Mi Kim, also work to "dena-
tionalize" Asian American literature and to reinforce its oppositional
relationship to Western culture. The poems critique not only Western
literary traditions and stereotypes, but also the English language in
which Kim writes her poetry. In "Into Such Assembly," the Korean
American narrator struggles with her relationship to the English language as a tool of forced assimilation: a line in Korean [*Sung-Bul-Sah,
geep eun bahm ae*] is followed by "neither, neither // Who is mother
tongue, who is father country?" (18). The unintelligibility for non-Korean speakers of the line in Korean obfuscates also the line which follows ("neither, neither"), but at the same time bears it out: the translit-
eration of the Korean from a Hankul alphabet into a Latin one renders
it intelligible neither to Koreans nor to non-Korean speaking Americans. In this way the poem playfully resists appropriation by non-Korean-
speaking Americans. The poem juxtaposes racist American stereotypes
about Korea with the Korean-born narrator's experience of it:

Do they have trees in Korea? Do the children eat out of garbage cans?

We had a Dalmation
We rode the train on weekends from Seoul to So-Sah where we grew grapes

We ate on the patio surrounded by dahlias (18)

The beauty, comfort, and elegance of the narrator's memories of Korea counter the questioner's assumptions of dirt, ugliness, poverty, and neglect. Kim's poem mourns the dissolution of Korean land and identity, and connects it to the loss of Korean language through sustained water imagery. The effect of this difficult poem is to cut the reader adrift from both the United States and Korea and to expose the English language as a tool of hegemony. If the narrator speaks in an American English tongue, she does not do so freely, nor do we see her finding a sense of belonging with other Asian Americans. What the narrators in Chin's and Kim's poems share is their alienation (or alien/nation).

While the narrators in these poems speak from an American location, subsequent narrators speak from Asian settings, or from locales that prove difficult to identify. The presence of "On Such a Day," written by Korean Song-jook Park and translated by Hyun-jae Yee Sallee, suggests that Asian works translated by Asian Americans constitute a part of Asian American literature. Also included are stories and poems set in Japan, China, India, Korea, and the Philippines, among others, and the anthology presents these shifting terrains without exoticizing, idealizing, or explaining them. As in *Making Waves*, the inclusion and presentation of this literature counters the anthology's American or Asian American nationalist strains. While Americans dehumanize Korea and Koreans in America in Kim's "Into Such Assembly," her poem which follows, "A Rose of Sharon," details American men's acts of rape and murder, as well as the effects of America's military presence in Korea. This first section of poetry demonstrates the dissolving of national boundaries, as it also cautions against a dehistoricized, decontextualized celebration of border crossings.

The meanings as well as the locations of the literature in *The Forbidden Stitch* defy readers who do not possess a nuanced understanding of the particular histories the writers evoke. In the poem "Higashiyami Crematorium, November 16, 1983," as Lynne Yamaguchi Fletcher describes a Buddhist burial, she alludes to Kokugo, which she glosses in a note as "'national language.' What the Japanese call their own language among themselves, believing no foreigner can ever truly master it" (121). What Fletcher provides here is a note on the impossibility of access, rather than a translation providing access. While in *Making Waves* the editors seek to explain and draw connections among the experiences of different groups of immigrants, refugees, and American-born Asians, in *The Forbidden Stitch* the editors defiantly present these diverse histories without explanation and without drawing any explicit connections among them.

The Accessibility of the Alien

The anthology's refusal to make its literature accessible, to translate or explain it, paradoxically results in its granting almost equal access to all readers—Asian American or otherwise—willing to do their homework and to establish connections with the range of women *The Forbidden Stitch* encompasses. The anthology bears out Lim's introductory contention that the category "Asian American women" includes "entire racial/national/cultural/sexual preferenced groups, many of whom find each other as alien as mainstream America apparently finds us" (10). While the anthology plays up the bewildering and often alienating nature of this heterogeneity, it is up to individual readers to come to terms with it. In its refusal to historicize or translate itself, *The Forbidden Stitch* is a forbidding work, and as in *Making Waves,* its concentration on internal otherness works against establishing any clear us-them dichotomy.

Thus the anthology destabilizes the identity politics that underwrite it. In addition to thematizing the otherness within the category "Asian American women" without then working to overcome it, the anthology also admits non-Asian American women as reviewers, and it includes contributors who write about the ways in which Asian American women feel themselves to be inauthentically Asian (see, for example, Diana Chang's "The Oriental Contingent"). Furthermore, while it takes as its premise an Asian American identity, however problematical, the anthology emerges out of cross-racial alliances between the Calyx collective and the guest editors.

Against a Backdrop of White

At the same time, in the anthology itself, pieces which establish alliances among Asian Americans and other women of color constitute but a thin thread of the anthology's fabric. Lim states in her introduction that the writers in *The Forbidden Stitch* "are striking new notes and registers in their exploration of subjectivity as gendered and identified against the backdrop of white 'otherness'" (12), and the literature and the artwork in the anthology in fact position Asian American women more often in relation to dominant society and white racism than in relation to other women of color.

The book review of *This Bridge Called My Back* by a white contributor, Julia Watson, obliquely seems to comment upon *The Forbidden Stitch*'s relationship to other women of color. Watson finds that Asian American women in *This Bridge* "don't seem as strongly represented as Afro American or Latina women" (254). She contends that "*Bridge* is a powerful and persuasive book of continuing value, but [that] where Asian American women are concerned, it points to the need for a collection exclusively on Asian American women" (254). The inclusion of Watson's argument suggests the editors' endorsement of it, and *The Forbidden Stitch* implicitly stands as the sort of collection Watson calls for to combat the underrepresentation and diminishment of Asian American women. While *The Forbidden Stitch* exposes and denounces white racism, it leaves the relations among Asian American women and other women of color virtually undiscussed, slipped into only one review written by a white woman. Given the absence of such a discussion, *The Forbidden Stitch* is positioned largely in relation to a white framework.

An Outlaw (to) Feminism

If the largely invisible backdrop against which the anthology is situated is white, the interactions and pieces within the anthology itself are implicitly women-centered ones, as well as Asian American. Like *Making Waves*, *The Forbidden Stitch* provides a counterpart to masculinist anthologies such as *Aiiieeeee!*, and it, too, does this without directly opposing these anthologies or othering men. The anthology is more outspokenly feminist than *Making Waves*, however, and, while it does not participate explicitly in gendered debates within Asian American studies, neither does it attempt to heal divisions between Asian American men and women, as *Making Waves* does. Although *The Forbidden Stitch* contains a few pieces critical of Euro-American or Asian men, Asian American men are largely absent from the anthology. *The Forbidden Stitch*'s refusal to enter into existing debates and its lack of attention to Asian American men pose perhaps greater threats to Asian American men than would explicit opposition, since the effect is to render Asian American men irrelevant to, rather than embattled with, Asian American women.[38] The anthology's silence on this front, especially when combined with its outspoken feminism, contributes to its outlaw status.

Compared to *Making Waves*, *The Forbidden Stitch* takes a stand that is more firmly feminist, and one that breaks down the equation that feminism necessarily entails assimilation to white America. In fact, the feminism of much of its literature is anchored strongly in its contributors' specific Asian American cultures. In Valerie Matsumoto's story "Two Deserts," the protagonist, Emiko, is threatened in her home both by a scorpion and a racist neighbor making sexual advances. Using a

shovel "like a *samurai* in battle," she kills the scorpion, and simultaneously wards off the white male intruder. Afterwards, she "wipe[s] her
brow on her arm, like a farmer, or a warrior" (52). Matsumoto's metaphors make clear that Emiko's feminist assertion comes not only from
the skills she has developed farming desert land in the United States
but also from her Japanese heritage. Furthermore, Emiko acts to protect
herself and her daughter from white racism and sexism, rather than accommodate herself to white American society.

In keeping with the anthology's thoroughly diasporic perspective, as
women in *The Forbidden Stitch* critique white sexist and racist society
from a feminist perspective, they also expose "shameful" secrets about
Asian men and cultures, exploring taboo subjects such as infanticide
and molestation. For example, Shirley Geok-lin Lim's poem "Pantoun
for Chinese Women" begins with a quote from *The People's Daily* in
Peking about the killing of girl infants. As the poem expresses empathy
for a woman about to kill her girl baby because "they say a child with
two mouths is no good" (204), it provides an implicit critique of the
forms patriarchy takes in China.

While some of the literature in *The Forbidden Stitch* stands in defiance
of Asian cultures, some pieces, often simultaneously, also defy feminist
orthodoxies.[39] Stories such as Kyoko Mori's "Yellow Mittens and Early
Violets," set in Japan, and Anjana Appachana's "My Only Gods," set in
India, detail subjects such as women's suicide and nervous breakdowns
without giving any clear feminist analysis or contexts to account for
them. Other literature delves into women's capacities for cruelty to one
another. In Mei-Mei Berssenbrugge's "Chronicle," a poem set in China,
the speaker discloses that when she was born, her mother, who considers herself "the family's 'First Son,'" "took one look at me/and lit
out/on a vacation to Sumatra" (148), leaving the speaker's uncle and
grandparents to care for her. The loving attention of the uncle and
grandfather destabilizes gender roles and complicates the workings of
a patriarchal society. In these and other positions it plots, the anthology
stands in an outlaw relationship not only to Asian Americans, who
might view feminism as a form of assimilation, but also to feminists
who valorize women and their relationships.

The Forbidden Stitch includes a few powerful and passionate pieces
written from an explicitly lesbian point of view, further differentiating
it from *Making Waves,* and extending its outlaw status. Ultimately, however, it confirms lesbianism to be that which is continually excluded
from Asian American as well as dominant cultural paradigms. Donnelly and Lim, for example, fail to credit the 1987 *Between the Lines: An*

Anthology by Pacific/Asian Lesbians of Santa Cruz (although they reference it in the bibliography) when they proclaim *The Forbidden Stitch* to
be the first Asian American women's anthology (15). Similarly, in titling her poem "Untitled," Woo presents lesbianism as that which remains unnameable, and without adequate language.[40] Contributor Alison Kim (a co-editor of *Between the Lines*) also titles her sculpture, a
figure of indeterminate gender, "Untitled," and in her accompanying
statement she explains, "I continually struggle with the coming out
process, whether as a lesbian, as a writer, or as an artist" (182). With
this statement, which links artistic and sexual expression, and presents
both as forbidden, Kim encourages her audience to read these struggles
into the sculpture, again with the effect of underlining lesbianism as
that which remains nameless as it is played out in and through the
body. Thus, as *The Forbidden Stitch* evokes a lesbian existence and sexuality, it also conveys its contributors' sense of the unspeakability and
the nameless quality, the taboo nature of lesbianism.

The *Forbidden Stitch* also includes Kit Quan's review of Elaine Kim's
and Janice Otani's *With Silk Wings: Asian American Women at Work* (published by AWU). Quan denounces the book from an explicitly lesbian
(and working-class) point of view: "It was a nightmare of assimilationist attitudes that was poorly written and reflected very little of my experience as a Chinese American immigrant and lesbian or of the existence of other Asian American women workers that I know" (253).
Quan's review provides a rare instance of open dissent among Asian
American women in *The Forbidden Stitch* (and in Asian American wom-
en's anthologies in general). It reflects the anthology's willingness to
take on controversy directly within a community of Asian American
women, and to open up a space for a distinctly lesbian (and, however
fleetingly, working-class) point of view.

Class: The (Un)Common Thread

Quan's critique of the class bias in *With Silk Wings* is also one that can
be leveled at *The Forbidden Stitch*, for its radical heterogeneity and outlaw status only go so far. The anthology does not claim to be, and is not,
representative of the range of Asian American women's experiences,
and the art and literature it includes express viewpoints primarily of
economic and educational privilege. The overall effect of *The Forbidden
Stitch* is to position Asian American women similarly in terms of class,
and to confirm the myth of Asian American (economic) success. The
depictions of China, Japan, and India are mostly of wealth. For exam-

ple, Myung Mi Kim's poem "Into Such Assembly" portrays Korea as a place of comfort and elegance, and, while this provides a necessary balance to the usual clichés of poverty, it does not leave room to address that poverty or the reasons behind it, which in fact include U.S. imperialism. While I do not mean to suggest it is Kim's responsibility to provide such a viewpoint, the dearth of such viewpoints in *The Forbidden Stitch* certainly limits its range as an Asian American women's anthology.

Furthermore, *The Forbidden Stitch*'s chronicles of immigrant experience in the United States contain few accounts of material hardships or even of work. Even one of the two pieces to thematize the labor of immigrant workers, Talat Abbasi's "Sari Petticoats," confirms the Asian American success myth and the myth of America as the land of equal opportunity and self-making. In Abbasi's story the narrator and her husband come from Lahore to New York and find the streets riddled with bullets, rather than paved with gold, as they had hoped, and they live in an apartment the size of their servant's quarters at home. As the narrator, who begins sewing saris, thrives, her husband despairs: "He paced the floor for months exclaiming tragically, 'A Master's in Persian poetry from Punjab University is sewing *sari* petticoats!' I could not see the tragedy for the dollar bills" (219). At the story's end, the now-wealthy narrator sits in her luxurious apartment and contemplates sending money to her husband, who has returned to Lahore. While the tone of the story is sardonic and the representation of the narrator's "success" ambivalent, it nevertheless details a rags-to-riches narrative.

This story, as do others in the collection, upholds the success myth for Asian Americans. It illustrates the complexities of class for recent immigrants who come from backgrounds of wealth and education to find themselves doing working-class jobs, but who, owing to their backgrounds, may not identify as working-class. This might help to account for the deemphasis of work, and for the way in which the privilege of engaging in artistic work (necessary though it is to a community's survival) goes unacknowledged in *The Forbidden Stitch*. The biographies confirm the privilege of the anthology's contributors: of the 60, 15 identify themselves as professional writers, 19 as academics, and 20 as having graduate degrees. In addition, 46 contributors mention mainstream or academic funding, rewards or publications, while only 4 mention non-professional employment.

The few exceptions to this general tendency in *The Forbidden Stitch* provide glimpses into the lives of poor or working-class Asian Americans or thematize class divisions among Asian Americans. One of these is Alison Kim's "Sewing Woman," which gives voice to a woman too overworked to eat, let alone learn to write a poem in English: "I like crack-seed / After I married / I no like. / I like only sewing. / Too busy for eat anything" (203). This poem implicitly comments upon the anthology's limitations in relying upon written English to represent the range of Asian American women. In including only literature written in English, the anthology can admit only first-generation immigrants with educational and economic privilege and later generations of Asian Americans who have benefited from the labor of previous generations. This limitation is by no means unique to *The Forbidden Stitch*, or to Asian American literature; *The Forbidden Stitch* however, makes less of a project of addressing it (by introducing oral histories or transcribed conversations) than do the editors of *Making Waves, Home Girls, This Bridge Called My Back*, and *Calling Home*. Instead, as *The Forbidden Stitch* adheres to more conventional definitions of art and literature, the class bias of doing so goes largely unacknowledged.

Putting L.A. on the Map of Asian America

The undercurrents of class consciousness which may be detected in *The Forbidden Stitch* surface and become a focal point in Lim's 1993 preface to the inaugural issue of *Asian America: Journal of Culture and the Arts*. Lim's comments are triggered by the Los Angeles uprisings following the verdict in the Rodney King case, an event which made class divisions among Asian Americans and racial and class divisions between Asian Americans and other people of color explosively evident. Writing during the aftermath of this uprising, Lim attempts to confront and heal some of these divisions. After detailing the frustrations and rage fueling the violence in L.A., she shifts to a discussion of *Asian America*, in which she refutes the idea that the journal is "an elitist production, a middle-brow project for middle-class Asian Americans seeking cultural legitimation."[41] Contending that the journal responds to the needs of cultural workers, Lim asserts, "*Asian America* is the product of volunteer and minimum-wage labor: none of our contributors are paid, all of our editorial work is undertaken voluntarily, and one editorial assistant labored under minimum wage conditions to help us physically produce the copy. While the journal's form . . . appears middle-class, its materialization is the result of community striving and low or no wages, as historically has been the case with Asian American small businesses" (7). To suture over the differences between small businesses and an academic journal, Lim must overlook the fact that virtually all academic journals are produced this way, and that participants are able to work on them because, unlike small business owners, their means of subsistence lies elsewhere. The inadequacies of Lim's argument here testify movingly to the difficulties of forging alliances across classes for Asian Americans, and to the urgency Lim feels both to justify academic work and to override class divisions in the wake of the violence directed against first-generation Korean Americans in Los Angeles.

Having tenuously allied Asian Americans across the related divides of education, immigration, and class, Lim struggles with their relationship to other racial and ethnic groups. In a discussion that complicates any easy division between the dominant white society on the one hand and people of color and marginalized others on the other, Lim positions whites and non-Asian American people of color together as insiders who oppose Asian Americans. She concludes, "We need to ask, what has gone unsaid, unshared, uncommitted between Asian Americans and other ethnic groups who have again and again expressed the fear that they are being hurt by our presence?" (8). Lim's efforts to confront and heal ethnic and class divisions in *Asian America* not only among Asian Americans, but also among Asian Americans and other racial and ethnic groups, illustrate the painfulness and difficulties involved, and the lack of an adequate theoretical language or conceptual framework for doing so.[42] Lim's preface suggests that the white backdrop that accompanies works such as *Making Waves* and *The Forbidden Stitch* will increasingly become a multiracial one. Both the violence in Los Angeles and Lim's preface point to the need for more nuanced theories of class, within and across different ethnic groups, that can articulate the importance of factors such as language, education, location, generation, and citizenship status in the United States, in addition to factors of race, gender, and sexuality.

Asian America, with its dual focus on nationalization and denationalization, expands and develops the projects of both *The Forbidden Stitch* and *Making Waves.* The journal's multilingual, multinational approach expands the class boundaries for Asian Americans and their literature, and makes interlocking forms of analysis necessary. With their insistence on giving voice to the heterogeneity within Asian Americans, *Making Waves* and *The Forbidden Stitch* not only forge models for a nonexclusionary politics of identity, they also begin to make such analysis inevitable.

5

(Un)Common Class Identities in the United States and Britain

Calling Home and *The Common Thread*

> Begin with the material. Pick up again the long struggle against lofty and privileged abstraction. Perhaps this is the core of revolutionary process, whether it calls itself Marxist or Third World or feminist or all three.
> —Adrienne Rich, "Notes Towards a Politics of Location (1984)," p. 213

> Class has been the invisible issue for far too long.
> —Julie Cotterill and Jeanne Wilding, introduction to *The Common Thread*, p. 9

If the L.A. uprisings signal a racial crisis that includes the threats to, as well as the continuing need for, solidarity among people of color, they also emerge from and speak to a class crisis that cannot be understood solely in terms of race or ethnicity. Indeed, this class crisis, based as it is in the increasing numbers of people in this country who are materially dispossessed, is precisely what is breaking apart and transforming categories of race and ethnicity. Over the course of the Reagan and Bush years, class became a pressing concern in the United States, disrupting the coherence of identities within as well as across categories of race, gender, and sexuality.[1] During these years the wealthy elite became even more so (one-third of the wealth in the United States is presently owned and controlled by 1 percent of the people), the middle class shrank (many workers lost jobs as a result of "down-sizing" and subsequently—now—are patching together a living), and growing numbers of people came to live a paycheck away from the street or in poverty (over forty million in 1991, most of them white women and children).

In the academy, critics are increasingly noticing that while it is often evoked as part of the "race, class, and gender" triumvirate, class is generally either overlooked or subsumed within analyses of race or gender, especially in practices of identity politics. The other anthologies in this study, which have either understood class as a part of a racial identity (*This Bridge, Haciendo Caras,* and *Home Girls*) or have chosen not to focus on it (*The Forbidden Stitch, Making Waves,* and *Nice Jewish Girls*), provide some evidence for this claim. In addition, critics in North America and Europe have noted that "identity politics emerges from the demise of class politics attendant upon post-Fordism or pursuant to May '68,"[2] and a few have gone so far as to argue that, in fact, identity politics occurs only with the dismantlement of class politics. Wendy Brown, for one, suggests that "the political purchase of contemporary American identity politics would seem to be achieved in part *through* a certain renaturalization of capitalism which can be said to have marked progressive discourse since the 1970s" (206). Brown poses the rhetorical question: "To what extent do identity politics require a standard internal to existing society against which to pitch their claims, a standard which not only preserves capitalism from critique, but sustains the invisibility and inarticulateness of class, not accidentally, but endemically?" (208). While other critics such as Stanley Aronowitz, Constance Coiner, and Cornel West do not necessarily find identity politics and class discourse to be at odds, they call for attention to class as a means for overcoming the fragmentation and separatism engendered by identity politics.[3]

Some U.S. critics, however, have formulated an identity politics that makes class a primary focus. One such critic, Janet Zandy, does so in editing *Calling Home: Working Class Women's Writings.*[4] This 1990 anthology marks the growing consciousness of an American working-class identity in an age of identity politics. Zandy sets out in this anthology to make class identity central, and to create a place of belonging for North American working-class women and their literature. As such, the anthology provides a way both to explore the possibility for an identity politics that takes class as its primary concern and to test the limits—and limitations—of identity politics. From her position in the academy, Zandy works to make a home for herself and other working-class women both inside and outside the academy, and she insists on a common identity for working-class women that transcends differences including those of education, income, occupation, race, ethnicity, geography, sexual orientation, age, and generation. Faced with the amorphousness of working-class identity in the United States, Zandy confronts the dual projects of defining and uniting working-class women and their literature. Her strategy for doing so—insisting on working-class women's commonalties across a range of differences—often makes the basis for working-class women's community a bewildering one; the contradictions Zandy's anthology encompasses and attempts to gloss over continually threaten to undermine the community she works to create. At the same time, I would argue, her insistence on understanding class through the rubric of a claimed and shared experience provides a compelling glimpse of how identity politics may be deployed to work against the class structures so operative in the United States—structures in which the authoritative abstraction and elitism of theories such as Brown's are implicated.

After a consideration of *Calling Home* in the first half of this chapter, I turn to *The Common Thread: Writings by Working-Class Women*, the 1989 British anthology edited by The Common Thread Collective.[5] Published in a country in which class already serves as a primary marker, *The Common Thread* anthology works within firmly established class structures that liberate The Common Thread Collective to foreground and celebrate working-class women's differences, rather than their commonalties, and defiantly to assert themselves against the middle-class and male-dominated working-class institutions that oppress them. The striking contrasts between *Calling Home* and *The Common Thread* demonstrate that any conclusions we may draw about the possibilities and limitations of identity politics are contextual and embedded in a particular history, as are any understandings of class. I also look, in the conclusion of this chapter, at the black British women's anthology *Charting the Journey*, to consider the way particular class- and race-based identities mutually construct, inform, and deconstruct one another, and national identities as well. Considered together, *Calling Home, The Common Thread*, and *Charting the Journey* verge on undoing the categories of identity upon which they and the other anthologies in this study depend. At the same time, these British and U.S. anthologies together provide another way of mapping and exploring further the significance of the current challenges to national boundaries traced in chapter 4, and also the transnational alliances and practices of identity politics that contribute to and can result from these challenges.

Defining Class in a "Classless" Society

In naming her 1990 anthology of working-class women's literature "Calling Home," editor Janet Zandy indicates the distance she feels from her working-class origins, and suggests that representing or articulating working-class experience involves separation from these origins. Unlike Barbara Smith, who, with her title "Home Girls," firmly grounds her anthology in her and other working-class contributors' homes, Zandy's attempt is to get back home. Through her anthology, she calls home from another location, namely, the Rochester Institute of Technology where she teaches. In her preface, Zandy explains herself as follows: "I write from a double perspective: from the inside working-class consciousness of my childhood and from the outside perception of formal education. My purpose is to align these two views to provide a place where the lives and voices of working-class women can be seen and heard" (n.p.). Zandy thus revises Paul Lauter's assertion that working-class people, "to improve their lot, must either move in solidarity with their class or leave it."[6] In attempting to move in solidarity with the class she has left, Zandy reaches toward both her working-class home and the university. She complicates the clear-cut nature of Lauter's alternatives by acknowledging what the anthology itself enacts—the difficulty not only of calling home, but of leaving home for another class location, in this case the academy. Neither of the two locations offers Zandy a real home. As *Calling Home* strives to make working-class women visible, and to celebrate their literature under the rubric of their class identity, it embodies some of the complexities and contradictions of defining working-class as a social identity and as a literary category.

Class, as Zandy points out in her introduction to *Calling Home,* is a category both operative and invisible in the United States: "The British working-class has one advantage over the American: it is, at least, named. . . . [In America] class is masked, hidden behind a national mythology of rugged individualism, social mobility, and political equality. Class consciousness is thwarted by institutionalized confusion of democracy and capitalism" (2). This national mythology not only instills the belief that, like Horatio Alger or Benjamin Franklin, one can move from rags to riches by way of ingenuity and hard work; it also works to stigmatize economic hardship as laziness or shiftlessness, thus leading people to deny their working-class existence or culture, unless, of course, they can narrate it as a condition that has been overcome.[7] This silencing further enables those with class privilege to deny that a class system even exists in this country. Class is, as Paul Fussell says, "America's dirty little secret."

When working-class existence is claimed or acknowledged, defining this existence presents its own problems and complexities. Not only is class under-theorized in the United States, but, as E. P. Thompson states at the outset of his treatise on English working-class formation,

"'Working classes' is a descriptive term which evades as much as it defines."[8] Much work on class in the United States takes the form of sociological studies. In the "strata approach" to class—which entails perceiving classes as layers stacked according to factors including wealth, occupation, level of education, and indications of social status—the relative importance these factors assume changes over time and place, making class identity difficult to determine. Earned income, for example, used to be a reliable gauge of class belonging, but some skilled "blue collar" workers today earn more than some "white collar" professionals. Coordinates including race, region, family history, education, and gender, further complicate or render chaotic understandings of class. Marxist conceptualizations of class, in which people are either capitalists, workers, or petty bourgeoisie, have also broken down in the postindustrial era. As Paul Gilroy notes, "Class has been shorn of the positivistic certainties which came to be associated with it when industrial production was ascendant."[9] This is particularly true as the number of people without jobs or homes grows. Generally speaking, the meaning of class fluctuates depending upon the context in which the term is used.[10]

For women, issues of class definition are particularly vexed. Because "working class" is so often coded as white and male,[11] definitions and discussions of working-class people often exclude, and are unable to address, questions and issues particular to working-class women, particularly women of color. For example, theories of class seldom consider the distinctions and contradictions between class and racial identity or affiliation, whether or not a woman must work for wages to be working class, or what the interrelations are for women between productive and reproductive labor. Because the very definition of "work" in the United States is gendered male, it obscures the lives of working-class women, whose private and public lives—and unpaid and paid labor—so often overlap. Feminist scholars are beginning to engage such questions, particularly by way of case studies,[12] but at the moment, as Zandy comments, the lives of working-class women "are obscured and erased; their work is barely visible" (5).

Basic problems of erasure, invisibility, and definition are compounded in the case of working-class women who, like Zandy, become academics. Because the unspoken norm in the university is middle-class, and because in academia neither language, dress, nor lifestyle provides a reliable indicator of a person's class background, class differences are often obscured.[13] Because all academics in such an environment are assumed to be either middle-class or part of the professional-managerial, or

"New" class,[14] many working-class academics explain that entry into the academy puts them at odds with their sense of working-class belonging. As Lillian Robinson points out, "The cultural euphemism for the working class is the 'less well-educated.'"[15] "Higher education," as Sharon O'Dair has put it, "is, perhaps, the best route out of working-class life, [but it] also helps keep the majority of the working class firmly embedded there."[16] As such comments suggest, to be a working-class academic in our culture presents a contradiction in terms, one that can prove particularly painful to working-class people who manage to gain entry into the academy. Once there, people of working-class origins receive little institutional support for, and opposition to, studies of their working-class backgrounds. In *Strangers in Paradise*, a collection and analysis of narratives by academics from the working classes, Jake Ryan and Charles Sackrey conclude *that the academic work process is essentially antagonistic to the working class, and academics for the most part live in a different world of culture, different ways that make it, too, antagonistic to working class life.*[17]

In U.S. universities, generally speaking, race and gender are seen as more "obvious" and recognizable categories than class, both as identities to rally around and as objects of study. Or, as Zandy puts it, "Class identity is easier to obscure and deny than gender and race identity" (2). Hence the past few decades have seen the development of women's studies, ethnic studies, and, albeit less commonly, lesbian and gay studies programs, without the development of comparable programs on class. As Zandy notes, "The epistemology of working-class lived experiences is not part of the institutionalized construction of knowledge."[18] As an identity and as an area of study, class often falls through the cracks, or becomes subsumed by gender and/or race. Middle-class feminist theorists such as Wittig or Christine Delphy who claim and focus on women as an oppressed class, and/or focus on middle-class women, often exclude working-class women and their concerns.[19] And while white middle-class academic feminists have begun to position ourselves more consciously in terms of race and class, this has not resulted in a much greater understanding of, or attention to, working-class women and their concerns. Both white academics and academics of color often study class status as determined by, or secondary to, race.[20] Although the two are of course closely linked in the United States, approaching class through race eclipses an understanding of how class operates inter- and intraracially, and what working-class women across races do or do not share. A race-based focus may lead to the erasure of white working-class women, whose experiences may differ profoundly from working-class women of color, but no less profoundly from white middle-class women. Thus, it is perhaps not surprising that most of the efforts to highlight working-class identity in the academy have come from white women, Zandy included, who have done so by way of writing and/or compiling narratives which make visible and lay claim to their own and other women's working-class origins.[21]

Such projects, with their emphasis on class genealogy, enable women in the academy to counter those theories of class and, more recently, of identity politics, that leave them and their literature invisible. In the past, for the most part, academics who have concentrated on class as a category of analysis have not considered working-class women and their literature. Marxist literary theorists have traditionally ignored women and their issues, and have often maintained a focus on canonical (middle-class) literature.[22] Working-class culture in general, and working-class women's literature more specifically, constitute largely unexplored—if not entirely unacknowledged—subject matter. Paul Lauter's 1980 article, "Working-Class Women's Literature," marked one of the first attempts to stake out a definition for and a bibliography of U.S. working-class women's literature. In fact, in her 1990 anthology, Zandy expresses her debt to this article, and draws on many of its sources and definitions. Zandy's anthology remains part of a terrain that is just beginning to be charted. Among anthologies of the past few decades organized around identity, for example, Zandy's is the first to make class primary. In politicizing working-class identity, and in claiming it as the basis for a shared culture, *Calling Home* builds on, and points to the exclusions of, practices of identity politics based primarily upon race, gender, or sexuality.

Towards Calling the Academy Home

At the 1991 MLA convention, as a participant on a panel entitled "American Working-Class Women's Writing," Gloria Anzaldúa stated that, as an academic, she can no longer lay claim to her working-class identity. She expressed the conviction that her work as an intellectual removes her from her origins, from the working-class into which she was born.[23] Tillie Olsen, a panel respondent, passionately contested Anzaldúa's claim. She asserted that, as someone who writes about and articulates a working-class consciousness, Anzaldúa not only represents the working-class, she fulfills that class's potential.

The clarity of Olsen's response to Anzaldúa was complicated by her asking, in her opening exchange with the audience, which audience members were the first in their family to attend college. By posing the question, she was ostensibly asking the audience a question about class belonging, and suggesting that, at least for previous generations, working-class belonging was incompatible with a university education. Anzaldúa's message to the audience was also a multivalent one, with her body language contradicting her words. She gave her MLA address while standing on a chair, thus expressing her refusal to conform to the academy and its class-based conventions. Anzaldúa and Olsen's exchange dramatizes some of the contradictions and instabilities of class definitions in this country, in particular for working-class women who enter the university. How, for instance, does receiving an education associated with class privilege change one's working-class identity? Does one, or can one, maintain a working-class identity as a professional academic with a middle-class income and predominantly middle-class colleagues? If so, would one, or could one, pass this working-class identity on to one's children? Does representing or articulating working-class experience entail, as Anzaldúa implies it does, separation from this experience, or even from a working-class identity? To what extent do academics constitute a class of their own, one that precludes working-class belonging?

While panel participants discussed the ways in which a university education and an academic career entail the potential dislocation from one's working-class origins, the panel's context at MLA dramatized working-class women's dislocation in the university. The enthusiasm of the audience that crowded into a tiny conference room at 8 A.M. for the MLA's only panel on working-class women's literature seemed to me symptomatic of the lack of space and attention granted working-class women and their literature in the university. It also suggested working-class women's urgent desire to make their literature and themselves more visible.[24]

The same desire motivates Zandy's *Calling Home*, where she and other contributors dramatize the questions and contradictions working-class women encounter in the academy. Of her project of mapping out working-class literature, Zandy concedes, "We do not know where the borders of working-class literature are nor how much of it exists. Judging from the yield of my research and the many contemporary women who are worker-writers, I suspect there is a rich but submerged lode" (7–8). In characterizing working-class literature as a "submerged lode," Zandy attributes the indeterminacy of its boundaries to inadequate research rather than to the category itself. To assert the category of working-class literature as valid, Zandy juxtaposes works from disparate genres and time periods (ranging from 1910 to the present), contending: "To try to fit this literature into the neat academic categories of genre or period is like squeezing a wilderness into a cultivated park. Despite its diversity and unconventional literary forms, working-class literature is not a mass of dangling parts but a collective body of work" (9).

While Zandy claims the unconventionality of working-class forms of literature and its defiance of academic categorizations, she also attempts to assert this literature's unity and legitimacy. In doing so, she ends up with an organizational structure that, in its thematic progression, is ultimately fairly conventional. Her comparison of working-class literature to a wilderness, for example, evoking as it does Elaine Showalter's formulation of the by now well-landscaped field of feminist criticism, begins to tame the wilderness even as she asserts it. While insisting on the breadth and uncertainty of its boundaries, Zandy nevertheless works to give the category of working-class literature solidity.

Zandy's designation of working-class women writers as "worker-writers" achieves a similar effect. The vagueness of this term gives Zandy maximum flexibility in defining the literature, and it suggests that a writer-worker is occupied both with writing and some other "real" work.[25] Rather than proceeding by "neat academic categories of genre or period," Zandy divides *Calling Home* into three sections she describes as being "by," "about," and "for" working-class women: "Telling Stories," "Bearing Witness," and "Celebrating Solidarity." She subdivides each section thematically, including in each a mix of songs, poems, oral and written autobiography, speeches, reportage, short stories, and excerpts from novels and research projects written by women from different time periods, age groups, races, ethnicities, and geographical regions. Zandy uses this mix of genres to demonstrate the range of working-class literature as she simultaneously argues for the literature's unity.

Working-class literature, Zandy argues, is characterized by its accessibility and by its thematic grounding in material conditions. "The literary antecedents of the texts in [*Calling Home*]," she explains, "come from material existence rather than canonized literature" (11). The anthology's artwork consists of snapshots of anonymous working-class women, emphasizing the anthology's rootedness in the lives of everyday working-class women. Entries describe, and often attempt to convey through form and style, working-class women's work. Hazel Hall's poem "Puzzled Stitches," with its sing-song rhythm and simple rhyming scheme, reflects the sort of reverie that might accompany sewing: "Needle, running in and out, / In and out, in and out, / Do you know what you're about, / In and out, in and out?" (96).

Accompanying her characterization of working-class literature's connection to material conditions are Zandy's claims, and those of many of the *Calling Home* contributors, regarding this literature's usefulness to other working-class people. Contributor Florence Reece explains the origins of "Which Side Are You On?," her song protesting the conditions of coal miners: "It was the night Sam had sneaked in through the cornfields and I was a-watchin' for the thugs to come after him. That's when I wrote the song. We didn't have any stationery cause we didn't get nothing, we was doing good to live. So I just took the calendar off the wall and wrote that song, 'Which Side Are You On?'" (62). In addition to Reece's utilization of everyday materials, her song is informed by her urgency to protest workers' conditions and her desire to make a protest in which others can easily participate. Judy Grahn also wants her art to reach and be useful to a large (working-class) audience. She celebrates the fact that her "Common Woman Poems" "were reprinted hundreds of thousands of times, were put to music, danced, used to name various women's projects, quoted and then misquoted in a watered-down fashion for use on posters and T-shirts" (315). For Grahn, these poems succeed *because* they become the property of "the masses." Their popularity and popularization constitute for Grahn not appropriation or cheapening, but good use, the fulfillment of her expectations for a practical art that many women ("common women") can relate to and make their own.

As *Calling Home* puts forth a distinctly working-class literature and aesthetic, it challenges the reigning academic criteria which demand that literature be difficult, expressive of individual uniqueness or genius, and dense in allusions. In celebrating texts that literature departments often denigrate or dismiss as propaganda, as popular, or as source material for historians or ethnographers, *Calling Home* also exposes the upper/middle-class biases of modernist definitions of what constitutes literature, raises questions about the purpose and value of literature, and points to its participation in enforcing and creating class distinctions.[26] In working to make a place for working-class women's literature, Lauter asks "whether the expectation, the demand for denseness and speculative play in a work does not disable critics from apprehending other virtues, of transparency in structure, of immediacy in language, and of feelings deeply engaged by symbol."[27] In evidencing the values of simplicity, repetition and accessibility, *Calling Home* implicitly responds to this question.

Calling Home and its authors do not, however, simply cast aside accepted forms and aesthetic criteria as irrelevant, or as the exclusive province of the middle and upper classes. The anthology instead juxtaposes working-class forms of the kind literature departments typically exclude (i.e., oral narratives, popular songs, reportage) with more canonical writing. In the context of *Calling Home*, correspondences emerge between Olsen's use in *Yonnondio* (excerpted in the anthology) of modernist techniques that dramatize the mechanized frenzy of factory work and Hall's use of simple rhymes and repetitions. In this way Zandy breaks down, rather than reinforces, hierarchized binaries between literature and popular culture, and between scholarship and propaganda or politics. Similarly, though the anthology in some ways privileges forms of oral expression over written forms, it also works against the hierarchized boundary between the written and the oral by interspersing oral narratives with written ones.

When There's No Place Like Home

Zandy works in *Calling Home* to make a place in the university for both working-class women's literature and working-class women themselves. At the same time, she attempts to use the anthology as a way to (re)connect with her working-class home outside the university. Zandy and many of the other contributors who write professionally express the sense that, as their working-class backgrounds isolate them within the university, writing often puts them in opposition to, rather than in alliance with, their working-class communities. Zandy's solo editorship and the dearth of material written specifically by friends and/or colleagues for *Calling Home* suggest to me the isolation, and most probably the budget constraints, that working-class women face as writers and academics.[28]

In fact, for many of the women in *Calling Home* writing entails not only separation from their working-class communities but a betrayal: the sense that they act as voyeur-accomplices, exposing working-class secrets to a middle-class audience. Zandy herself reveals such a view of her writing and anthologizing at the close of her introduction: "My journey away from the factory that faced my home has taught me how great the divide is. Books alone cannot bridge it. Economic justice will bridge it. Until that justice comes, let us *pry* open the doors, see the divisions, remember the possibilities, the promise of home" (13, emphasis added). Zandy reveals her sense that writing of home (or collecting such writing) involves an act of voyeurism, of forced or surreptitious (re)entry. Although Zandy here stresses the positive aspects of her working-class home, both she and other writers find themselves, in portraying their working-class homes, exposing the oppressive conditions of these homes. Contributors repeatedly portray their working-class homes as places from which they desire to escape, as well as loci of love and strength. Psychic and physical enclosure converge in many of these narratives. Sandra Cisneros writes of her home on Mango Street, "It's small and red with tight little steps in front and windows so small you'd think they were holding their breath" (69). Cy-Thea Sand evokes a similar atmosphere of claustrophobia when describing her childhood home: "My father's irritability marked the boundaries of my childhood like the fence of our tiny backyard" (29).

Such pieces exist alongside and in uneasy tension with Zandy's claims regarding the collective nature of working-class writing, and her inclusion of pieces that thematize and/or embody a working-class collectivity. In her introduction she argues that, given its purposes in expressing class solidarity, "a collectivist rather than individualistic sensibility is a key difference between bourgeois art and working-class art, as the handful of critics who study working-class literature attest" (12).[29] The anthology culminates with "Celebrating Solidarity," a section demonstrating Zandy's contention that "The working-class writer/artist uses her skills in service to her community" (269), and writers throughout the anthology echo or illustrate this claim. In "What It Is I Think I'm Doing Anyhow," Toni Cade Bambara discusses the different kinds of writing she does, including her work as neighborhood scribe. Poems by Marge Piercy and Meridel Le Sueur stress the need for collective consciousness and action. In her reportage "The Strike," Olsen (then Lerner) writes in solidarity with longshoremen and other workers involved in the General Strike of 1934, presenting herself as both witness and participant in their collective uprising. The oral narratives included in *Calling Home,* involving as they do collaborations between a writer and narrator(s), exemplify another collective format open to working-class literature.

Zandy's claims for collective writing, and the examples she presents, provide her with a means to counter the alienation she and other writers who have migrated from their working-class homes experience, both within these homes and in the university or other middle-class environments. The format of *Calling Home,* wherein works from disparate genres are placed side by side, often with little or nothing in their introductions to place them as fiction, or oral or written histories, serves to equalize the various positions of the writers and speakers. Through it Zandy shapes a community of writers that includes both academics like herself and women who can neither read nor write. And in introducing oral history as "a collaborative effort where the literary skills of the listener are joined with the memories of the teller" (11), Zandy unites academics with women who have not left their working-class communities.

While this strategy works against ranking women in *Calling Home* in terms of how "authentically" working-class they are, thus bypassing the kind of debates in which Anzaldúa and Olsen engage and, instead, allying contributors across differences in education and income, it also forecloses on any exploration of the inequities or negotiations such differences may result in, both in general and among the contributors. The juxtapositions of genres such as autobiography and scholarship on working-class women, for example, blur the distinctions Zandy establishes by structuring the anthology into sections that are "by," "about," and "for" working-class women. The effect of this is to collapse differences between literature in which working-class women appear as subjects and literature in which they appear as objects. Furthermore, the way Zandy presents the oral narratives smoothes over the potential inequities and/or tensions between "speaker" and "listener," terms which downplay the latter's power as editor and writer. Instead, the anthology presents the relationship between them in the most idealized terms, often leaving the listener's class background and relationship to her narrator unspecified. Zandy thus avoids exploring aspects of the kind approached by Sherna Berger Gluck and Daphne Patai in their analysis of the feminist practice of oral history: "In addition to the empowering aspects oral narrative has for a teller," they point out,

> narrators typically are not true partners in the process. Whatever control they exercise during the interview, when they are able to negotiate the terrain, usually ends once the session is completed. This shift in control over the narrative reveals the potential for appropriation hiding under the comforting rationale of empowerment.[30]

As Gluck and Patai indicate, oral narratives consist of negotiations for control on the part of both narrator and listener/scholar. While a narrator may employ a variety of strategies to tell (or not tell) her story, it is the scholar—who does not necessarily belong to the narrator's community—who usually has the final say over, and ownership of, this story.[31]

As Zandy equalizes the relationship between scholar and narrator in the body of *Calling Home*, the contributors' biographies evidence and reinforce the inequities of these roles. These biographies include the "listeners" and not the "speakers" from the oral narratives. For example, Zandy excerpts Mary Hammond's "I'm in the Sliced Bacon," as told to Betty Burke, from Ann Banks's *First Person America*. While Banks (whose class status is not given) and Burke appear in the contributors' biographies, Hammond does not. While Zandy's reasons for excluding narrators from the biographies are most probably practical, since so many of these women are probably dead or otherwise unreachable, their exclusion, even if necessary, highlights the way in which oral narrators remain invisible in a way scholars do not, and the way in which narrators' stories become the property of scholars. *Calling Home*, in its attempts to forge a community among women regardless of their education, fails to provide a satisfactory interrogation of the relationship of class and education.

Working against Time

Juxtaposing work from disparate time periods is another strategy Zandy adopts to unite working-class women and assert a place for them and their traditions in the academy. In including the work of women from previous generations, Zandy calls attention to an ongoing history of working-class women writers and a working-class women's culture, and draws on periods, especially the 1930s, when workers' identities were more clearly and collectively defined and claimed. In her clearest "intrusion" in the contributors' biographies, Zandy pays tribute to Olsen and Le Sueur, calling them the "spiritual and literary foremothers of this anthology" (346). As Zandy and other contributors honor writers and other working-class women from previous generations, they also link—even attempt to merge—their writing and politics with the work of these foremothers and past periods characterized by collective class struggle.[32] *Calling Home* counters the isolation and invisibility working-class women experience in the academy, and, as I will later discuss, provides a challenge to the elitism and exclusions of academic feminism. In her introduction, in arguing for the continuity of working-class women's concerns across time, Zandy states, "The writers in this collection are saying: I am, they were; we can be. The movement is in time but not linear; it is circular or spiraling" (10).

One disadvantage of melding time periods in this way is that it takes *Calling Home* into a position where class transcends history. Despite Zandy's stated intention in her introduction to demonstrate E. P. Thompson's conception of class as "relational, dynamic and situated in a specific history and culture" (5), the anthology's organization—in juxtaposing writers and writings from different time periods—and its contents work to dismiss considerations of class formation as a process that changes over time. Zandy's presentation of Agnes Smedley's "The Fall of Shangpo," which she uses to open the section "On Making a Revolution," is one such example. She introduces this piece by explaining, "In her description of the wealth of the landlords, the plight of the poor, the use of opium as a cash crop and as a means to numb the people, Agnes Smedley could be writing about the South Bronx or Detroit, instead of Shangpo, China, autumn 1931" (283). For me, this attempt to merge time and place provides an exaggerated instance of the way that the anthology in some ways empties out, rather than fills in, the term "working class."

In Search of Solidarity

In evoking a tradition of working-class women, and in allying contemporary working-class women with women of the past, Zandy and other contemporary contributors to *Calling Home* do not attempt to fit working-class women—either themselves or women from the past—into a contemporary feminist framework. In her poem "Downtown Women," Julia Stein divorces herself from a white middle-class feminist tradition: "I come from Bessie Abramowitz, / the Russian Jewish factory girl; / not Elizabeth Cady Stanton, / the WASP judge's daughter" (103). In establishing a lineage of working-class women, Stein avoids, as do Zandy and the other contributors, using the term "feminist." Bracketing any discussion of feminism within *Calling Home* enables Zandy to emphasize the commonalties among working-class women regardless of their views of feminism, and allows her to avoid bringing out the antagonisms that exist between working-class women and middle-class feminists. It also entails a deferral of questions of importance to establishing community, or alliances, among women along—or across—class lines.

The unity Zandy forges among working-class women relies not upon a recognizably feminist vocabulary, but a socialist one that emphasizes terms such as "solidarity" and evokes a tradition of unions and strikes. As Lauter says of the term "solidarity," it "is not simply a slogan or an abstraction that happens to appeal to many people who work. It is, rather, a way of describing the culture of people who have been pushed together into workplaces and communities where survival and growth enforce interdependence."[33] Zandy entitles the concluding section of her anthology "Celebrating Solidarity," and, in the introduction to this section, she privileges strikes as "moments of collective definition in the memories of workers, and in their common effort to fight for economic justice" (269). "Strikes," the first subdivision of "Celebrating Solidarity," ranges from Bertha Hendrix's account of the 1929 Gastonia Strike to a poem by Donna Langston about a contemporary strike. A language of solidarity and an emphasis on unions and labor movements runs throughout *Calling Home*, sometimes accompanied by an endorsement of communism or socialism (see, for example, Olsen's "I Want You Women Up North to Know"). In presenting visions antithetical to capitalism alongside pro-union ones which formulate struggle within capitalist structures, Zandy stresses not the conflicts and divisions inherent in these different visions, but their commonalties.

In evoking and unifying these traditions, Zandy also extends *Calling Home*'s vision of collective struggle to working-class men, and in fact shows the concerns of working-class men and women to be inseparable. Women in *Calling Home* such as Le Sueur, Smedley, Olsen, and Reece not only depict working-class men and women in struggle together, but often attribute their involvement in class-based activism to male family members. Many contemporary contributors, including Zandy, pay similar tribute to men workers.

Zandy's explanation that the anthology focuses on the literature of working-class women rather than working-class men and women because of space considerations serves to mute any feminist agenda she may have, and to suggest, in fact, that any divide the anthology establishes between men and women is an arbitrary one.[34] Furthermore, by including a few pieces by men that stress the connections among working-class men's and women's literature and lives, she makes permeable the boundaries between them. The anthology includes poems transcribed and written by Ross Talarico as part of an oral history project, oral narratives from John Langston Gwaltney's *Drylongso: A Self-Portrait of Black America*, a song written by Pete Seeger and Malvina Reynolds, and even an excerpt on motherhood from steelworker Thomas Bell's 1941 novel *Out of This Furnace*.

In forging a sense of unity among working-class men and women, Zandy complicates feminist formulations in which men, particularly white men, are positioned as oppressors/Other; she combats both the silences surrounding and the stereotypes particular to working-class men. As Zandy asserts of her father in her essay "Labor Day," he "was no blue-collar chauvinist" (156). And in her preface to the anthology, she establishes her concern with working-class men as well as women. She opens the first section, "Telling Stories," with a subsection "Identity," which begins with Bobbie Louise Hawkins' piece, "My Daddy Was a Good-Looking Woman Chaser." Other pieces in this section underline the connection between contributors' fathers and their sense of self. Carol Tarlen begins her poem "White Trash: An Autobiography" with her father's story. And, in "A Question of Identity," Sand speaks of her own and other white American or Canadian working-class women's "psychic/emotional links to the outside world being tied up with our fathers" (32). When she attended university, she confides, "I walked those corridors as my father's daughter" (35). Zandy entitles a section of the anthology "Parents," and, if anything, the section emphasizes the importance of fathers over mothers as role models, and the sense that a working-class identity is passed on through the father. In the opening piece, "The Father Poem," Sue Doro expresses a mix of emotions for her father but blames his meanness on "profit hungry factory owners." She ends the poem by asserting the need for solidarity with him. Other contributors similarly put their criticism of husbands or fathers in a socioeconomic context that allows them to ally themselves with these male figures.

The anthology's inclusion of men helps promote working-class men's and women's shared struggles against common oppression, but in doing so it fails to probe the material and historical conditions that might have led to many contributors' reliance on their fathers rather than their mothers as role models and transmitters of class identity. Generally speaking, the anthology smoothes over all tensions between working-class men and women. Only five years after the publication of *Calling Home* does Zandy open up some space for such explorations. In the collection *Liberating Memory,* she includes a poem by Doro entitled "Focus," which addresses Doro's having been molested by her father. The poem is accompanied by a note on how Doro came to write a poem that contrasts so extremely with "The Father Poem": "I began to understand that my own personal political beliefs did not contradict my right to hold him accountable."[35] Although the opportunity exists here, Doro does not (and neither does *Calling Home* nor *Liberating Memory*) link critiques of men's roles in the domestic sphere to the history of sexism in unions, or to the sexism in socialist and communist movements.[36]

Calling Home's structure and its position regarding men also contribute to its heterosexual bias, which amounts to an erasure of lesbian sexuality. Literature about sexuality is placed in a section entitled "Sex, Marriage, and Birth," and the linkage of the three categories is explained only in another section ("Bearing Witness"), where Zandy states: "Being an 'old maid' is an economic luxury" (89). Ultimately, the anthology supports heterosexual and patriarchal institutions without allowing much room for criticism of them or alternatives to them—indeed the very term "old maid" itself forecloses a lesbian identity. Although many of the depictions of the domestic relationships between men and women are far from idealized, the overall effect in *Calling Home* is to suggest the inevitability, hence the justification, of traditional gender roles. This position is particularly evident in Thomas Bell's "Mary," a romanticized portrait of Mary as a grief-struck widow who lives as a martyr to her husband's death. A victim with no agency of her own, she depends upon her son to save her. Zandy includes the piece without contextualizing it, suggesting her support for such a representation of the woman and her marriage.

While the anthology contains accounts of women surviving domestic hardships and abuse at the hands of working-class men, *Calling Home* contains few pieces that critique or provide alternatives to—either through fiction or analysis—the ways working-class women are oppressed not only as workers but also as wives and mothers. All told, the only writings to represent lesbian relationships are Sand's "A Question of Identity" and Barbara Smith's "Home." Although the anthology includes pieces by Moraga, Grahn, Piercy, Dorothy Allison, and Nellie Wong, all writers who thematize lesbian feminism in other publications, the work Zandy selects for *Calling Home* does not do so.[37] While this group of writings does provide a glimpse of working-class women's lives that diverge from the otherwise heterosexually oriented narratives in the book, because they are so few in number, and because they are positioned and introduced in a way that highlights not their gender politics but other aspects of their working-class identities, the alternatives they represent are muted, and differences among working-class women—and among working-class women and men—remain glossed over.

Classifying Race

Race and ethnicity make up an area of special concern for Zandy as she works to unite working-class women. Zandy is aware, as Michael Omi and Howard Winant point out, that the racism of white workers (not just of capitalist institutions) has long been a divisive factor in the working class. As Omi and Winant explain:

With the end of Reconstruction in 1877, an effective program for limiting the emergent class struggles of the later nineteenth century was forged: the definition of the working class *in racial terms*—as "white." This was not accomplished by any legislative decree or capitalist maneuvering to divide the working class, but rather by white workers themselves. Many of them were recent immigrants, who organized on racial lines as much as on traditionally defined class lines.

. . . Thus the very political organization of the working class was in important ways a racial project. The legacy of racial conflicts and arrangements shaped the definition of interests and in turn led to the consolidation of institutional patterns (e.g. segregated unions, dual labor markets, exclusionary legislation) which perpetuated the color line *within* the working class.[38]

While contemporary studies show this legacy to be an ongoing one, and one specific to women's work cultures as well as men's,[39] in *Calling Home* Zandy sets herself against it. She opposes this history of "divide and conquer" in part by countering the idea that whiteness automatically entails privilege, and by attempting to make a place for white working-class women within current practices of identity politics.[40]

One of Zandy's strategies for forging cross-racial unity is to use class-related themes to group together literature by women of different races and ethnicities. This organization suggests the existence of a working-class identity that encompasses, even transcends, women's racial and ethnic identities. In fact, much of the literature is not marked or introduced in a way that makes contributors' race or ethnicity evident. When contributors address their racial identities, Zandy organizes their writing in ways that stress cross-racial similarities. For example, Zandy places an excerpt about blues singer Sippie Wallace from Daphne Duval Harrison's book *Black Pearls* after "Clara Sullivan's Letter," a song by Malvina Reynolds exposing the conditions of coal miners in Perry County.

Calling Home also promotes cross-racial solidarity by including anti-racist pieces by white women, pieces by women of color expressing the need to transcend racial divisions, and pieces from anthologies organized primarily around contributors' racial identities. Including these previously anthologized pieces enables Zandy to highlight the class dimensions of that writing and the anthologies in which they initially appeared. Thus, for example, the working-class qualities of Cherríe Moraga's poem "The Welder" and Barbara Smith's essay "Home" emerge more strongly than they do in *This Bridge* and *Home Girls*. Lines such as Moraga's "I am a welder. / Not an alchemist. / I am interested in the blend / of common elements to make / a common thing" (326) achieve a new emphasis, working to forge a specifically working-class solidarity. This shift in emphasis complicates the presentations in *This Bridge* and other anthologies of white women as the oppressive and implicitly middle-class Other. For example, in the introduction to *Haciendo Caras,* Gloria Anzaldúa remarks of white feminists, "Yet in their eager attempt to highlight similarities, they create or accentuate 'other' differences [between women of color] such as class."[41] In suggesting here that class neither divides women of color nor can conjoin white women and women of color, Anzaldúa does not allow much room for a class-based politics, or for white working-class women to address their class oppression. Zandy combats such a position when she includes in *Calling Home* pieces from *This Bridge* and *Home Girls* (and other anthologies as well). She puts her anthology in alliance with these others, and white working-class women in alliance with women of color.

However, promoting cross-racial alliances as Zandy does necessitates smoothing over, at least provisionally, the racial tensions that exist among working-class women. Furthermore, at times *Calling Home* also presents class and race concerns as interchangeable. While stressing the similarities between these categories reveals connections between them, it also presents problems and questions as well. It becomes difficult, for example, to assess the ways that, as Omi and Winant point out, "class and race work off and sometimes contradict each other."[42] This becomes evident in Zandy's own "Class Quartet," an essay in which she describes her response to a speaker at an MLA panel who justified "racialism": " 'Oh,' I blurt out in a voice deliberately unbleached of its working-class color, 'is that why we are in these rooms giving papers and other people are in our hotel rooms cleaning toilets?' " (85). In equating racism and classism, Zandy has no room to address the distinction that white working-class people can "pass" in the academy (can bleach their voices to match their skin), as Zandy is able to do. Furthermore, when Zandy introduces the section entitled "Telling Stories," she begins with a quote by Toni Morrison taken from *Black Women Writers*: "My single solitary and individual self is like the lives of the tribe" (17). In shifting the context of Morrison's remark to apply to working-class women rather than African Americans, Zandy posits their interchangeability. Zandy's use of this quote by Morrison raises a great number of questions. Why, for example, do both black and working-class cultures claim to be characterized by collectivity? What different forms does collectivity take between black and non-black working-class women? Between working-class and middle-class African Americans? Can all African American, or all working-class women, be said to share a common culture? And finally, under what circumstances does applying remarks about race to speak to issues of class constitute an act of appropriation? In not addressing the ways in which class and race identities may contradict or compete with each other as well as overlap, the foundation the anthology establishes for an interracial community of working-class women is an uncertain one.[43]

That most of the contributors to Zandy's *Liberating Memory* are white suggests that the associations of "working-class identity" and whiteness remain in place, and continue to be an obstacle towards establishing a more inclusive working-class identity. At the same time, many of those contributors directly address and contest their own experiences with racism in white working-class movements,[44] and to that extent Zandy and the contributors lay the groundwork for a working-class movement that, in addressing the divides of race, can cut across them. The deployment of identity politics in both *Calling Home* and *Liberating Memory* suggests that, while race and class structure our society in complex and contradictory ways, they also open up space for formulating alliances across these and other categories of identity—in ways that can be used to resist social and economic inequities and injustices. And while constituting such alliances depends upon attention to, not a suspension of, the complexities of class, suspending these complexities may nevertheless prove to be a necessary first step.

When Calling Home Becomes an Occasion

While the inclusiveness of Zandy's *Calling Home* obscures the different forms class may take, as well as its divisions and the way in which it changes over time and place, this same inclusiveness also provides a starting point for unity among disparate groups of women and promotes solidarity among working-class women and men. *Calling Home*'s inclusiveness in terms of what constitutes working-class literature works against a territorial notion of it. This inclusiveness also allows readers from across classes a means for exploring the complexities and questions of class identity, and for thinking about the way class informs literature and our understanding of it. In this way, *Calling Home* provides an occasion, within the university, for dialogue about class, including dialogue about the possibilities and dangers of studies such as my own.

I suspect that one of the more difficult relationships for *Calling Home* to establish is the one between working-class academics and women with no access to written language, regardless of how "accessible" or grounded in material conditions the literature is.[45] In the introduction to *Calling Home*, Zandy expresses her hope that the anthology will serve as "an invitation to women in similar circumstances to tell their own stories and to seek opportunities for expression within the contexts of their communities or jobs" (6).[46] Zandy's choice of the verb "to tell" functions to extend her invitation to women who may not be able to read or write. Yet the practical inability of these women to receive this invitation demonstrates the basic limitations of *Calling Home,* and of writing in general, as a means for calling home to the range of working-class women Zandy seeks to reach (and whom she does include by way of the anthology's oral narratives). The fact that not all the women included in the anthology can read "their own stories" poses a problem Zandy does not address within *Calling Home.* Zandy had already disclosed one strategy for overcoming the limits of a textual "call," however, at the same MLA panel on working-class literature mentioned above. At the panel, Zandy distributed fliers advertising a reading of *Calling Home* that would take place in a San Francisco community building. Such a reading provides a way to begin to reach a range of working-class women, and it provides women from working-class backgrounds at the MLA conference with the occasion to call home, to invite their families to participate in a community that extends beyond the textual and beyond the academy.

A Language of Their Own/"No Language but Their Own"

The concern of the editors of the British anthology *The Common Thread: Writings by Working-Class Women* is not to call home, nor is it to define and create community among working-class women; instead they draw upon—and rework—an established history of working-class women's writings and organizations, and of working-class women's consciousness of themselves as an already-defined—and often negatively stereotyped—group. In her introduction to *Life as We Have Known It* (1930), a collection of Women's Co-operative Guild members' accounts of their lives as working-class women, Virginia Woolf writes,

It cannot be denied that the chapters here put together do not make a book—that as literature they have many limitations. The writing, a literary critic might say, lacks detachment and imaginative breadth, even as the women themselves lacked variety and play of feature. Here are no reflections, he might object, no view of life as a whole, and no attempt to enter into the lives of other people. Poetry and fiction seem far beyond their horizon. Indeed, we are reminded of those obscure writers before the birth of Shakespeare who never traveled beyond the borders of their own parishes, who read no language but their own, and wrote with difficulty, finding few words and those awkwardly. And yet since writing is a complex art, much infected by life, these pages have some qualities even as literature that the literate and instructed might envy.[47]

While the characteristic irony that attends Woolf's description of the inadequacies of the writing she introduces obfuscates her own position—indeed she begins by attributing the point of view she presents to a

male literary critic—this description nonetheless stands in the introduction, and is reinforced by her movement to a first person plural ("we
are reminded"). Furthermore, while Woolf imagines women writers of
the past as the genius sisters of Shakespeare, she imagines her working-
class contemporaries as fixed by their class position in some remote
and primitive *pre*-Shakespearean past—in a different class altogether
than that of "women."

Published fifty-nine years later, *The Common Thread* in many ways
builds upon the Women's Co-operative Guild's *Life*, while implicitly
refuting the main tenets of Woolf's introduction. A 1989 multi-genre
anthology of writings by British working-class women, *The Common
Thread* critiques the distinction Woolf adopts between working-class
language and the language of fiction and poetry, which Woolf evi-
dently views as unmarked or universal. *The Common Thread* exposes the
class biases of Woolf's distinctions and refutes them by presenting
fiction and poetry, as well as personal narratives, letters, diary entries,
essays, and artwork, in distinctly working-class forms. Furthermore,
unlike *Life*, the anthology need not rely upon an introduction by an
upper-class writer of great renown such as Woolf to justify its existence;[48] instead *The Common Thread* is introduced by a collective which
shares the anthology's name.

In addressing Woolf and her introduction in this way, I do not mean
to place myself "above" Woolf and her class biases. While the different
historical moment in which I write enables my critique of her position
vis-à-vis working-class literature, I nevertheless share many of Woolf's
criticisms of the failings of the literature of *Life* (and, by extension, *The
Common Thread* and *Calling Home*), although I am well-trained enough
to know that this venture into a discussion of "quality" is dangerous,
that any understanding of "quality" is shaped by competing ideologies.
I also share the discomfort Woolf feels in her relation to working-class
women. In the introduction to *Life*, Woolf describes her participation at
a Guild conference in the following way: "There is no life blood or urgency about it. However hard I clap my hands or stamp my feet there
is a hollowness in the sound which betrays me. I am a benevolent spec-
tator. I am irretrievably cut off from the actors" (xx). Such detachment
is often critiqued in the anthologies in this study, including *The Common
Thread*, as the problem with academics. For this reason, and because I
write during a time when the very possibility of benevolent spectatorship is suspect, I understand all too well Woolf's discomfort regarding
her position outside the community she observes and then introduces.
However, because writing inevitably entails the exposure of one's own

class position, investments, and biases, and because, after all, class identity is established relationally, across as well as within classes, this study of *The Common Thread* becomes for me a means to move beyond both "benevolence" and "spectatorship" into a position where I can try to understand—and where others can trace—my own class position as well as that of British working-class women's. I hope, in other words, to work from a position of discomfort that will be productive and instructive, for myself and for others. Furthermore, while this chapter does not focus on detailing and interrelating British and American formulations of nation, a comparison of *The Common Thread* and *Calling Home* does suggest the extent to which class identities cannot be understood apart from—but rather exist in a dialectical relation to—national identities and formations.

While *Calling Home* must struggle to assert the concept of working-class culture in the United States, *The Common Thread* negotiates clearly delineated understandings of British working-class culture and history. E. P. Thompson indicates just how far back British working-class history goes: "The outstanding fact of the period between 1790 and 1830 is the formation of 'the working class.' This is revealed, first, in the growth of class-consciousness: the consciousness of an identity of interests as between all these diverse groups of working people and as against the interests of other classes. And, second, in the growth of corresponding forms of political and industrial organisation. By 1832 there were strongly-based [sic] and self-conscious working-class institutions . . . , working-class intellectual traditions, working-class community-patterns, and a working-class structure of feeling."[49] These specifically working-class structures have continued into the twentieth century. According to Raphael Samuel, "The working class developed as a separate estate, with their own political party (Labour), their own forms of shopping (the Co-ops, whose membership doubled between the wars), and to an increasing degree their own forms of holiday making and entertainment."[50]

Working-class literature testifies to and helps shape the working-class institutions Thompson and Samuel reference. As Mike Featherstone notes, "the audience for accounts of working-class life has a long history going back to Engels and Charles Booth in the nineteenth century."[51] However, these accounts, which include, for example, Richard Hoggart's classic narrative about his Leeds childhood (*The Uses of Literacy*, in 1958), largely reflect and perpetuate the sexism of working-class culture and the marginalization of working-class women.[52] The Common Thread Collective cites the Virago Press 1977 reprint of *Life* as one of the "few books published in this country which have tried to re-claim our place in feminist history" (4). *Life* was initially published at a time when the Guild (founded in 1882) was at the height of its powers. By 1930, the Guild, "one of the first separatist organisations of working class women," and "an articulate and influential protagonist for wom-en's rights as well as a vehicle for personal and communal develop-ment,"[53] had nearly 1,400 branches and 60,000 members. In addition to *Life*, the Women's Co-operative Guild also published "Working Women and Divorce" in 1911, and, in 1915, "Maternity: Letters for Working Women," a collection which "received considerable public attention, both in Britain and America, and, despite the war, two editions were sold out within months of their appearance."[54] *The Common Thread*, then, not only defines itself against a male-centered working-class his-tory and identity, but also builds upon working-class women's organi-zations and writings, in particular, the Women's Co-operative Guild and its publications.

What distinguishes The Common Thread Collective from the Wom-en's Co-operative Guild and other working-class organizations is its explicit feminism and unequivocal focus on working-class *women*. When the Co-operative movement went into decline after WWII, the Women's Co-operative Guild was forced to choose between directing its energies to a working-class movement or a women's movement. The Guild chose the former (though its change of name in the 1950s to the Co-operative Women's Guild, as it marked its change in focus, perhaps also registered some resistance to this change). While writings by the Women's Co-operative Guild have been used since by both working-class organizations and feminist ones (the feminist press Virago repub-lished their early books), The Common Thread Collective, in its refusal to choose between or make separable their working-class and feminist concerns in *The Common Thread*, creates a model for working-class fem-inists interested in organizing and speaking collectively.

Edited by The Common Thread Collective, an organization of work-ing-class women, and published by Mandarin, a press committed to working-class women's concerns, *The Common Thread* demonstrates a sense of politicized autonomy and belonging to an established move-ment which remains inaccessible to Zandy, who edits *Calling Home* alone and from within the university, and publishes the anthology with a university press. While the energy of Zandy's anthology comes from its position between working-class and middle-class (university) lo-cales, the energy of *The Common Thread* comes from its firmly defined position outside middle-class institutions and ideologies, and outside male-dominated working-class institutions. In his study of working-class boys in the British school system, Paul Willis makes a claim for the "often unrecognised potential that working class cultural creativity and insight really does have." In his view, "the working class is the only class not inherently structured from within by the ideological intricacy of capitalist organisation. It does not take nor, therefore, need to hold the cultural and social 'initiative' and is thus potentially freer from its logic."[55] Whereas a consideration of *Calling Home* suggests that this claim does not extend to the United States, where class divisions blur to a much greater extent, *The Common Thread* substantiates and begins to realize Willis' claims regarding the potential for working-class cultural creativity and insight. In comparing the two anthologies, the liberatory potential as well as the constraints of a more fixed class structure for British versus U.S. working-class women become clear. Furthermore, *The Common Thread* contributors' status as women, and often as lesbians, gives them an even greater liberatory potential than the boys in Willis' study (Willis does not fully consider the ways cross-class constructions of masculinity help keep the boys in their place), even as this same status simultaneously accounts for their lack of power. While a position "in the margins" or "outside" may engender a stronger call for rebellion and unique forms of cultural creativity, the powers of these expressions to effect institutional change remain in question and help explain the combination of daring, despair, revolutionary optimism, and cynicism that characterizes *The Common Thread*.

Complicating and Claiming the Common

While Zandy in *Calling Home* works against the dominant perception of a classless American society, struggling to overcome the invisibility of working-class women and to forge a definition for them, the Collective in *The Common Thread* takes issue with the definitions and stereotypes that the upper and middle classes use to oppress working-class women. In countering these stereotypes, contributors insist on their right to self-definition: "This book speaks of working-class women's lives as they are. It is saying that *we* are the experts on working-class life, because *we* are the ones who live it" (5). The anthology's introduction and the introductions to six of the anthology's seven sections begin by denouncing the stereotypes which oppress working-class women. But rather than arrive at a definition for working-class women (which could be appropriated by middle-class readers), the anthology emphasizes the process of self-naming and self-definition. As Julie Cotterill and Jeanne

Wilding state in the introduction, "This book . . . contains the voices of many different working-class women, so when we ask, 'Who is working-class?', *perhaps* they give the beginnings of a definition" (6; emphasis added). In leaving open the possibility for a general definition of "working-class," *The Common Thread* enables contributors to define themselves without allowing working-class identity to become solely a matter of self-definition, or an indeterminate category altogether. In this way, the anthology guards against the position it refutes and attributes to the middle classes—namely, the perception that "we all are working class"—as it enables maximum diversity.

Heterogeneity is central to the political vision, and the politicization, of working-class identity that *The Common Thread* promotes. The anthology insists on the diversity of working-class women in terms of their education, shape, size, nationality, age, race, ethnicity, sexuality, physical abilities, politics, and attitudes. It expresses its opposition not only to classism and capitalism, but to racism, homophobia/heterosexism, sexism, and a wide range of other forms of discrimination. Its cover, a collage of photos of women of various ages and races, introduces the reader to the anthology's commitment to a diverse body of women. The five Collective members present themselves as characterized by the diversity they promote: June Burnett situates herself in relation to her black father and white mother; Julie Cotterill identifies herself as 31, white, able-bodied heterosexual/married, and the product of a Catholic upbringing; Annette Kennerly, as a lesbian mother; Phoebe Nathan, as a 73–year-old Jewish lesbian; and Jeanne Wilding, as a 40-year-old white lesbian mother. This heterogeneity extends to the nearly one hundred women the anthology includes: contributors discuss being old, young, single, married, heterosexual, mothers, lesbians, disabled, black, white, Irish, Jewish, fat, thin, vegetarian, etc. While *Calling Home* encompasses a diverse group of contributors, but elides their differences to establish the existence and unity of working-class women, *The Common Thread* foregrounds differences among contributors in order to challenge upper- and middle-class stereotypes of working-class women.

In making the anthology's name coterminous with the name of their collective, members of The Common Thread also work to extend their ongoing community to the women in the anthology, and to forge a textual collectivity based upon what working-class women have in common, what joins them together, in all their heterogeneity (their "commonness"). Not only in name do the boundaries between the collectivity and the text blur: the anthology sets into motion interactions between contributors that extend beyond its covers. As Cotterill and Wilding explain in the introduction:

It's taken about four years to put the collection together. In that time, we've organized a number of open meetings and readings of working-class women's work in different parts of the country, encouraged individual women to write, and the setting up of working-class women's groups, made hundreds of contacts, contributed to other anthologies, written articles, participated in conferences and challenged classism in a range of different ways. (6–7)

Thus, they value the book not only as end product, but as the means for bringing together and politicizing working-class women.

As they emphasize their diversity, the women of The Common Thread downplay any sense that their differences may create divisions among them. Cotterill and Wilding allude to, but do not make clear, the possibility of divisions among working-class women in their introductory remark: "The collective has never been static, and, until this last year, had twelve or so core members. For all sorts of reasons, as the book went to press, we were down to only five" (8). The notes on contributors, which list Collective members under the unwieldy subheading "The Common Thread Collective as the book went to press," further emphasizes the Collective's provisional and shifting make-up. The reasons for the Collective's fluctuations in membership remain unarticulated, although the likelihood that these difficulties have a strong if not exclusively economic base would make them interesting ones to explore. The pieces the Collective chooses to include show working-class women engaged in struggle with working-class men, and with middle-class men and women, but not with one another. Furthermore, the work in *The Common Thread*, for all its claims to diversity in attitudes and beliefs, maintains a consistently rigorous stance against racism, sexism, and other forms of oppression besides classism. In this way, the anthology maintains its focus on what binds working-class women together, and excludes views which might unravel their ties.

However, if the Collective members do not elaborate divisions among working-class women and the difficulties of working collectively, neither do they present collective work as "natural" for, or even characteristic of, working-class women; instead, they present such collectivity as a goal to work towards, one the anthology helps to set in motion. The collage on the anthology's cover brings together pictures of individual women (with the exception of one mother-child portrait), and the women in these snapshots and portraits become linked only through art, through The Common Thread Collective's efforts as editors. This effort to make individual women part of a collectivity recurs throughout the anthology: rather than listing contributors and the titles of their writings in the table of contents, for example, the Collective presents only the anthology's various themes. Thus contributors are presented first as a unified body, and only second as individuals, when their names precede their individual pieces in the body of the text, and when they are listed in the contributors section at the back. The arrangement contributes to the collective—and socialist—vision in *The Common Thread*.

Contributors to *The Common Thread* also express their belief in collective action in their writings, but for the most part, they present it as something to strive for, something which, though it might be textually arranged or imagined, does not yet exist. In the introduction to "Survival and Resistance," Wilding states, "Until we organize together, create networks of support, refuges, resistance etc., that fight [against exploitation] will be no more than it often is here—individual statements, angry letters, witty remarks to keep the pain at bay—private solutions" (301). As *The Common Thread* itself enacts the organizing it calls for, and makes "private solutions" public, it calls attention to the limitations of a textually arranged collectivity and activism, and moves towards a form of resistance that takes place outside of (though it may be enabled by) writing. Working with an already established category of identity, *The Common Thread* need not rely on *Calling Home*'s idealization of collectivity (an idealization it in many ways is unable to realize), and can instead confront and attempt to overcome the obstacles to collectivity.

The Common Thread Collective uses the anthology not only to establish a model and a means for realizing its goal of collectivity, but also to assert—and so help create—class pride in working-class women. The success of the anthology rests on its gestures beyond the limits of language, beyond what can be said in the anthology itself. Unlike *Calling Home*, in which pieces sometimes probe the shame working-class women may feel about their class belonging, The Common Thread anthology contains no reference to working-class shame. If class shame in the United States results from a linkage of the lack of capital with a judgment of moral deficiency, in *The Common Thread*, by contrast, it is viewed as a property of the middle class. In the cover collage, the women in the photos face forward, and, with only one exception, greet the reader with a smile. This upbeat representation establishes the mood the Collective strives to create in the anthology. One entire section of the anthology, "Class Pride and Celebration," is dedicated to the effort, despite the fact that, as Wilding acknowledges in the introduction to that section, "Pieces celebrating our class identity were few"

(263). Wilding accounts for the dearth of writings expressing class pride when she explains:

> The reasons for class pride are elusive, slippery and difficult to express. From birth, we face less opportunity and choice and for most of us, life is a continuous struggle.
>
> And yet, none of the hundreds of women who sent us their writing spoke of wishing to be other than working-class. We may not be able to say why, but all of us are glad, proud to be who we are—with our resilience and energy, our capacity to survive, to hope, to be creative, to maintain a sense of humour and a vision of beauty. (263)

Wilding here introduces class pride as a quality which defies reason or articulation, as one evidenced by a lack of comments to the contrary. She also reads expressions of survival and hope, humor and beauty as standing in for class pride. Thus, the Collective includes under the rubric of class pride pieces such as Sarah Hunter's "The Witchery of the Ocean," a meditation on the beauty and wonder of the sea. Class pride, in this section at least, comes to be characterized as the ability to transcend class, to share in concerns (i.e., the sea) that appear to be unmarked by, or outside of, social structures. Furthermore, entries wherein humor, hope, or assertions of survival form the basis for class pride raise the question of whether pride exists in spite of, or owing to, one's working-class standing. While the anthology as a whole works to inspire pride in working-class women readers and to stand up to middle-class ones, both the section's brevity and its specific entries suggest some of the difficulties associated with asserting a pride that is specific to, rather than transcendent of, the hardships and deprivations of a working-class existence.[56]

The pride and self-definition of the working class vis-à-vis the middle class is developed from a long history in Britain of firm divisions between the classes. Given working-class people's long history of struggle against class oppression, the relationship of the women in *The Common Thread* over and against middle-class women readers is strikingly more hostile and defiant than it is in *Calling Home*. While *Calling Home* contributors represent their struggles with middle-class colleagues, lovers, and friends, *The Common Thread* contributors represent middle-class people largely as mouthpieces for classist stereotypes and ignorance against which they may forge a sense of class pride. Nickie Roberts concludes "Frozen Smiles," an address to a middle-class couple who disapprove of her interactions with their son, "Most of all, I'm scared / he'll end up repressed / like you" (206). In a similar spirit, Theresa Verlaine concludes her poem directed at those who dismiss her with the phrase "people like you" with the lines: "'People like me' I said / looking her squarely in her hoity-toity middle-class eyes / 'People like me' I said / 'will rise up in their millions one day and wipe / People like you,' I said, / 'off the face of this bloody earth'" (310). Middle-class people are represented in the anthology as repeatedly failing or refusing to understand working-class women and their own privilege in relation to them.

Furthermore, whereas *Calling Home* admits middle-class contributors who speak "for" working-class women, in *The Common Thread* the lines are more sharply drawn. The only middle-class woman *The Common Thread* admits, Hilary P., is included for her response to an article by Marlene Packwood. The Collective makes clear that including her involves a violation of editorial policy. The views Hilary P. expresses are both patronizing and ignorant, and it becomes evident that the Collective makes this exception not to blur boundaries or to establish cross-class alliances, but rather to unite working-class women and to define more clearly what/whom they are up against. In *The Common Thread*, defying the pain of middle-class contempt becomes the grounds for pride and solidarity, although this stance also entails categorically denying middle-class people's subjectivity or sensitivity, and thus reinforces class divisions.

Taking (the) Education out of the Academy

The Common Thread's opposition to members of the middle-class extends even more forcefully to male-dominated and middle-class institutions. The Collective expresses opposition to the academy in particular, and uses the clearly delineated class hierarchies that have worked to exclude working-class women from the academy to their own advantage. While *Calling Home,* in some substantial ways, emerges from an academic community and attempts to reform that academy from within, *The Common Thread* attacks the academy from an outsider's position, rejecting its middle- and upper-class structures and ways of knowing. As Evelyn Tension puts it in the title to her 1979 pamphlet, to which collective members often refer: "You don't need a degree to read the writing on the wall." Contributors to *The Common Thread* often denounce academics as middle-class men out of touch with working-class women's lives, or as engaged in exploiting working-class women's stories and labor. In "The Sociologist," Verlaine writes, "The sociologist / looks down on me / through a vast microscope / of mis-understanding / non-understanding" (15), all the while making money from her and other women's stories. "Then / when he has finished exorcising his guilt / at my expense / he turns his back / and waits, / SILENT / as I clean his house" (16). As contributors describe the hierarchized division between working-class women and academics, they subvert it: not only do they portray academic men's knowledge as irrelevant and/or illegitimate in contrast to working-class women's, but they show how, because of the blindness of these men to working-class women's subjectivity, working-class women can learn the secrets and—literally and metaphorically—expose the dirty laundry of those who exploit them.

Despite this opposition to academia, as a middle-class, often male institution, the anthology simultaneously makes evident the complex relation that in fact exists between working-class women and the academy. Over twenty contributors mention their university educations, and others may have simply chosen not to mention it. Furthermore, many argue on behalf of working-class women's rights to a university education and refute the belief that higher education lies outside their province, attributing such beliefs to middle-class ignorance and exploitation. Jenneba Sie Jalloh in "I Am at the End of 85-Contradictions," is one of the few contributors to address the contradictory relationship she has to the university. Her poem dramatizes the way in which *The Common Thread*'s antagonism to the university emerges not only out of contributors' exclusion from the university, but from their experiences within it.

Contributors resolve the contradiction Sie Jalloh articulates by claiming a university education but then getting out of the university itself. Unlike some of the *Calling Home* contributors, the women in *The Common Thread* do not work as professional academics, and they view their working-class identities as wholly at odds with a university position, if not with a university education. While in *Calling Home* many contributors struggle to find a place as working-class women in the university, in *The Common Thread* contributors present passing as middle-class in the academy as a necessity which they ultimately refuse or condemn. Burnett expresses a typical position when she says that through education, "I had, I suppose, 'bettered myself,' but on my own terms and without surrendering the identity I had matured with" (276). While contributors value education (albeit ambivalently), they uniformly express their refusal of the limited possibility of assimilation into the middle classes that it offers them.

In and against Language, and the Body Language Beyond

Just as *The Common Thread* works to assert the compatibility between higher education and working-class identity, it vigorously asserts the compatibility between being working-class and being articulate (being a writer). While in *Calling Home* the amorphousness of class in the United States leads Zandy and other contributors to explore the split they perceive between their identities as writers and members of the working-class, in the *The Common Thread* the Collective presents this split as the product of middle-class attempts to silence working-class women. As Wilding states, "The image of us as inarticulate allows others to continue to determine what's good for us" (314). Not only do the members of the Collective compile their anthology to refute this image, but they argue against it in their individual pieces as well, at times by positing the compatibility between a working-class existence and writing, as Burnett does in the cartoon accompanying Kennerly's "About to Speak." In this cartoon, a business woman tells the woman scrubbing her office floor about her impending promotion. The woman responds, "That's nice dear. Did I tell you I'm having my first novel published in two weeks?" (349). Another cartoon by Burnett exemplifies *The Common Threads*'s alternative presentation of working-class women's relationship to writing. This cartoon, placed at the start of the section entitled "Identity," has a caption that reads, "I think poor Mary's having an identity crisis. She asked me if she was working-class or middle-class. I sorted her through. I told her she was a poet" (12). Here, as in Hunter's poem about the ocean, the category "writer" exists outside of, or as irrelevant to, class identity. In moments such as these, *The Common Thread* argues against the notion that one's class determines one's relationship to authorship or powers of articulation.

The anthology also makes clear, however, both the ways in which language is a structure defined and controlled by the middle-classes, and the obstacles faced by working-class women writers. Packwood's "The Colonel's Lady and Judy O'Grady—Sisters under the Skin?" historicizes working-class women's exclusion from reading and writing, and claims the ongoing effects of this exclusion: "Following on from this [history], even when working-class women can write, they are discouraged from being heard (i.e. published), unless they conform to the established principles of traditional writing and literature" (319). Packwood's article is one of the few pieces in *The Common Thread* that adheres to what she calls "established principles of traditional writing"; it is also one of the few previously published pieces *The Common Thread* includes. As the Collective provides a forum for working-class women writers whose writing doesn't conform to these principles, The Common Thread's decision to include "The Colonel's Lady" suggests their desire not only to comment on, but to counter the absence of, analytical writings by working-class women.

Rather than reject or dismiss analytical writing as middle-class, the Collective calls attention to the need for working-class women to overcome the obstacles to engaging in it. The Collective views the scarcity of analytical pieces they received in response to their call for submissions as symptomatic of the material conditions militating against working-class women's writing: in the introduction, Cotterill and Wilding state, "It was unfortunate, but perhaps not surprising, that an analysis of class represented such a very small percentage of the writings we received" (5). And in the introduction to "Survival and Resistance," Wilding explains, "Frequently the analysis we did receive was contained in correspondence. Sometimes it was angry, sometimes good-humoured, but however expressed, it was only a beginning" (301). The extreme brevity of the pieces in *The Common Thread* (the anthology contains 153 entries in 350 pages) and the fragmentary or unfinished nature of many of them further testify to the material and psychological constraints working-class women face as writers, as does the fact that only twelve contributors mention previous publications. Barbara Collins' "Diary" is typical in its truncated and fragmentary nature; her piece covers five weeks in just over one page, and in her contributor's note, she explains, "I write endlessly in my head but battle with even holding a pen to put things down on paper" (354). Writers in *The Common Thread* do not celebrate the formal qualities that mark their writing as working-class, nor do they present them as strategic or subversive; instead, the anthology evidences the ways in which working-class women have been denied access to written language, and demonstrates some of the costs of this denial.

In other ways, however, contributors work to transform the middle-class properties of language. In exploring the relationship of working-class boys to the middle-class institution of education, for example, Willis finds: "Part of the reaction to the school institution is anyway a rejection of words and considered language as the expression of mental life. The way in which these creative insights are expressed, therefore, is one of expressive antagonism to the dominant bourgeois mode of signification—language. In a real sense of the working class the cultural is in a battle with language" (124). *The Common Thread* manifests the different forms this battle may take. In negotiating working-class women's relation to language, the anthology vacillates between, on the one hand, claiming working-class women's abilities to utilize traditional forms of expressions, and, on the other hand, dismissing these forms as middle-class, and instead celebrating other working-class forms.

In challenging the middle-class biases toward prevailing configurations of what constitutes articulation, contributors to *The Common Thread* valorize specifically working-class forms of expression, ones which, when recognized by the middle classes at all, have been denigrated by them. Packwood, for instance, claims that despite the fact that a lack of education often leads to inarticulation over the range of the whole English language, "I think working-class women are more articulate than middle-class women in using a combination of language, anger and emotion in order to be understood" (317). The form working-class articulation takes, she goes on to say, emerges from a tradition "more verbal than written" (318). Other contributors attempt to incorporate distinctly working-class idioms into their writing, as Janice Galloway does through dialogue in "Two Fragments." However, while *The Common Thread* alludes to and provides a glimpse of working-class women's verbal traditions, the anthology itself cannot fully embody them, and suggests that in translating working-class women's voices into writing, they become infused with middle-class linguistic forms.

Furthermore, although contributors evoke a language of the (female) body which accompanies and constitutes a part of working-class speech, this language itself cannot exist in writing. Unlike Hélène Cixous' notion of writing woman's body, *The Common Thread* suggests a form of women's bodily expression that is resistant to writing. (This is not to say that the body is celebrated in *The Common Thread*; in ways I explore later, the anthology relentlessly presents working-class women's bodies as sites of oppression.) Billie Hunter's "Mothertongue" testifies to this alternative language of the body, which finds its expression in physical labor. She claims poems are

for the men to write,
the doting father poems of six pm baby life.
For the women, tied as they are
by soaking clothes and salty tears
and smiles that make your heart go tight inside,
the poems are there,
minute by minute,
written by chapped hands in words of Persil foam,
pouring out with the PG Tips

and the bathwater
unobserved
undefined
I wrote you a poem a minute
my gladeyed boy
my raspberry rascal
but they had no words
there are never words for such extremities. (101–102)

Her own poem belies her gendered division between men writing poems
and women enacting them, but cannot itself represent the poems she
"wrote" her son. Anne Cunningham also, paradoxically, relies upon
writing to testify to a bodily form of knowing that defies articulation.
In "Power Play" she writes,

So when you ask
how I know my class
I am speechless to describe
how I feel it
deep inside my blood
running like fire. (267)

The form of knowing that Cunningham alludes to, grounded as it is in
her female working-class body, through its very resistance to translation into words provides Cunningham with a means of resisting appropriation by, or assimilation to, the middle-class reader she addresses
in the poem.

Women in *The Common Thread* portray their silences—their states of
inarticulation—as sites of power, as a means for opposing middle-class
readers. In "About to speak," Kennerly affirms that keeping silent can
entail pride, self-respect, wisdom, and understanding—a way of "Keeping my culture and beliefs from your analytical claws / In my silence /
I can define myself / My background / And my class" (349–350). Kennerly does not, however, render this silence as sufficient. She concludes
the poem with, "In my silence / I am like a mountain in the sun / And
when that sun burns down / Look out for the avalanche / As I begin to
speak my words" (350). Here, as in the above examples, the form of articulation she envisions is not represented in the writing that exists on
the pages of *The Common Thread*. In adopting a disparate array of strategies that are often contradictory—both within themselves and in relation to each other—the anthology reveals working-class contributors'
ambivalent relationship to language, and the Collective's resistance to
limiting or defining working-class forms of expression. It at once val-

ues and proclaims working-class women's ability to manipulate traditional (middle-class) forms of language and writing, and reveals and
protests the costs of the limited access working-class women have had
to these forms. The anthology simultaneously posits a distinctly working-
class women's realm of expression that, in exceeding definition within
the covers of *The Common Thread,* both demonstrates the limitations of
the anthology itself and becomes a means for working-class women to
elude appropriation by middle-class readers and containment within
middle-class forms of expression.

A Feminism of Their Own

In their relation to feminism, members of The Common Thread adopt a
similar strategy: they neither abdicate feminism to middle-class women,
nor do they uncritically endorse it. As they proclaim themselves feminists, they simultaneously critique the classism of Britain's feminist organizations and work to create a feminism that is specifically working-
class, one that exists independently of middle-class feminism. Enabled
by its contemporary focus, a history of working-class women's organizations, and contributors' clearly delineated outsider status as working-class women (and often as lesbians as well), the feminism the
women in *The Common Thread* adopt is feisty and outspoken, and draws
on working-class women's senses of humor. Sue Vodden gives voice to
this feminism as she uses humor to critique a women's Psychic Development Course: "I got really pissed off on the Journey, though. / Diana
said, find a meadow, / and I couldn't think what the fuck a meadow
was / —that's because I'm working-class" (200). In "Is There Something in the Coffee?" Lizzie Demdyke's feminism depends upon a similar irreverent humor. Finding no slot for herself as a working-class lesbian in a women's magazine, she creates her own slot, and asks to be
put "'in touch'" with someone like herself, a "lazy, unattractive, striving anarcha/feminist / lesbian (25), a daughter and a son, a dog and /
a cat. Disenchanted with motherhood, scared of / dying in the nuclear
holocaust . . ." (249). In contrast to *Calling Home,* where feminism implicitly remains middle-class, Demdyke's poem illustrates working-
class women's impetus in *The Common Thread* to create their own feminist community, one which excludes no aspect of their being, and
which employs humor to fly in the face of middle-class norms and
niceties.[57]

Demdyke's poem—and her name—also signal another way in which
The Common Thread departs from *Calling Home:* through its emphasis on

lesbianism. In *Calling Home*, the heterosexual focus seems to be the product of Zandy's need to establish the historical reasons for women's dependence on marriage, and her need to portray the ways in which working-class women and men have worked together. *The Common Thread*, on the other hand, combines a working-class agenda with a radical feminist one, one that draws not only on Collective members' lesbian identities but also on their involvement in specifically lesbian working-class organizations. *The Common Thread*'s highly politicized lesbianism demonstrates once again the way the women's clearly established position outside both middle-class and male-dominated working-class institutions enables them to stand outside both middle-class and working-class society in other ways as well. About one-fourth of the contributors (twenty-four) identify themselves as lesbians, and the names some of them adopt reflect the unabashed nature of their lesbian feminism (as well as the anthology's anti-academic position). In addition to Demdyke (who tells us in her contributor's note, "I poached my name from one of the Pendle witches murdered in the 17th century" [355]), other contributors have also chosen subversive names for themselves: Viv Acious, Chaucer Cameron, Dolores, Susan Evasdaughter, Caron Freeborn, Eve Featherstone, Liza Rymer, and Tina Wildebeest. Other contributors, in identifying themselves as heterosexual, work to combat the heterosexism that usually makes that position an unmarked one.

The Common Thread's depiction of motherhood reflects the anthology's lesbian focus. As is the case in *Calling Home*, many of the women in *The Common Thread* are mothers (about half identify themselves as such). However, while *Calling Home* emphasizes the roles of fathers as well as mothers, and renders motherhood exclusively within the confines of contributors' heterosexual existence, *The Common Thread* posits a working-class culture that is women-centered and matrilineal, one wherein fathers are most often absent or abusive. Many single mothers in *The Common Thread* depict narrators entrapped in abusive or stifling marriages that their contributors' notes make clear they themselves have escaped. *The Common Thread* also celebrates depictions of motherhood unencumbered by the constraints of marriage or heterosexuality. The many contributors who represent themselves as lesbian delineate in *The Common Thread* a feminism wherein motherhood may flourish, where it may even contribute to the feminism the anthology promulgates.

As its depictions of motherhood suggest, *The Common Thread* paints, with few exceptions, a negative portrait of working-class men. Whereas

Calling Home emphasizes solidarity between working-class men and women, in *The Common Thread* the introduction addresses everyone *but* working-class men, and the literature details working-class women suffering a range of emotional and physical abuse by working-class men. Gill Newsham, in "We Have It All," wryly comments on how, as working-class men struggle against class oppression, they participate in oppression of women at home: "This generation, my generation—what do I know of the Working-Class? . . . Visions of lines of men, ten thick or more, rebelling against the Tory's stringent assault on their communities—strong, proud, etc., etc. . . . Or is it, perhaps, these same men denying power en bloc in their unions, and the same, perhaps, at home, to their wives, their sisters and their daughters? Is this working-class unity?" (261). Unlike *Calling Home,* where ambivalence regarding the domestic relationships between men and women does not extend to the realm of working-class political movements, *The Common Thread* establishes a continuity between the two spheres, and condemns men's behavior in them both.

Perhaps because the silences surrounding working-class existence and activism are fewer in Britain than in the United States, especially for working-class men, *The Common Thread* focuses on cross-class ways men oppress women. In *The Common Thread,* working-class men emotionally and physically damage women at home through violence or through sex, with sex represented, in its heterosexual expression in the anthology, as either a form of violence or a means of enslaving working-class women to men and children. Jennifer Bauer, for example, in "Where the Houses Are Bleak," makes connections between being a working-class wife and being disabled: her narrator literally has been paralyzed by her husband's drunk driving. The section "Our Bodies" paints an unremittingly negative picture of men as agents of physical harm to women. The section includes a series of pieces which depict men molesting, raping, and battering women.

The exceptions in the anthology only serve to reinforce such portrayals of men as oppressive to working-class women. Mandy Dee's poem "Event on an Andean Mountain" is one of the few pieces that expresses solidarity between working-class men and women. In it, the man who shares in the struggle with two women to climb a mountain has tin legs and National Health crutches. Only disabled, and in a nonsexual alliance, the poem suggests, can men companionably exist with women. The other instances of solidarity in *The Common Thread* between men and women occur when black women call for men and women to work together against racism as they struggle over sexism. Burnett's poem

"Father 1947–86" explores her father's oppression as a black man and the ways in which war and England destroyed him. And in "Superior Equality," Sie Jalloh refuses to be divided from black men: "I want to fight with you. See me as I am, / your comrade, your sister, your equal / I AM WE" (42). The relative newness of blacks' struggles against racism in England seems to enable, at least the *The Common Thread*, these racial struggles to take precedence over gender divisions.

Class and Race: A Search for the Common Ground between Them

As the inclusion of poems such as Burnett's and Sie Jalloh's indicates, *The Common Thread* confronts and begins to link class and race struggles in Britain. Willis finds that racial division "provides an evident underclass which is more heavily exploited than the white working class, and is therefore indirectly and partially exploited by the working class itself. . . . Racism therefore divides the working class both materially and ideologically" (152). Gilroy concurs, but argues that the struggles of blacks (who, in the British context, include not only people of African and Caribbean descent, but other peoples of color as well) work to bridge these divides:

In our view of class formation, the racist ideologies and practices of the white working class and the consequent differentiation of "the blacks" are ways in which the class as a whole is disorganized. The struggles of black people to refuse and transform their subjugation are no simple antidote to class segmentation, but they are processes which attempt to constitute the class politically across racial divisions.[58]

The Common Thread not only portrays black women engaged in the struggles Gilroy describes, but also shows white and black women struggling together against racism. The white Collective members as well as the one black member, Burnett, address race in their writings about class, and convey the sense that blacks and working-class women share a similar basis for oppression, one located in the white upper and middle classes. The one piece in the anthology to discuss the racism of white working-class women does so in an optimistic way, in the letters white Collective member Wilding and black *Common Thread* contributor Maria Noble wrote to a working-class women's magazine challenging its racism. By including these letters, which lead to positive changes on the magazine's part, the Collective presents a situation wherein white working-class women's racism results from their anti-racist intentions, and wherein white and black women work together and find a positive resolution.

The deeper ways in which race divides working-class women remain unarticulated in *The Common Thread*. While in part this omission seems strategic, it also indicates the dearth of work on how class and race relate to one another in Britain. In *"There Ain't No Black in the Union Jack,"* Gilroy claims blacks' history remains hidden in Britain, and that "the marginalization of 'race' and racism has persisted even where cultural studies have identified themselves with socialist and political aspirations."[59] In attempting to consider the intersection of racism and classism, then, The Common Thread Collective does not have much of a foundation upon which to build, and they profess themselves and other contributors not yet ready to take it on. While Wilding acknowledges elsewhere that "the oppressions of classism and racism, though twins with much in common, are not the same, and should surely not be lumped together" (329), the anthology does not provide much analysis of the way these oppressions overlap and diverge. By including pieces by black and white women which address race in each of the seven sections, yet by placing these pieces together within each section, the anthology establishes racial identity both as central to, and yet as set apart from, class identity. In many of these pieces, women convey their class subjugation by way of their status as colonized others. However, while the parallels between being a colonial subject and a working-class subject are implicitly posited, they are not explored. Such a study remains relegated to the future. In the introduction to "Survival and Resistance," Wilding informs her readers, "Two of us in the Common Thread have already agreed to co-edit a second book in which we will seek out land where we, along with other black and white working-class women with different experiences, sexualities and ages, can come together to explore our identities and the links we might forge" (301).

Interestingly, the links in *The Common Thread* between class and race emerge most suggestively in contributors' relationships to women of color in the United States. In "Private Memoirs," Lesley Summers narrates her experiences visiting the southern United States. While there, she encounters African Americans who have certain expectations of her as a black woman. While she initially persists in claiming her race as "English," and in resisting black or white classification because she is both, she comes to understand the need for identifying herself as black. Just as Summers' racial identity as black emerges in the context of the southern United States, the class identity of U.S. women of color—African American women in particular—is what British working-class women foreground in claiming these women as role models. The Col-

lective quotes Alice Walker's poem "Women" in the anthology's introduction, and in "Survival and Resistance," Wilding cites Walker again.
Black contributors in particular evidence the influence of Walker and
also Audre Lorde: Sie Jalloh utilizes Walker's term in calling herself a
"womanist," while Maria Noble quotes from Lorde, and pays tribute to
her. Anthologies by U.S. women of color also emerge as models for *The
Common Thread*, and in looking to these anthologies, the Collective highlights their class concerns. In their introduction, Cotterill and Wilding
explain, "Ironically, though, it has been from America, where the notion of a classless society is strongest, that some of the most challenging
writing by working-class women has come—often from black women,
in anthologies like *Home Girls . . .* and *This Bridge Called My Back . . .*" (4).
Wilding again evokes these anthologies in "The Power of Letters and
Articles": "Before 1983, little had been written and published by working-
class women about our experiences of class exploitation and oppression, or our sense of ourselves. There had been [only] a few American
anthologies and pamphlets, and some particularly inspiring writings
by black women, which dealt, almost in passing, with class" (311).

"Almost in Passing"

These remarks in *The Common Thread* and analogous moments in *Calling Home* suggest the extent to which class and race can stand in for
and/or obscure one another, and, therefore, also reflect the potential for
each to unfix the other. In the movement from the United States to
Britain, concerns of race in many ways translate to concerns of class.
Racial identity in the United States becomes, in some respects, analogous to class identity in Britain. Both race in the United States and class
in Britain have a relative solidity of definition which provides a foundation upon which to establish a politics of identity. The reverse for-
mula also holds true: class in the United States resembles race in Britain
as a contested and thus unstable category of identity. While in the
United States, as *Calling Home* demonstrates, women are in the process
of constructing their working-class identities, race in Britain is, like
class in the United States, in the process of being constructed.

Since World War II, people of Asian, West Indian, African, and Med-
iterranean descent have migrated in significant numbers to Britain,
where they have been largely confined to unskilled or semi-skilled labor,
and where they have confronted racism in all arenas of their lives. Governing bodies in Britain have worked systematically to play these
different racial and ethnic groups against each other, as well as against

members of the white working class. In response, Avtar Brah details the way in which a black identity was

adopted by the emerging coalitions amongst African-Caribbean and South Asian organizations and activists in the late 1960s and 1970s. They were influenced by the way that the Black Power movement in the USA, which had turned the concept of Black on its head, divested it of its pejorative connotations in racialized discourses, and transformed it into a confident expression of an assertive group identity.[60]

Activists in Britain adopted the term "black" with some striking differences from black Americans: as Brah explains, they did so "to foster a rejection of chromatism amongst those defined as 'coloured people' in Britain."[61] Unlike the Black Power movement, the movement on the part of blacks in Britain is a multiracial, multiethnic one.[62] In contrast to its situation in the United States, black identity in Britain is not synonymous with racial identity (as it is for African Americans). In fact, just who this identity includes is continually contested: debates occur in Britain over whether Iranians, Palestinians, Filipinos, or Irish people are black.[63] It is through this self-conscious nonreferentiality, however, which it achieves while resisting erasure of its constructedness, that the term "black" as used in Britain retains its political charge.

Charting the Journey: From Black in Britain to Back in the U.S.A.

Racism and struggles over racial identity are currently complicating and reconfiguring understandings of class identity in Britain.[64] While juxtaposing *Calling Home* and *The Common Thread* underlines the indeterminacy of class in the United States in relation to its relative solidity in Britain, a cursory exploration of the 1988 anthology *Charting the Journey: Writings by Black and Third World Women* suggests the pressures being placed on Britain's class structure—and indeed on its national cultural identity—as people from Britain's former colonies immigrate in significant numbers to Britain. As Stuart Hall notes, "In the very moment when finally Britain convinced itself it had to decolonize, it had to get rid of them, we all came back home. As they hauled down the flag, we got on the banana boat and sailed right into London."[65] *Charting the Journey* conveys some of the consequences of this "return," and considering the anthology alongside *The Common Thread* and *Calling Home* makes it possible to sketch a few specific intersections and divergences of identities of race, class, and nation, and to see how each identity informs the other.

   Charting the Journey, edited by Shabnam Grewal, Jackie Kay, Liliane

Landor, Gail Lewis, and Pratibha Parmar, was published just one year before *The Common Thread*. The anthology provides a place to see a British black women's movement in the making, as in the process of constructing a black women's movement, its editors find that "there is no structure (as opposed to *number* of women) from within which to find unknown women, women 'out there,' and thus solicit pieces."[66] The editors of *Charting the Journey* look not to British working-class women's movements for models and alliances, but to an African American lesbian feminist movement. *Charting the Journey* manifests the influence of *Home Girls* and its contributors even as it works to differentiate British black women and African American women, to create a space that is distinct to British black women.

Charting the Journey shares with *Home Girls* (and other U.S. anthologies) its thematic movement from articulating oppression to self-naming and celebration, to anticipating revolution. It also shares *Home Girls*'s multi-genre form, its equation of writing and activism (the editors claim that writing is a "weapon in this process of collectivization and harmonization" [4]), and its basis in identity politics. Throughout, contributors cite African American feminist writers (usually lesbian feminists) as models, Lorde and June Jordan in particular. The anthology also includes "Wild Women Don't Get the Blues," a conversation between Walker and Maud Sulter, and an interview of Lorde by Parmar and Kay, carried out trans-Atlantic and on tape. In the interview, Lorde, Parmar, and Kay share information about their respective black feminist communities, with Lorde assuming the role of mentor, telling Parmar and Kay, "You should be proud of yourselves. You should also recognize how much you've done" (127). Her concluding statement in this interview, "But all of our strengths together are going to turn this whole world around," inspires the anthology's concluding section, "Turning the World Upside Down."

At the same time, the women in *Charting the Journey* resist the silencing of black British women through what Barbara Burford calls the British publishers' "Hollywood-style star system," in which they promote the work of a few black American women writers such as Walker but do not publish black British women. Burford's critique of this star system in fact precedes the interview with Walker; in this way, the editors of *Charting the Journey* introduce Walker as different from black British women, while making clear that the critique of the "star system" is not a critique of Walker and other "stars," but of the publishing industry itself. The way that the editors incorporate quotes by African American women similarly works against any easy equivalence between African American and black British identity. They conclude their preface with some lines from a poem by Jordan: "Come then into our house for a reflection of yourself. Glance at a snapshot which attempts to capture the process of a movement of transformation in which 'I was born a Black woman / and now / I am become a Palestinian'" (6). In quoting Jordan's poem, the editors enact the alliance-building they (and Jordan) call for, and, in the context of their anthology—which does not make black women Palestinian, but Palestinian women black—they put into practice the poem's proclamation of identity as constructed, strategic, and shifting in nature: they both claim and reverse the process Jordan celebrates.

As *Charting the Journey* focuses on creating a black women's identity and community, the issue of class drops out of the equation almost entirely. Whether contributors view themselves as working-class and how they view their relationship to white working-class women in Britain remain questions in uncharted territory. However, as *Charting the Journey, The Common Thread,* and *Calling Home* all draw on African American women in constituting their communities, the fluidity and interconnectedness among race, class, and also nationality becomes evident, as does the difficulty of keeping both racial and class identities in play simultaneously, without one unfixing or subsuming the other. Tracing the relationships between these American and British anthologies thus reveals the fluidity of race, class, and national identity, and indicates how the practice of a politics of identity involves the construction and transformation of these identities. Exploring these interrelations not only illuminates constructions of class and race in the United States and Britain, but also suggests ways in which transatlantic exchanges are unsettling national boundaries and forging new identities and alliances—and possibilities for identity politics—across these boundaries.

6

Around 1996

Re-Placing Identity Politics from the "Racial Paradise" of Hawai'i

> For most of us, any heritage is much more complicated than simply pointing to a map.
> —Sharon Lim-Hing, introduction to *The Very Inside*, n.p.

> we are what has happened here
> —Annette Arkeketa, "Quincentennial Ghostdance Song," p. 5

I began this project as a graduate student at UC Berkeley and re-visioned it after becoming an assistant professor at the University of Hawai'i at Mānoa.[1] The university at Mānoa sits at the bottom of a valley, up against intensely green and jagged volcanic mountains. Sometimes, trade winds sweep the scent of plumeria into my office. The ocean, never far away, is imaginable at all times, immensely blue. Random rains come down daily, sometimes from still-blue skies crossed only by rainbows. I awaken to the clattering of birds, a tropical sound. It is possible, as an outsider with an unnuanced sense of Hawaii's seasons, to confuse June and February. It is possible to bracket time, to picture paradise.

Imagining Hawai'i as paradise entails, however, sticking strictly and selectively to the scenery—to the sun, water, and sand. I have not, for example, described the dilapidated building that my office overlooks, nor the sounds of car alarms, nor the insurgent shouts in response to the cutting of Hawaiian language classes from the university. I have left out the concrete, the cars, the dissonance of the architecture. I have distilled the "natural" elements, left out the people and history that impact these elements, that construct this place.

155

This closing chapter constitutes an attempt to mark both time and place, an effort to trace the ways in which identity politics undergoes continual revisioning given the coordinates of time and place. I both review the preceding chapters and try to provide a way to re-open this book, suggesting ways to reconfigure this project from the perspective of a different time and place.

Paradise (Re-)Visited (Hawai'i Take Two)

When I first flew into Honolulu two years ago to give a job talk, to assess and be assessed by the University of Hawai'i English department for a position teaching ethnic American literature, I worried that the talk that I was to give on *The Forbidden Stitch* would be fraught with dangers. Given the large Asian American student population at the university, I assumed that many of the faculty and students attending my talk not only would be Asian American, but would also have an expertise in Asian American literary studies, and that they might be less than enthusiastic about a white person discoursing on this topic. I also knew enough about Hawai'i to know that my continent-based study might seem entirely wrong or even offensive to a local audience. In particular, I began to worry once more about the relationship between Asian Americans in Hawai'i and Asian Americans in the continental United States, and, more generally, about the relationship between Asian Americans and Pacific Islanders.

Questions regarding these relationships had arisen for me during my initial research on *Making Waves* and *The Forbidden Stitch*, when I encountered a variety of terms: "Asian American," "Asian/Pacific American," "Asian American/Pacific Islander." I remember looking at maps and trying to figure out which region, exactly, constituted the Pacific, and which islands the American Pacific. I looked at several maps, all of them different, none of them particularly helpful. While a few of them had the faces of Captain Cook, Magellan, and other "adventurers" pasted across various groups of islands, thus making clear the range and arrogance of Western imperialism, none of them gave me more than the most general understanding of the geopolitics of the Pacific. After puzzling over this issue for a few days, I decided to follow the lead of *Making Waves* and *The Forbidden Stitch*, and not to confront the relationship of Pacific Islanders to Asian Americans as a problematic.

When I got the call from Hawai'i, and the request for a talk on *Making Waves* and *The Forbidden Stitch*, I returned to this problematic, concentrating specifically on the site of Hawai'i. Would people of Asian descent there consider themselves Asian Americans, Pacific Islanders, or both? And what about Native Hawaiians?

I went to Berkeley's Asian American studies library, where I remembered seeing several books about Hawai'i, and read through the 1986 anthology of Hawai'i writing *The Best of Bamboo Ridge*. Edited by Eric Chock and Darrell Lum, and concluding with Stephen Sumida's essay "Waiting for the Big Fish: Recent Research in the Asian American Literature of Hawaii," the anthology clearly had an Asian American emphasis; I could not, however, tell if Native Hawaiian contributors were included in the community of Hawai'i writers it claimed as "Local."[2] From my location in Berkeley the anthology's use of the term "Local" seemed to present a way out of the Asian American/Pacific Islander dilemma, but the inadequacy of this solution became apparent to me already on the plane ride over, as I read sections from Michael Kioni Dudley and Keoni Kealoha Agard's *A Call for Hawaiian Sovereignty* (also from Berkeley's Asian American studies library), and I have since come to learn that Bamboo Ridge's Local Asian emphasis and representations of Native Hawaiians constitute key points of contention in the local literary scene. In relation to Hawaiian sovereignty in particular, the slash between "Asian" and "Pacific" seemed to signal more of a divide than a joining, one that could not be sutured over by the term "Local."

I had many hours of ocean to turn this problem over. I even had time to worry that not only would my understanding of Asian American studies be totally inadequate in the context of Hawai'i, but that I also might be required to wear a bathing suit, that my winter-white, white-no-matter-what-the-season skin would mark in yet another way my lack of belonging. That, even with sunscreen, I would scorch and burn.

I worried in vain. As it turned out, my flyback to Hawai'i did not entail beaches and bathing suits, but a more standard set of academic activities and attire. And at my talk, I addressed an almost entirely white audience, whose questions pertained to market capitalism and feminist theory, not to my work's relationship to a Hawai'i or Pacific context.

However, if I did not have to address my status as a *haole* on this trip, the initial comfort that this provided me is now precisely the problem that I and my white colleagues from the continental United States face. Becoming yet another white faculty import on a campus where the student population is approximately 60 percent Asian and only 8 percent Hawaiian (a percentage considerably below the 20 percent estimated by the State Census),[3] and becoming, moreover, the employee of a university that sits on ceded land, land to which Hawaiians hold clear legal and ethical claim, my identity as a white American is very much at issue each and every day. And while I had spent my graduate career at UC Berkeley struggling with identity politics—both in writing my dissertation and in teaching composition and ethnic literature to a racially diverse and highly politicized student body—in Hawai'i the struggles over identity politics were thrust upon me with a new and painful immediacy and complexity. Whereas in multiracial Berkeley it is possible to feel unmarked much of the time as a white person and as an American, in Hawai'i, where whites are a numerical minority and where colonial and plantation histories continue to be negotiated and contested, there is no space in which whiteness goes unmarked, and everyday encounters are fraught in complex and unstable ways along lines of race and nationality. In particular, teaching ethnic American literature in an English department that Local writer Rodney Morales has termed "the literary heart of the colonialist enterprise,"[4] identity politics cannot be wished away with a poststructuralist sleight of hand.

However, if the importance of identity politics remains centrally at issue in Hawai'i, it operates differently here than in the continental United States. Being here has complicated, and in some ways undone or reconfigured, the identities that the anthologies I study in the previous five chapters articulate, as well as my analyses of those identities. And if the importance of location in shaping and defining identity, in constructing coalitions, and in deploying identity politics, has become fully evident to me only upon relocating to Hawai'i, this understanding is reinforced, and made all the more illuminating by the turn in the 1990s by many cultural critics from a politics of identity to a politics of location.

My move to Hawai'i has coincided with cultural critics' "discovery" of the importance of location: in fact, a politics of location has come to replace—but grows out of and is intimately connected to—a politics of identity. In her piece "Locating Identity Politics," Liz Bondi considers the role spatial metaphors currently play in the academy, contending, "One consequence of the spatial metaphor is that the question 'Who am I?' evident in some versions of identity politics becomes 'Where am I?'" The concern with locale, she argues, "turns a politics of identity into a politics of location."[5] As Bondi implies, a politics of location entails not a break from identity politics, but a recasting of its central premise to the argument that one's standpoint determines one's identity, politics, and potential alliances. Identity remains very much at issue, but place, rather than race, sexuality, gender, or class, becomes the primary focus through which these other components of identity are understood.

In this chapter, as I explore the relationships between a politics of location, in its several senses, and a politics of identity, I foreground this book's mapping of regional and national concerns. While chapters 2–5 trace the increasing centrality during the course of the 1980s of identity-based anthologies in questions of nationality, this chapter theorizes reasons for this development, and also addresses recent identity-based anthologies which depart from those studied in previous chapters in their highlighting of questions of nationality, and in their emphasis on location. Many recent anthologies problematize national identity by way of establishing diasporic communities that disregard the importance of national boundaries altogether, and that locate contributors' identities in the movements between different nations and locations, thus employing what I will be calling a diasporic politics of location. Other anthologies employ what can be called a place-bound politics of location by positing a local, and often indigenous, identity, one inextricably bound to a particular location, and one that often resists or reconfigures geopolitical borders. Taken together, these anthologies reflect the importance a politics of location has come to assume, as well as the inextricability of such a politics, whether place-bound or diasporic, from a politics of identity. They also offer a way to explore the interrelations of diasporic and place-bound deployments of a politics of location. While a politics of location has been linked more often and explicitly to diasporic than to place-bound or indigenous formulations, one of my projects here is to tease out the possibilities and limitations of these different, and at times opposing, articulations of such a politics, and also to consider how they inform, coincide with, and, implicitly, critique current discussions in the academy of location and the local.

The Timeliness of Place

One of the earliest articulations of a politics of location, and the most influential, is Adrienne Rich's "Notes toward a Politics of Location (1984)."[6] In "Notes," Rich begins "with the geography closest in—the body" (212), or, to be more precise, her own body, and thinks about "the places it has taken me, the places it has not let me go" (216). As Rich thinks through these questions, she comes to understand that her geographical location, and her movements from one location to another, are inextricably related to her social location, to her bodily experiences of being female, white, Jewish, lesbian, middle-class, etc. For Rich, practicing a politics of location entails interrogating and taking responsibility for her whiteness as well as her geographical location in North

America, points of location whose centrality she had previously taken for granted. Although Rich's "Notes" appeared in 1984 (and thus works against any clear-cut chronological ordering of identity politics and a politics of location), it was not widely taken up until the 1990s. However, the frequency with which "Notes" is now cited, in disparate and overlapping areas of study including those of nationalism, transnationalism, postcolonialism, globalization, feminism, ethnic studies, and American literary studies, suggests the importance that this new understanding of location, and particularly a politics of location—however differently defined and deployed—has come to assume.

In the field of American literary studies, scholars are approaching location by way of a renewed interest in regionalism, whether they posit it as a possible alternative to a nationalist framework if critically deployed (Paul Lyons, Anne Goldman, Jacqueline Shea Murphy) or charge it with reinscribing such a framework (Roberto Mario Dainotto, Amy Kaplan).[7] The concern with location is also evidenced by the multitude of references to "mappings" and "re-mappings" that are national and transnational in scope. For example, the 1995 *American Literature* forum, entitled "American Literary History: The Next Century," is devoted in large part to unfixing and contesting "American" and other geopolitical borders, and mapping is its guiding metaphor. Eric Sundquist introduces the forum with the statement, "All the papers, one might say, are informed by a new sense of mapping the literary history of the United States."[8] Similarly, Carolyn Porter's massive essay "What We Know That We Don't Know: Remapping American Literary Studies" addresses the impact of a "politics of location" on the reconstellation of what constitutes "America," and what comprises literary studies. As Porter notes, the "remapping" of America and American literary studies results in part from the challenges African American, Native American, Asian American, and Chicano/a studies have issued to understandings of what makes up both "American" and "Literature."[9] Gregory Jay dismantles both of these terms in "The End of American Literature," one of the essays noted by Porter, and Jay's urging that "America" be more precisely termed "US" is enabled by his reading of Rich's "Notes."[10] I believe that anthologies of the 1990s, as I demonstrate below, also constitute an important part of this remapping. At its best, such a remapping issues a powerful challenge to forms of U.S. colonialism (internal and external) that have become as naturalized as the borders around and between the 50 states; at its worst, it continues an imperialist project, both by casting all countries as American subjects, and by erasing the specificity of particular struggles inside and outside U.S. borders.

The reconfiguring of borders in American literary studies results not only from challenges issued by those aligned with feminist and ethnic studies, but also from the pressure being put on national borders and identities by those engaged in studies of nationalism, transnationalism, postcolonialism, diaspora, world systems, and globalization. Scholars across a range of disciplines and theoretical perspectives discuss the increasing instability, porousness, and ambivalence of constructions of national identities, and the growing interdependence among nations (e.g., Kaplan, Gilroy, Dirlik, Anthony King, Homi Bhabha, Immanuel Wallerstein, Arjun Appadurai, Masao Miyoshi, Etienne Balibar, and Armand Mattelart), often claiming that identities are now postnational, transnational, and/or diasporic, as must be any responsible scholarship. As I am not the first to note, such accounts, especially when they are overly celebratory, can falsely dispense with the idea of nationalism as an ongoing power—both insurgent and repressive—and with the uneven flow of "global" capital and other resources. Furthermore, these accounts are often inattentive to concerns of gender (while gender is often acknowledged in passing as important, determining how it is important is usually left as work for "others" to do), and frequently make totalizing generalizations that more precisely illuminate the theorist's own—unacknowledged—situation than that of the rest of the world.[11]

The attention, then, to location and local sites of resistance, attention which emerges alongside—and comes out of—studies of transnationalism and globalization, not only serves to acknowledge local movements as "a pervasive phenomenon of the contemporary world,"[12] but also effects a crucial intervention into theories of global systems or transnationalism that, in their abstraction and totalizing reach, can further neocolonial agendas. Joan Dayan comments on the way internationalist perspectives can reinforce hegemonic power relations as she suggests the need to pay attention to specific locations: "Under the pretext of trendy internationalism, the need for local knowledge is circumvented, making it possible—yet again—for those who wield the terms to construct a 'receptacle for that race of men.'"[13] Dayan forcefully articulates the contrast between the "borderless world" (to borrow Masao Miyoshi's term) enjoyed by both multinationals and academics, and the strength and violence of national borders for refugees and for some immigrant populations: "As national borders become harsher in daily life—with shootouts on the Arizona and Mexico border—the multinational corporations' borders become ever more permeable—as does the multicultural rhetoric of the academy."[14] Identity-based anthologies of the 1990s published in the United States increasingly include contributors who cross national borders, and identity-based anthologies have become more firmly located in the academy (see chapter 2). In order to maintain an oppositional edge, then, these anthologies must keep in firm focus both the locations from which they emerge, and the site-specific struggles that exist in tension with the border crossings of cultural capital.[15] The final sections of this chapter, in addition to tracing this dynamic in readings of the 1994 anthologies *The Very Inside: An Anthology of Writing by Asian and Pacific Islander Lesbian and Bisexual Women* and *Returning the Gift: Poetry and Prose from the First North American Native Writers' Festival*,[16] consider ways in which identity-based anthologies resist and/or make resourceful use of commodification through attention to specific locations, including the locations—and occasions—which lead to their production.

Critics often conjoin discussions of the local and the global, in acknowledgment of their inextricability and also in recognition of local sites and movements as sources of resistance to transnational capital, as well as to repressive and—despite the power of globalization—still-operative nationalisms.[17] Discourses of globalization or transnationalism call with increasing frequency and urgency for site-specific analyses, attention to the local, and a politics of location, although all too often such calls, in their abstraction, produce a "local" that circulates in as ungrounded a way as the global does.[18]

Rob Wilson and Wimal Dissanayake make the interrelations between global and local movements the subject of their 1996 collection, *Global/ Local: Cultural Production and the Transnational Imaginary*. As contributor Mitsuhiro Yoshimoto comments, "While national boundaries are increasingly blurred in the new global formation, transnational capitalism has paradoxically given rise to an increasing obsession with place or specific site."[19] Contributors to *Culture, Globalization and the World-System* make similar claims. Reflecting on people's sense of being unable to grasp, or grapple with, the global, Stuart Hall theorizes that, "The return to the local is often a response to globalization."[20] He also attributes the power of the local to the transformations effected by identity politics, claiming, "The most profound cultural revolution has come about as a consequence of the margins coming into representation" (34). At present, Hall contends, "It may be that all we have, in bringing the politics of the local to bear against the global, is a lot of little local politics."[21] Hall's endorsement of what he calls "the cultural politics of the local" resembles Dirlik's call for "critical localism"[22] and Wilson's in *Global/Local* for "critical regionalism," and each of their place-based analyses articulate with what feminist theorists are calling a politics of location, be it diasporic or place-bound. What differentiates many transnational or global/local formulations from explicitly feminist ones is that while transnational or global/local theorists often place more emphasis on the need for a local that is canny about global/local dynamics and dialectics, they also, with a few exceptions such as Hall, usually bracket gender, and tend neither to address the ways in which the personal is political (and the political—or theoretical—is personal), nor do they name the ground from which they themselves speak.

Recovering Ground

The foregrounding of location and the interest in traversing or otherwise challenging national boundaries and categories of belonging are embedded in anthologies of the 1980s, and in earlier ones as well. The centrality of location, for example, is evident in the very titles and/or names of the editorial collectives of the following anthologies: *Between the Lines: An Anthology by Pacific/Asian Lesbians of Santa Cruz, California; Making Waves*, edited by Asian Women United of California; *Sowing Ti Leaves*, edited by Multi-Cultural Women of Orange County; and *Gathering Ground: New Writing and Art by Northwest Women of Color*. The following anthologies similarly cross lines of national identity in asserting communities based on some shared combination of gender, race or ethnicity, sexual orientation, or class: *Nice Jewish Girls* and *Tribe of Dina: A Jewish Women's Anthology*, which include contributors writing from and about Israel; *Making Waves* and *The Forbidden Stitch*, which blur the lines between the United States and the disparate countries that comprise Asia; *Compañeras: Latina Lesbians*, a 1987 anthology inclusive of women from ten different countries that editor Juanita Ramos dedicates to "Latina lesbians everywhere"; and *Gathering of Spirit: Writing and Art by North American Indian Women*, which includes Native women from the United States and Canada. In their introductions, anthologies of the 1980s also call for transnational alliances among third world women (*This Bridge* and *Haciendo Caras*), black women (*Home Girls*), U.S. women of color and black women in Britain (*Charting the Journey*), working-class women in Britain and black women in the United States (*The Common Thread*), or working-class women from the United States and Canada (*Calling Home*). Earlier identity-based anthologies, too, particularly those from the Harlem Renaissance and the Civil Rights Era, have included contributors across national lines, and/or derive their oppositional identities through alliances with those in other countries who share their racial oppression.[23] Such anthologies include *Negro* (1934), *El Espejo—The Mirror: Selected Chicano Literature* (1969), *Roots* (1971), *Time to Greez! Incantations from the Third World* (1975), *Counterpoint* (1976), *Sturdy Black Bridges* (1979), etc. Thus, while I would still maintain that anthologies produced in the United States shift from a more strictly domestic focus in the early 1980s toward an increasing interest in either highlighting identities that are constituitively diasporic or transnational, or in putting forth alternative national or local identities, any arguments about the newness of this shift must be carefully qualified and contextualized, as must any claims regarding its revolutionary possibilities.[24]

What seemed new to me upon moving to Hawai'i and reading theory (both recent and not-so-recent) about location and nation has, in fact, been present in this study all along, and I have been tempted to revise the earlier chapters in ways that might emphasize the concerns of location and nation already present both there (in muted forms) and in the anthologies of the 1980s. For example, were I to rewrite chapter 3, on *Nice Jewish Girls* and *Home Girls*, I would begin by evoking Gilroy's discussion of diaspora in the last chapter of *The Black Atlantic*. There Gilroy suggests that:

the concept of diaspora can itself provide an underutilised device with which to explore the fragmentary relationship between blacks and Jews and the difficult political questions to which it plays host: the status of ethnic identity, the power of cultural nationalism, and the manner in which carefully preserved social histories of ethnocidal suffering can function to supply ethical and political legitimacy. These issues are inherent in both the Israeli political situation and the practices of the Africentric movement.[25]

In my look at *Nice Jewish Girls* and *Home Girls*, I was unable to find a basis for exploring relations among blacks and Jews. Beginning with Gilroy's arguments, however, would have provided me with a framework for teasing out the intersections and divergences between black and Jewish diasporic identities. The newly envisioned chapter 3 would include a more sustained discussion of *Nice Jewish Girls*'s formulation— via its section on Israel—of a diasporic identity, and a more sustained comparison of *Nice Jewish Girls* and *The Tribe of Dina*, an anthology that focuses more on Israel than *Nice Jewish Girls* does. Such analysis also would require re-reading these anthologies in light of the recent elections in Israel and the renewed commitment to increasing numbers of settlers in disputed areas. The chapter then would consider continent-crossing precursors to *Home Girls*, from the Harlem Renaissance (e.g.,

Nancy Cunard's *Negro*[26] and Alain Locke's *The New Negro*) to the Black Power Movement (e.g., Amiri Baraka and Larry Neal's *Black Fire*, and Steve Henderson's *Understanding New Black Poetry*) and beyond (e.g., Roseann Bell, Bettye Parker, and Beverly Guy-Sheftall's *Sturdy Black Bridges*). It would also include an exploration of why *Home Girls* departs from earlier anthologies' transatlantic scope in order to adopt a more strictly domestic one, a departure I would read as part of its refusal of a masculine-gendered nationalism.

Taking up different deployments of a diasporic identity, or the refusal of such an identity, would have resulted in a different, more timely, discussion of identity politics, one guided by the current preoccupation with location and nation. And such an approach might have been enabling in ways Bondi suggests when she argues that "the emphasis on *where*—on position, on location" encourages "a concern with the relationships between different kinds of identities and therefore with the development of a politics grounded in affinities and coalitions, rather than some pristine, coherent consciousness."[27] On the one hand, I disagree with Bondi's suggestion that a politics of identity is not coalitional; after all, the anthologies explored in this book all formulate identities that are in and of themselves coalitional (i.e., "women of color"), and, as Bondi herself makes clear, a politics of location can be every bit as essentialist as identity politics. On the other hand, I agree with Bondi that a focus on location makes it possible to rethink questions of identity in ways that might allow for affinities and coalitions that are less restrictive, and based more on shared affinities, than those enabled by identity politics. In fact, a politics of location might be one way to get where Bernice Reagon and *Home Girls* want to go, the direction pointed to in the anthology's concluding essay, "Coalition Politics: Turning the Century."

If a politics of location enables new forms of affinities and coalitions, however, it also potentially eclipses, or at least displaces, others. In framing chapter 3 with Gilroy's *Black Atlantic*, a discussion of transnationalism (which, to be crude, but also to the point, is dominated by male theorists who tend to ignore gender) would take the place of one, domestic in scope, about lesbian feminism and coalitions concerned with home. And if such a discussion would encompass more of the world and make more of a place for those who are not black or Jewish lesbians, the focus on the particular identities and concerns that the anthologies promote—which continue to be marginalized ones in every sphere, especially that of transnationalism—would be diminished. My sense that concerns of gender, sexuality, and race would be displaced does not derive simply from the fact that theories of transnationalism have tended to be male-dominated and insensitive to gender. I also have in mind the slippage of these concerns in transnationalist work that positions itself as feminist. In part, I attribute this to the difficulty, if not the impossibility, of keeping multiple categories of analysis in play. Nevertheless, I also think that, counter to Adrienne Rich's intentions, a politics of location can enable critics, especially white critics, to overlook differences (most often, of race) which can be sources of discomfort and division as these critics proclaim alliances based on shared political objectives. In the introduction, I made a similar argument in relation to work that is being done by Cornel West and others under the name of a "new cultural politics of difference," a politics that has arisen concomitantly with a politics of location and which, with its postmodernist multiplications of difference, shares much with it. What distinguishes a cultural politics of difference and a politics of location for me, however, is the fact that if a politics of location loosens its hold on race, class, and gender as central categories, it offers geographical location as a way to ground its exploration of multiple differences and alliances. For this reason, along with my attraction to a politics that allows for alliances that do not depend upon a shared identity of race, class, gender, or sexuality, I count myself among those drawn to a politics of location. At the same time, I feel the need to strike a cautionary note when I see the number of white critics who forward a politics of location without identifying the ground upon which they themselves stand, or without feeling the need to locate themselves in terms of race, class, gender, or sexual orientation. Such deployments of a politics of location leave behind the lessons of identity politics and cut too quickly to dismissals of identity politics as crude or essentialist. They also can, in their focus on space, leave time and history off the map.

Such tendencies are discernible even in Caren Kaplan's careful and rigorous transnational feminist work. In "The Politics of Location as Transnational Feminist Critical Practice," despite Kaplan's urging that "feminists with socioeconomic power need to investigate the grounds of their strong desire for rapport and intimacy with the 'other,'"[28] her own socioeconomic power goes unexplored, as does her geographical location, and her racial, sexual, and gender identity. This lack of positioning weakens the alliances she forges and the politics of location that she promotes. In her discussion of recent deployments of a politics of location, Kaplan contrasts those by Michele Wallace and bell hooks—whose chosen position in the margins Kaplan endorses—to those she finds "at the very center of academia," where "a different reading of

Rich's politics of location takes place, a practice that can be most generally described as an Anglo-American feminist poststructuralist reading" (144). Here, as exemplified by Elizabeth Meese and Nancy Miller's
work, Kaplan finds "a relativism that masks appropriation" (144). In
positioning "good" theorists of color in the margins against "bad"
Anglo-American theorists in the center of academia, Kaplan falls into
the kind of spatialized binarization she otherwise works to resist. While
Kaplan's own position implicitly complicates this binary, since she, as
an Anglo-American poststructuralist aligns herself with hooks and
Wallace, Kaplan does not locate herself in this essay in terms of race or
address the complexity of her own position (to what extent does she—
can she—occupy the margins? and are they the same margins hooks
occupies?).[29]

Kaplan's lack of positioning works both to unground and to replicate
the problems she finds in her critique of Rich's "Notes." Kaplan ad-
monishes Rich for attributing her awakening to her racial privilege to
her experiences of international travel rather than to her domestic negotiations with women of color. Kaplan concludes, "In its first articulation as a term, therefore, a politics of location could be seen as a sup-
pression of discussions of differences between white women and
women of color within the geographical boundaries of the United
States in favor of a new binary—North American white women and the
victims of North American foreign policies" (140–141). Kaplan's more
recent articulation of a politics of location, however, is open to the same
critiques as those she levels at Rich, in part for the very reason that she
seems to leave behind the early 1980s formulation of a politics of location as a "method of interrogating and deconstructing the position,
identity, and privilege of whiteness" (139). In this essay, as Kaplan's
whiteness goes unaddressed, so does the way her own politics of location is informed by her own negotiations with women of color in the
United States (including, for example, the co-editing of *Scattered Hegemonies* with Inderpal Grewal),[30] and her spatial metaphors operate
much as Rich's descriptions of travel do: in Kaplan's essay, difference all
too often resides in discrete locations scattered across the globe rather
than embedded within particular locations. For example, when Kaplan
claims that a politics of location enables "the historical roles of mediation, betrayal, and alliance in the relationships between women *in diverse locations*" (139; emphasis added), what undergoes erasure is the
texturedness, the layers within given locations that are themselves sites
of struggle.[31]

By rendering relations among women spatially and eliding the specificity of her own location, Kaplan's transnational mapping of a politics of location can flatten factors of time and history and work against her interest in "a politics of location that investigates the productive tension between temporal and spatial theories of subjectivity" (138). Despite the careful historical framing that Kaplan provides in the introduction to her essay when she traces the trajectory from Virginia Woolf's concern with location and space to Rich's politics of location, Kaplan's own historical location is present only at the level of inference. And when the politics of Kaplan's own location remain unmapped, so, too, do the dynamic interrelations of history, location, and identity.

These concerns of time return me to the decision not to reframe the earlier chapters of this book in terms of a politics of location. This decision, in part, comes from my desire to keep time visibly in play, even at the expense of not being timely. By maintaining a sometimes "dated" approach, I hope both to preserve my sense of respect for the concerns—and women—that have guided this project from the outset and to make an argument for their continuing importance, and also to preserve the narrative embedded within this study of my own movements through time and space. In foregrounding these issues that pertain to time and timeliness, I am inspired by Laura Lyons' work on ephemera, and by her insight that the line between theory and ephemera is by no means a clear-cut one—that, like ephemera, theory is dated in a way that can provide important insights into the given time and place from which it emerges.[32] I am also interested in trying to convey structurally the importance of process, and the open-endedness and provisionality of any politics, lessons the anthologies in this study have taught me through their form and contents.

Anthologies of the 1990s: Putting New Identities on the Map

In the 1990s, identity-based multi-genre anthologies by women continue to proliferate. At times, the increasingly specific identities put forth by many anthologies of the 1990s comprise those that earlier anthologies may have overlooked or subsumed. For example, the editors of the 1993 *Our Feet Walk the Sky: Women of the South Asian Diaspora* explain that women of South Asian descent constitute a relatively new group in the United States, by and about whom not much has been written, and whose specificity is often elided in organizations focused on women of color or Asian Americans. The anthology's title—"Our Feet Walk the Sky"—suggests the diasporic nature of contributors' experiences: not rooted in the United States, as are many other women of color (e.g., *Home Girls*), they cross continents not by way of water—a form of travel evoked by *Making Waves* and other Asian American collections such as *Strangers from a Different Shore*—but instead traverse continents by air (their feet "walk the sky"). While anthologies such as *Our Feet Walk the Sky* highlight new or previously marginalized identities, other anthologies promote identities that earlier anthologies worked to realize. In the introduction to *Third Woman: The Sexuality of Latinas,* editors Norma Alarcón, Ana Castillo, and Cherríe Moraga explain, "In 1984 Third Woman decided to pursue the publication of a Chicana/Latina lesbian issue. However, such an issue has yet to materialize. In part this is due to the fact that very few professional writers— be they creative or critical—have actively pursued a lesbian political identity" (8). Although initially there was not enough material for a lesbian issue, the attempt and the resulting 1989 anthology arguably laid the foundation for the formulation of Chicana and Latina lesbian communities. It also helped make possible both the 1991 *Chicana Lesbians,* also published by Third Woman, and the 1994 Routledge reissuing of *Compañeras: Latina Lesbians,* a 276-page anthology edited by Juanita Ramos and initially published in 1987 by the Latina Lesbian History Project.[33]

As anthologies of the late 1980s and 1990s become more particular in terms of the ethnic and/or sexual identities they advance, they often simultaneously become broader—less located, in some sense—in terms of contributors' national and geographic locations. *Our Feet Walk the Sky, Third Woman,* and *Compañeras*—along with other 1990s anthologies including the 1991 U.S. and Canadian anthology *Piece of my Heart: A Lesbian of Colour Anthology,* edited by Makeda Silvera, and *The Very Inside*—can be distinguished from many anthologies published in the 1980s in their attention to contributors' diasporic identities, and/or in their testing or refusal of national boundaries. The editors of these anthologies establish what I have referred to as "coalitional communities": they emphasize the coalitional nature of contributors' ties without surrendering their claims for community. The anthologies sometimes forward diasporic formulations of identity or transnational ties between contributors that are abstract or unspecified rather than tied to particular locations, but in their insistence on contributors' positions between locations and nations (a betweenness that at once makes them at home nowhere and in multiple places) the anthologies illustrate the spatialization of identity outlined above, and emphasize the importance of location in determining identity. Furthermore, these anthologies demonstrate their engagement with a politics of location by highlighting the locations and occasions that lead to their conceptualization, and that ground them and the identities they promote.

In order not to preclude the insights afforded by a politics of location, and also to consider how formulations of diasporic or multinational coalitional identities relate to deployments of identity politics and a politics of location, the remainder of this chapter focuses on a few of these anthologies from the 1990s. I have chosen anthologies that involve Hawaiian and/or other Local contributors, not only because doing so allows me to situate this study from my present location, but also because attention to Hawai'i makes the importance of location and nation obvious and immediate, not only for those living in Hawai'i, but, albeit in different ways, for everyone on the continental United States and in the Asian and Pacific regions.[34] As both the fiftieth state of the United States and the homeland for Hawaiians struggling for the recognition of their never-relinquished sovereignty, Hawai'i is, to borrow (and slightly redirect) Candace Fujikane's phrase, "between nationalisms."[35] The fact that many Hawaiians' self-defined nationality conflicts with the one imposed upon them by the U.S. government enables Hawaiians' inclusion in—but also their disruption of—a number of coalitional identities: U.S. women/people of color, Asian American, Native American, Local, and Pacific Islander. Hawaiians' relations to each of these groups raise complex questions regarding at whose expense— and in whose interest—different coalitions and identities can be constituted.

In perusing anthologies of the 1990s organized around the coalitional identities listed above, I have, in a provisional way, been tracing the presence—or absence—of Hawaiians in them. Hawaii's status, however disavowed or unwanted, as America's fiftieth state often seems to place Hawaiians outside configurations of Pacific Islander identity (Albert Wendt's Pacific anthologies *Lali* and *Nuanua,* for example, do not include Native Hawaiian contributors). In addition, their struggles for Hawaiian land as native people distinguish Hawaiians from Asian Locals, let alone other Asian Americans—a fact that Local anthologies such as Eric Chock and Darrell Lum's *The Best of Bamboo Ridge* and Asian American anthologies such as *Between the Lines,* gloss over. Native Hawaiians' geographical and genealogical remove from the native peoples of the Americas also places them outside the identity "Native American," and, often, in opposition to an American identity. This distance occurs not only from the point of view of Hawaiians asserting sovereignty, but also from the continental U.S.—just before I moved here, a relative commented, "Too bad you couldn't get a job in this country."

At the same time, Hawaiians have worked in coalition with Native Americans (see Joseph Bruchac's *Returning the Gift*) and others of the above groups in creative and mutually enabling ways. As indicated by the names of the editors listed above, attention to Hawaiians' presence in multi-genre anthologies has led me to those that include men as well as women. To advance an argument that I will develop in a discussion of *Returning the Gift,* I partially attribute this unity across gender lines to the fact that Hawaiians' participation in anthologies is so often linked to nationalist, land-based struggles. Hawaiians' inclusion in— as well as absence from—various coalitional identities illuminates for me the contradictions, possibilities, and problems that attend each of them, and the importance that factors of location and nation have in determining identities and possibilities for coalitions.

The two 1994 anthologies that I consider here—Sharon Lim-Hing's *The Very Inside: An Anthology of Writing by Asian and Pacific Islander Lesbian and Bisexual Women* and Joseph Bruchac's *Returning the Gift: Poetry and Prose from the First North American Native Writers' Festival*—thematize crossings between the continental United States and Hawai'i. *The Very Inside* does so to promote a diasporic Asian and Pacific Islander identity; *Returning the Gift* does so in the interest of promoting indigenous alliances that are produced by, but defy, American colonialism. At the same time, and in tension with the coalitional identities the anthologies establish, Hawai'i operates in these anthologies as a site of contested and competing nationalisms, complex interethnic relationships, and highly unstable categories of identity. In addressing Hawai'i, contributors challenge and disrupt the categories of identity upon which these anthologies and those I considered in the previous chapters depend. Taken together, *The Very Inside* and *Returning the Gift* illustrate the ways identity politics operate differently in different cultural and place locations. Juxtaposing the diasporic and indigenous coalitions in these anthologies also enables the exploration of the importance of a politics of location in view of increasing globalization and the privileging of models of diasporic or post-national identity that often accompanies this movement.

Grounding Diasporic Identities in *The Very Inside*

Published in 1994 by Sister Vision: Black Women and Women of Colour Press and edited by Sharon Lim-Hing, *The Very Inside: An Anthology of Writing by Asian and Pacific Islander Lesbian and Bisexual Women* holds the local and the global in productive tension: while its contributors come from various parts of Asia, Canada, and the United States, and while they do not always identify their present location or renounce any national identity as restrictive or inaccurate, the anthology also emerges from specific work Lim-Hing has done with groups in the United States. These include, in Boston, the Alliance of Massachusetts Asian Lesbians and Gay Men (AMALGM) and Asian Sisters in Action (ASIA), and, in Santa Cruz, California, the West Coast Regional Asian/Pacific Lesbian and Bisexual Network retreat, which she attended in 1993. The retreat, in particular, crucially shapes the anthology: Pacific Islanders' experiences of marginalization there led to a San Francisco-based committee formed to ensure responsible inclusion of Pacific Islanders in the anthology. As *The Very Inside* encompasses and dialectically engages the local or site specific and the global or transnational, it provides a way to trace a diasporic politics of location that emerges out of an identity politics framework.

The Very Inside's diasporic conception of identity and the links it establishes among its sixty-four contributors all depend upon a bracketing, even a dismissal, of the importance of nationality. What anchors contributors across their differences of nationality, as well as other differences including race, ethnicity, and sexual orientation, is, as the anthology's title metaphor suggests, their female bodies, and a resistance to or disregard for heterosexual norms. This 467-page anthology, published in Canada, is not reducible to any one national framework. Edited by a woman of Chinese origins who was born in Kingston, Jamaica, and moved to Florida at age twelve, it includes contributors presently living in the United States, Canada, India, Malaysia, and England. The majority of the anthology's contributors, who are Asian-born and now (many temporarily) living in Canada or the United States, highlight and often celebrate their diasporic identities. For example, while Joyoti Grech states in her contributor's note that she was born in Bangladesh, she does not include information about her present location; instead, she states that "her parents taught her the rich fluidity of culture and the changing nature of 'national' boundaries" (456).

In its promotion of a diasporic Asian and Pacific Islander identity, *The Very Inside* takes off in the direction pointed to in *The Forbidden Stitch*. It does not merely challenge the national framework from within, however, but rather, as its title makes clear, forgoes such a framework altogether. The national and geographic diversity of the anthology's "Asian and Pacific Islander" contributors and its descriptions of contributors moving between countries support Dirlik's argument that "the idea of Asian America today requires a different mapping of the U.S., Asia, the Pacific and the world than that which produced the idea less than three decades ago."[36] In the complexity and multiplicity of individual contributors' geopolitical locations, as well as in the diversity of these locations taken together, *The Very Inside* makes evident the inadequacies of maps that suggest stable correspondences among geographic borders, national identities, and (to draw on Benedict Anderson's phrase) imagined communities.

As it resists static mappings of identity, *The Very Inside* facilitates alliances among Asians of diverse ethnicities and histories, and between Asian Americans and Pacific Islanders, Native Hawaiians in particular. In using the term "Asian and Pacific Islander" rather than a term such as "Asian/Pacific American," the anthology works against reinscribing the colonization of Hawaiians and other Pacific Islanders, or inadvertently undermining their struggles for sovereignty. Within the anthology's rubric, discussions of Hawaiian sovereignty need not put Asian Americans and Hawaiians at odds, nor rupture the bonds the anthology establishes between them. Furthermore, contributors' transpacific connections undermine long-maintained divisions between "East" and "West."[37] This undermining coincides with what Dirlik notes are "radical changes in the United States' relationship to Asia, as expressed in the new language of the Pacific" that are themselves bound up in the demographic transformation of Asian America.[38] Dirlik predicts, and *The Very Inside* is at the forefront of substantiating this prediction, that these changes "may be in the process of constructing new ethnicities that are no longer containable within the national framework that earlier bounded thinking about ethnicity, . . . giving new meaning to older divisions as well."[39]

The creation of transnational ethnic identities is not, of course, necessarily progressive, since the formulation of such identities can work to perpetuate neo-colonial agendas. As Dirlik trenchantly argues, "There is a good case to be made here that the blurring of area boundaries plays into the hands of existing hegemonic constructions of globalism and 'multiculturalism,' rather than challenging them, which also reflects the needs of an Asian American elite in complicity with existing structures of power."[40] While Dirlik perhaps assigns too much conscious intention to the "complicity" of those in Asian American studies, he does provide a sense of the ways that projects such as *Making Waves* and *The Forbidden Stitch* can be seen inadvertently to reinforce existing power structures, to the extent that they blur area boundaries without addressing the persistence—even the deepening—of class, racial, and geopolitical inequities in an era of transnational capitalism.

The Very Inside, however, more carefully accounts for the unevenness of contributors' diasporic identities.

The Very Inside does not simply represent what Miyoshi refers to as "a transnational class of professionals who can live and travel globally, while freely conversing with their colleagues in English, the lingua franca of the TNC era";[41] largely through the inclusion of Southeast Asian and Pacific Islander contributors, the anthology also highlights the lack of choice and/or cultural dislocation that can accompany experiences of diaspora. Particularly in the first section, "Origins, Departures," contributors, in a way consonant with Rich's politics of location, carefully locate their experiences of diaspora and in many instances make clear the pain of forced removals. In Lê Thi Diem Thúy's poem, "shrapnel shards on blue water," the speaker describes herself and other refugees from Vietnam as "fragmented shards / blown here by a war no one wants to remember" (4). Still other contributors (for example, sansei, or third-generation, Japanese Canadian Midi Onodera, in "True Confessions of a Queer Banana") refuse to blur national boundaries as they, in claiming pan-Asian alliances from their particular locations in Canada or the United States, resist conventional mappings of national belonging and put into practice a diasporic politics of location.

Other contributors also keep the anthology's global perspective grounded and precise—utilizing, in other words, a politics of location—when they trace the economic and political circumstances that lead to present-day Asian and Pacific Islander diasporas. It is the attention to Pacific Islanders, Hawaiians in particular, that serves in *The Very Inside* to temper other, more celebratory or ungrounded, portrayals of diasporic identity such as the one found in Mona Oikawa's "Stork Cools Wings." This story, which traces the developing relationship between two Asian Canadian women who meet in a Tai Chi class, concludes, "'Til the light of dawn, we carry each other to the peaks of Tian Shan and Fuji-san, arms and legs in perfect harmony, two Asian women stroking and striding and flying together" (254). Here, love transports these women across continents and connects them to a romanticized (or, rather, orientalized?) "Asia."

In contrast to such erotically fueled imaginative flights, Hawaiian contributors' discussions of their diasporic identities engage concrete issues of land struggles, demonstrating the crucial connection they maintain between identity and land. Both because Pacific Islanders trace their genealogy to land (e.g., J. Kehaulani Kauanui's poem "olelo kupuna o hapa/kanaka maoli wahine," and "Tita Talk," which begins with the Kānaka Maoli[42] contributors sharing their genealogies), and because, for the most part, they have been forced from this land by governmental theft and economic necessity, their discussions of diaspora remain firmly in line with the politics of location outlined by Rich, and counter those that might, however inadvertently, support corporate versions of globalization. As Kehaulani Kauanui points out in "Tita Talk," "There's a relationship between them [rich non-Hawaiians] being on our land and us not being able to be on our land, these things are connected" (103). And in "The Challenges Facing Asian and Pacific Islander Lesbian and Bisexual Women in the U.S.," Trinity Ordoña explains, "The lopsided economy [resulting from tourism in Hawai'i] forced many Native Hawaiians to leave home for job and education opportunities on the continent. Today, over 100,000 Pacific Island peoples live in California alone, including half of the total Samoan and Chamorro population" (386). Given such demographic changes, Ordoña underlines the need for diasporic networks of Pacific Islanders that extend across Canada, England, and the Pacific Islands. The presence of Pacific Islanders, and of other contributors who address Pacific Islander issues, makes clear the harsh economic conditions, created largely if not entirely by colonialism, that lead to the creation of contemporary international diasporic identities and communities.

In some ways, the distinctions that Ordoña and other contributors maintain between Asians and Pacific Islanders (defined by Lim-Hing as "indigenous Samoans, Fijians, Hawaiians, Guamanians, Polynesians, and so on" [n.p.]) are by no means clear-cut ones. For example, Filipinas, who pose contradictions to the category Asian (see chapter 4 above) can also be considered Pacific Islanders. However, Filipina contributors, especially those working on behalf of Asian and Pacific Islander coalitions (e.g., Ordoña), consistently position themselves as Asian in *The Very Inside*. Or, to take another example, many Hawaiians are also of Asian (and/or Caucasian) background, and the contributors to *The Very Inside* are no exception: for example, while they identify as Kānaka Maoli, Desiree Thompson and Leolani M. discuss their Chinese and/or Japanese heritage, as does Lani Ka'ahumanu. Likewise, the anthology's association of diaspora with colonialism and painful displacement for Pacific Islanders brackets ways some Pacific Islanders have chosen "diaspora": in the Pacific, writers such as Epeli Hau'ofa present Pacific Islander populations as migratory and voyaging from their inception.[43] The oppositions this anthology, which is otherwise committed to challenging binaries, leaves in place between Asians and Pacific Islanders are strategically effective, even necessary, given the anthology's historical and geographic location. In preserving a "Pacific

Islander" identity rather than emphasizing ways it overlaps with an "Asian" one, *The Very Inside* creates a coalitional space for Kānaka Maoli contributors and other Pacific Islanders who are struggling with internal colonialism and against cultural and geographical dislocation.

Lesbian Cartographies and Female Geographies

Another way in which contributors employ a politics of location as they resist romanticized and over-generalized portrayals of diaspora is through their discussions that link global mobility or belonging and sexuality. V. K. Aruna's "The Myth of One Closet" provides an especially strong example not only of the class privileges of a free-wheeling global identity, but also of the heterosexual privilege of such an identity. Aruna's essay makes clear the costs and lack of choice behind her description of her position in the contributors' notes as "a nonimmigrant Black Feminist Lesbian of dual Tamil heritage, born and raised in Malaysia, currently living in the Washington, D.C. area" (454). In "The Myth of One Closet," she explains,

As a nonimmigrant, I am not free to cross borders openly as a Lesbian. Laws that allow visitors into the U.S. for conferences on AIDS do not apply to me. Hence, the question becomes: Does the politics of coming out invalidate the politics of a double identity? Particularly, when it is a myth that there is only one closet and one way to come out? (373–374)

She elaborates in a footnote on this double identity, and on the two types of closets with which she contends: "There are many lesbians who are 'illegal aliens.' There are many undocumented lesbians who are 'illegally married.'" (376). "Even as I am suspended between borders, between definitions of legal and illegal, resident and non-resident . . . alien . . . I survive by remembering that Going [*sic*] in and out of closets is a strategy for working to remove the conditions that make my closets necessary in the first place" (374).

In "All At Once, All Together: One Asian American Lesbian's Account of the 1989 Asian Pacific Lesbian Network Retreat," Ann Yuri Uyeda addresses the situation of those whose race and sexual identity do not suspend them between borders, but make borders impassable altogether. She tells of a Korean woman's inability to get past the INS either to attend the 1989 retreat or to visit Los Angeles for two weeks as an observer and reporter for an international lesbian group. Reflecting on this woman's situation, Uyeda asks, "For all 170 of us present at the retreat, how many other lesbian and bisexual API women were not at UC Santa Cruz? How many other women wanted to come to Santa

Cruz from their homes abroad but could not get past INS and so gave up quietly?" (116). Such accounts and questioning in *The Very Inside* establish the importance not only of race, class, and gender, but also of sexuality, in determining who can claim "international citizenship," or a diasporic identity.[44] As contributors in these accounts begin, as Rich suggests women do, with their bodies, and think from there about where they can and cannot go, they practice the politics of location that she advocates. By including such pieces, *The Very Inside* does not elide the ongoing force of nation-states, passports, and green cards, as it promotes a sense of the complexity and ambiguity of contributors' national identities.

Contributors' lesbian and bisexual identities also keep *The Very Inside*'s diaspora from being so broad that it is ineffectual or incoherent. In thinking about the movement towards globalizing Asian American studies, Sau-ling Wong has sounded some cautionary notes: "But the idea of an 'Asian diaspora' would be so inclusive as to be politically ungrounded (in fact ungroundable, given the vastly different interests and conflicted histories of Asian peoples), while the idea of an 'Asian American diaspora' is simply quite meaningless."[45] Lim-Hing herself is quite aware of the difficulties of an Asian diasporic identity. Towards the end of her introduction, she asks, "Are there enough reasons for 'Asians' in the North American context to come together as one heterogeneous group? Do these reasons hold for lesbians and bisexual women, and are there additional reasons?" (n.p.). Rather than provide any definitive answers to these questions, she states, "Celebrating the enormous variation and richness within this one, large group [of contributors] is now more important to me than defining Asian and Pacific Islander lesbians and bisexual women in opposition to other groups" (n.p.). In the process of editing the anthology, Lim-Hing has established affectional bonds with the anthology contributors, and, in large part, it is the ties among contributors, as well as their pieces expressing sexual love and desire for other Asian and Pacific Islander women, that hold the anthology, and the contributors, together.

Indeed, the contributors' love for other Asian and Pacific Islander women serves in the anthology to bridge a diasporic coalition and a grounded sense of community, to create what might be called a coalitional community. It is their sexuality, a sexuality rooted in women's bodies ("the very inside"), that holds the contributors together. In addition, while the anthology includes bisexual women as well as lesbians, it does not address the differences between the two; instead, the inclusion of bisexual women stands more as a corrective to former ex-

clusions of bisexuals from lesbian communities. As bisexual contributor Ka'ahumanu explains this, "I am sick and tired of lesbians who love
lesbians, not women" (452). In this coalitional community, bisexuality
exists on a continuum with lesbianism, and women-centered relationships, as something bisexual and lesbian contributors have in common,
are central. In Ka'ahumanu's words, "I am a woman loving women" (451).

The anthology's title, "The Very Inside," suggests this focus as it situates the anthology not in relation to a national, or even transnational
framework, but in relation to the female body. The collection's title
poem, Indigo Chih-Lien Som's "the very inside," bears out this argument as its speaker tells her lover she wrote her a love poem "that tastes /
like your very inside" (188), and in poem after poem in the anthology's
centrally placed section, "Waking from a Dream of Love," women's
bodies serve as anchoring places, as the oceans or bodies of land that
locate their lovers. In Vanessa Marzan Deza's "This Hunger in my Hips,"
the speaker thanks her lover for the experience of "treading deeply /
fully into / each other's secret oceans" (184). The speaker in Lê Thi Diem
Thúy's poem "Foresee" tells her lover of her dream of waking and "climb-
ing / with me / down / into the ocean" (213). The ocean in Tomiye
Ishida's "Akairo" is also created by women making love: "We collapse
together / this woman and I / in the warm, salty ocean" (259), and in
still other poems in this section women address their lovers or offer
themselves as an "enchanting forest" or a "private garden" (Brenda Joy
Lem, "Enchanting Forest"), or as "a landscape so pleasing and rare"
(Suniti Namjoshi, "When My Love Lay Sleeping . . ."). In her prose
poem, "Swirling Tales, and the Concept of Tea," Lisa Asagi muses, "It
has become impossible to adhere to visible landmarks to establish a
sense of placement in the current of general time. It has nothing at all to
do with maps, but it involves a lot of research into the understanding of
why we love to understand" (245). A writer from Hawai'i living in California, Asagi provides in this surrealist piece only the most casual
markings of location; instead she maps her relationship with a woman
who "was the world" (244). Together, the pieces in this section work to
anchor the anthology's Asian and Pacific Islander diaspora in the female bodies of its contributors. Poems in this section take familiar and
idealizing tropes of women and subvert them in the service of a lesbian
erotics that doubles as a practice of a politics of location.[46]

Taken together, this group of poems offers a reworking of a politics of
location, one that, as it presents women's bodies as geographical locations, and as it orients women in relation to these geographies, is cut
free from specific geographical locales and their histories. Such a poli-

tics of location, with its turnings inward, can potentially work to de-contextualize lesbianism, to relegate women—once again—to ideal-ized landscapes, and to reinscribe a separation of love and politics. However, as the above sections suggest, another politics of location also circulates in *The Very Inside,* one that more closely resembles Rich's: framing, and providing a context for, this middle section are other sec-tions that establish the particular locations from which contributors speak, and the importance of these locations in determining contribu-tors' identities and their connections to one another. Furthermore, the grounds from which the anthology is produced provide yet another way in which the anthology utilizes a politics of location: its transna-tional/global vision emerges from North America, most broadly speak-ing and, more specifically, from the sites leading to its production: Boston, Santa Cruz, San Francisco, and Toronto.

Retreats, Coalitional Communities, and the Significance of Santa Cruz

As Lim-Hing's introduction makes clear, most of the Asian and Pacific Islander women that the anthology includes are situated, however pro-visionally or temporarily, in North America. Of the eight Pacific Is-landers included in the anthology, all but one identify as Native Hawai-ian, or Kānaka Maoli (Ami Mattison says only that she is of Polynesian descent). Thus they have imposed upon them, however undesired, a na-tional identity as Americans, and, as do the majority of the Asian con-tributors, they live in the continental United States (in fact, seven of the Kānaka Maoli contributors reside in California, at least during the mak-ing of the anthology). The term "Asian and Pacific Islander" is itself more global in rhetorical effect than in actuality, since it really only makes sense in a North American context. As Dorothy Yin-yee Ko notes in *Moving Mountains,* "Only in America [or areas outside "Asia"?] can one be born an 'Asian'" (56). Because the term "Asian and Pacific Is-lander" does not make clear its locatedness in North America, it ges-tures toward the inclusion of more people than it actually encom-passes. At worst, then, this term may operate to falsely cast other parts of the world in accordance with North American imaginings, and to perpetuate the dominance of Western culture—and the English lan-guage—in the guise of globalism. It can also elide the importance of specific and still-operative national identities, and of geopolitical loca-tions, in the interest of forging a transnational, diasporic Asian and Pacific Islander identity and community.

In *The Very Inside*, however, Lim-Hing carefully locates and historicizes the use of "Asian and Pacific Islander" in her introduction, and explores the problems attached to it. Furthermore, by centering Asian
and Pacific Islander lesbian and bisexual women in North America, she
represents a "west" that, inflected by transpacific crossings and a queer
erotics, is far from hegemonic. As contributors to *The Very Inside* write
in English and locate themselves in Canada or the United States, they
mark English as a hegemonic language and/or claim it by imprinting
it with their own histories. Thus, Local Hawai'i contributor Donna
Tsuyuko Tanigawa switches between standard English and pidgin, or
Hawaiian Creole English, in "I Like Beef Wit' Words," a piece about
language as a tool of dominance and resistance. And in her poem "Just
once / before I die / I want someone / to make love to me / in Can-
tonese," Som simultaneously claims English as mother tongue as she
disclaims it and points to the trauma of a diasporic identity in her desire "to remember / language I've never / known" (261). Along with
other contributors to *The Very Inside*, Tanigawa and Som bear out Stuart Hall's arguments that, on the one hand, "global mass culture" "is
centered in the West and it always speaks English" (28), and, on the
other hand, "It speaks a variety of broken forms of English: English as
it has been invaded, and as it has hegemonized a variety of other languages without being able to exclude them from it."[47] If, moreover, lesbianism and bisexuality are "western" identities, as Cambodian contributors Peou Lakhana and Chamroeun suggest they are in "Tha Phi
Neah Yeung The. . . .? (Only the two of us . . . ?)," they are undoubtedly
empowering ones for those of *The Very Inside*'s contributors born and
living in Asian countries, whose inclusion in the anthology results from
their attendance at the Santa Cruz–based retreats to which they traveled in order to affirm these identities.[48]

Through the many pieces that reflect on the importance of these annual Santa Cruz retreats, *The Very Inside* highlights the extent to which
it—and contributors' identities and their coalitional community—
emerge from specific locations, and also from specific occasions. These
occasions and locations crucially determine the shape and exchanges
of *The Very Inside*, particularly its success in bringing together Asians
and Pacific Islanders. As Lim-Hing makes clear, it is the 1993 West
Coast Regional Asian/Pacific Lesbian and Bisexual Network retreat set
in Santa Cruz that enabled Hawaiian participation in the anthology. In
her introduction, she gives some background on this retreat, explaining
that women of Native Hawaiian heritage "spoke out against the pre-
sumptions behind the term API."

Out of the pain and self-examination of that conference, a committee formed in San Francisco in order to generate texts by women of Pacific Islander heritage specifically for this anthology. With input from Pacific Islander women, Asian women took responsibility for creating conditions within which Pacific Islander women might feel that their name was not being stolen and their issues suppressed. It was through this committee that most Pacific Islander contributors sent in their work. (n.p.)

In *The Very Inside*, some of these committee members and other contributors describe the process of coalition-building at these retreats. Trinity Ordoña provides a particularly detailed account of the 1993 retreat in her "Cross-Racial Hostility and Inter-Racial Conflict: Stories to Tell, Lessons to Learn." Ordoña explains how, at a workshop entitled "Specific Islanders: Inclusion vs. Appropriation, Coalition, and Hawaiian Sovereignty" (395), workshop leaders "Lisa and Kehaulani" (also contributors to *The Very Inside*) led her to realize that, for Asian/Pacific groups, "sameness and power over, instead of difference and coalition with, have mistakenly become the operational framework for our politics" (396). She then describes the process by which the Asian women in the workshop "decided to take responsibility to change this practice among ourselves. . . . The next day following the morning plenary panel, we took over the Retreat" (396). The resulting " 'guerrilla workshop,' " was, according to Ordoña, "the first open struggle within the APLBN against this kind of tokenism by Asian lesbians and bisexual women and the beginning process of reconciliation with our Pacific Islander sisters. This story is but one contribution" (396). Through the interviews, dialogue, and essays that constitute other such contributions, the anthology evidences a rich network of relations among contributors that can be traced to specific California and Boston organizations and, especially, to the Asian/Pacific Lesbian Network (APLN) Santa Cruz retreats. If the 1993 retreat serves as a site of activism and coalition-building, as Ordoña suggests here, narratives of this process and the circulation of these narratives by way of *The Very Inside* constitute other forms of coalition building that follow from this event.[49]

The Very Inside advances and strengthens the coalitional work of the 1993 retreat through its inclusion of other pieces that keep in play the important differences among Pacific Islander and Asian contributors, and also through its inclusion of pieces that call attention to the work involved in forging Asian/Pacific Islander coalitions. In "Tita Talk," Grech's interview of Leolani M., and various poems, Hawaiian contributors address issues such as sovereignty, tourism, and the Hawaiian language, and works like Kehaulani Kauanui and Ju Hui 'Judy' Han's

"'Asian Pacific Islander': Issues of Representation and Responsibility" exemplify the coalitional effort. Because the anthology's Asian contributors confront ways in which Asian/Pacific groups have subsumed concerns specific to Pacific Islanders, the anthology frees its Hawaiian contributors to focus on their own issues and experiences, and not only insofar as they intersect with Asian women's, but also in ways that suggest oppositions between these groups.

The transnational feminist practices of *The Very Inside* are informed by and embody a politics of location in the fullest sense of the term: Lim-Hing thematizes throughout the site-specific and more general locations that produce not only the anthology, but also contributors' diasporic identities; in addition, individual contributors emphasize that their identities must be understood in relation to their geographical locations and the histories and politics of these locations. While critics in postcolonial and transnational studies have recognized the importance of a politics of location, they often have overlooked both the connections of this politics to feminist theory and practices (including a politics of identity), and the contributions women, especially those who are sexual and/or racial minorities, have made in theorizing and establishing transnational alliances on the basis of a politics of location. And yet, because these contributions, as *The Very Inside* demonstrates, bring together the often occluded or dismissed concerns of sexuality and gender with those of race, class, and nation, they are particularly important ones, ones that challenge dominant formations of national and sexual identity.[50]

In *The Very Inside*, it is women who unsettle and move between dominant sexual and racial or ethnic categories who break up hegemonic formulations of nation and race, as well as those of gender and sexuality. Given Lim-Hing's privileging of contributors who at once embody and resist multiple categories of identity, it is not surprising that she concludes *The Very Inside* with Ka'ahumanu's "Hapa Haole Wahine." In this poem, Ka'ahumanu traces her discovery and claiming of her Hawaiian, Irish Catholic, Japanese, and Jewish cultural ancestry along with her feminism, lesbianism, and bisexuality, and she links these discoveries to her movements through the continental United States, Hawai'i, and Japan. With statements such as "Mixed race people threaten the core of a racist society" and "Bisexuals jeopardize the foundation of a / monosexual heterosexist culture" (451), Ka'ahumanu celebrates the revolutionary potential of her various identities, which connect her to a wide range of people as they serve to challenge various forms of oppression. Along with the other Pacific Islander contributors, Ka'ahumanu exerts a particular force in *The Very Inside*. These women play a crucial role in helping to fulfill the anthology's aims to challenge and unfix North American formulations of nation, race, ethnicity, and sexuality, and to establish new diasporic alliances across these categories.

Diaspora Reconsidered

Lim-Hing is not alone in privileging a diasporic model of identity and community—such a position has come to be the expected one in discussions of the late twentieth century as an era of transnationalism, globalization, postmodernism, or postcolonialism. In introducing the journal *Diaspora* in 1991, editor Khachig Tölöyan proclaims that "diasporas are the exemplary communities of the transnational moment."[51] Those advocating a politics of location from a postmodernist perspective usually endorse diasporic formulations of identity and dismiss claims to essentialist links between people and places. Michael Keith and Steve Pile exemplify this stance in their introduction to *Place and the Politics of Identity:*

Politically, there is a reactionary vocabulary of both the identity politics of place and a spatialized politics of identity grounded in particular notions of space. It is the rhetoric of origins, of exclusion, of boundary-marking, of invasion and succession, of purity and contamination; the glossary of ethnic cleansing. But there are also more progressive formulations which become meaningless deprived of the metaphors of spatiality. Debates around territorialized and diasporic politics and political authority are just two instances where opposing the reactionary and promoting the progressive is possible only if the spatializations on which they rest are unpacked and made explicit.[52]

As do Keith and Pile, Daniel and Jonathan Boyarin assert an opposition between reactionary, territorial notions of space and progressive, diasporic ones in their article "Diaspora: Generation and the Ground of Jewish Identity." They propose:

a privileging of Diaspora, a dissociation of ethnicities and political hegemonies as the only social structure that even begins to make possible a maintenance of cultural identity in a world grown thoroughly and inextricably interdependent. . . . Assimilating the lesson of Diaspora, namely that peoples and lands are not naturally and organically connected, could help prevent bloodshed such as that occurring in Eastern Europe today."[53]

As their capitalization of "Diaspora" indicates, the Boyarins at once mark their model of diaspora as distinctly Jewish, as they claim its value and relevance for all people and places.

From Hawai'i, the problems with such privilegings of diaspora, which have become all-too-commonplace, are especially evident. While "the lesson of Diaspora" that the Boyarins draw from Jewish history might have progressive applications in many places, the problems with the "assimilation" of such a lesson and, concomitantly, with their call for "the renunciation of sovereignty (justified by discourses of autochthony, indigenousness, and territorial self-determination)" (723) are particularly glaring in Hawai'i. Haunani-Kay Trask begins *From a Native Daughter,* her forceful and eloquent book arguing against colonialism and on behalf of Hawaiian sovereignty, "We are the children of Papa— earth mother, and Wākea—sky father—who created the sacred lands of Hawai'i Nei. From these lands came the taro, and from the taro, came the Hawaiian people. . . . The land is our mother and we are her children. This is the lesson of our genealogy."[54] In Hawai'i, to deny such assertions of the organic connections between people and land, and to urge the renunciation of sovereignty, would serve most readily to perpetuate the colonization and, quite arguably, the genocide of Native Hawaiian people.[55]

If, for Hawaiians living in the continental United States, participation in a diasporic Asian and Pacific Islander coalitional community can be enabling, in Hawai'i such a formation is more fraught and contradictory. First, Hawaiians have quite different claims to Hawai'i than do Local Asians who, if they have been in Hawai'i for several generations, came to work on plantations. Second, Asian Americans (including Asian Locals) and Hawaiians cannot be said to occupy a similar position economically or socially: while Asian Americans' current economic and political status is far from homogeneous, it is significantly better overall than that of Hawaiians, who have the highest level of poverty, the shortest life expectancy, and the highest infant mortality rate in the state. Third, significant differences exist between Asian Americans in the continental United States and Asian Locals, as well as Hawaiians, and if Asian Americans in the continental United States are able to use blurred national boundaries to their advantage, Hawaiians (and many Asian Locals) would have little grounds to establish progressive alliances with Asians regardless of nationality, especially given Japan's neocolonial relationship to Hawai'i.[56]

When Hawai'i becomes the mainland, as in Hawaiian poet Joe Balaz's claim that "Hawai'i / is da mainland to me,"[57] diasporic formulations of community and identity become decidedly less enabling ones for Hawaiians. What works, in other words, in one location does not necessarily work in another. Thus, while some Hawaiians in the continental United States are formulating productive coalitional communities with Asians, in Hawai'i, many are establishing coalitional communities with native peoples across the Pacific, and those on the North American continent. Based on indigenous rather than diasporic conceptions of identity, these coalitional communities often focus on struggles for the right to self-government, and on related issues such as water rights, fishing rights, waste disposal, or the protest of the mining, testing, and storage of nuclear weapons on native lands.[58] The largest sovereignty group in Hawai'i, Ka Lāhui Hawai'i,[59] employs a nation-within-a-nation model that draws on the American Indian model, and in the last two years Native American activists including Ward Churchill (Keetoowah Band Cherokee), and Sharon Venne (Cree) have come to Hawai'i to work with sovereignty leaders including Haunani-Kay Trask, who, in addition to authoring *From a Native Daughter,* is also professor and Director of the Center for Hawaiian Studies, a poet, and a leading voice for Ka Lāhui Hawai'i (her sister, Mililani Trask, heads this organization as kia 'āina, or governor).[60] Both Churchill and Venne also sat as members on the 1993 Kānaka Maoli Peoples' International Tribunal that found in favor of Hawaiians' rights to self-governance under United Nations guidelines, and they have edited a collection, *Islands in Captivity: The International Tribunal on the Rights of Indigenous Hawaiians,* that emerges out of this experience.[61]

Pacific Crossings and Indigenous Alliances in *Returning the Gift*

Alliances made between Native Americans and Hawaiians in the more strictly political realm are facilitated and deepened by cultural and literary alliances, and vice versa. In addition to her work with Churchill and Venne, Haunani-Kay Trask has been involved in other exchanges with Natives from North America that involve transpacific crossings, and that bridge the cultural and the political. One such exchange involves her participation in the July 1992 festival, Returning the Gift, a four-day gathering in Norman, Oklahoma, which brought together over 350 Native writers from North, Central, and South America.[62] The 1994 anthology *Returning the Gift: Poetry and Prose from the First North American Native Writers' Festival,* emerged from this festival. Edited by conference co-organizer Joseph Bruchac (Abenaki), the anthology includes contributions from ninety-one of the festival participants, both established and lesser-known or new. As with *The Very Inside,* the coalition forged in *Returning the Gift* is not strictly a textual one, but is occasioned by a meeting in a particular time and place. This grounded coalition then circulates more widely by way of *Returning the Gift.*[63]

However, while in both *Returning the Gift* and *The Very Inside* Hawaiian participation results from meetings that depend upon Pacific crossings, in *Returning the Gift* these crossings themselves are not constitutive of contributors' identities. In fact, what brings contributors together is a sense of their genealogical ties to specific, distinct geographies. In other words, *Returning the Gift* depends upon contributors' shared indigenous, rather than shared diasporic, conception of identity.

Oklahoma serves as a particularly apt site for the Returning the Gift meeting. Oklahoma has the second largest population of Native peoples in the United States and during the 1800s Oklahoma Territory served as the final destination for the forced relocation of some sixty nations. With the discovery of oil at the turn of the century, Indian reservation trust lands were "redistributed," and most reservations were disbanded a few years preceding the statehood of Oklahoma in 1907. Thus, not only is Oklahoma a site where many Native peoples can gather to find connections to their ancestors, it is also a land in which is embedded the violent history of Native peoples' forced dislocation and relocation.

Like *The Very Inside*, *Returning the Gift* engages in a project of challenging national boundaries, but if *The Very Inside* sets out to unfix these boundaries, *Returning the Gift* remaps them. The 1992 festival coincided with the Columbus Quincentennial, and while the contributors do not focus exclusively on colonialism and its legacies, the anthology nevertheless marks a response to Native Americans' position "500 years A.C.," as contributor Annette Arkeketa puts it (5). In part, this response involves its defiance of what festival historian Geary Hobson calls "the Johnny-come-lately Europeanized boundaries between what are today called the United States and Canada, the United States and Mexico, Guatemala and Belize, and so on" (xxvi). Although, unlike the conference, the anthology includes only North American writers, contributors invoke their feelings of connection to indigenous peoples from the "other" Americas, and claim solidarity with them (e.g., Gail Tremblay's poem, "An Onondaga Trades with a Woman Who Sings with a Mayan Tongue"). The anthology works as Hobson claims the conference did, to oppose and expose "the fiction of enforced, superimposed nationality that characterizes the so-called American democracies" (xxvii), and to assert the presence and kinship of the various Native nations "America" has displaced. *Returning the Gift* provides a mapping of the North American continent that resists U.S. imperialism and exposes the arbitrariness of its borders, as it simultaneously draws together (rather than disbands) the nations subject to American control.

In this spirit, the anthology asserts connections between Native Hawaiians and Natives from the North American continent. In the anthology's introduction, Bruchac tells how hundreds of writers from dozens of tribal nations came to the Festival, "spanning the continent from Alaska to Florida, from Maine to southern California, from the Arctic circle to the highlands of Mexico and Guatemala. Also included were representatives from South America and *even Hawaii*" (xx; emphasis added). In Bruchac's remapping, as he forges connections among Native peoples based on geographical contiguity rather than the mappings of empire, he also extends support to those who are joined solely by U.S. imperialism. His "even Hawaii," then, marks the fictionality, but also the real and brutal force, of U.S.-imposed borders.

The anthology includes several crossings between the continental United States and what contributor Barney Bush (echoing Joe Balaz) calls "the mainland of Hawaii" (66) in his tribute to festival participant Haunani-Kay Trask, and the poems by Trask establish strong interrelations and alliances among Hawaiians and Native Americans. Her first poem, "Returning the Gift," set in Oklahoma and dedicated to Linda Hogan, is clearly occasioned by the Festival after which she names the poem. The speaker, "an ocean and a half a continent away from home," finds "no scarlet mango or crusted / breadfruit for my Hawaiian / eyes, only a wet dark stain / on Indian earth, returning / the gift of song and sorrow" (290). Trask follows this poem with one simply entitled "Hawai'i." This poem, with its long set of explanatory notes, allows readers to discover similarities and differences between Natives' histories in Hawai'i and the continental United States. In her final poem, "Chant of Lamentation," Trask's reference to "the stained / and dying earth" (295) connects her ancestral land to the "Indian earth" of Oklahoma, with its "wet dark stain."

The anthology also includes Pacific crossings by continental writers. Luci Tapahonso sets her poem "The Pacific Dawn" in Hilo, where the speaker attends to Pele with corn pollen and a prayer. This poem admits the foreignness of Hawai'i as it suggests relatedness between the Navajo speaker and Hawaiians: "The huge flowers I couldn't have imagined, / the lilting songs of the throaty chanters, / the nurturing stories of long ago, / and those who spread luau before us / as if we have just come home" (280). In "A Tribal Situation," set in Alaska during the days of statehood, Mary Lockwood subtly evokes the Nashalook clan's resistance to statehood by describing the continuance of tribal life in the face of it. This piece ends with a moment of understated but suggestive solidarity between one colonized people and another:

"Dad brought out his guitar from our cabin and strummed lovely Hawaiian songs" (187). While a history of colonialism provides a common context for contributors, the crossings and alliances the anthology includes do not reduce the complexity of this history or the diversity of the many cultures and nations to which contributors belong.

The emphasis on location and on the reclamation of land and nation in *Returning the Gift* sets it apart from an anthology such as *A Gathering of Spirit: A Collection by North American Indian Women*. In *A Gathering of Spirit*, editor Beth Brant (Degonwadonti) is less concerned with challenging geopolitical borders than she is with establishing a community for Native women. Brant, a Bay of Quinte Mohawk from Desertonto, Ontario, who now lives in Detroit, includes contributors from both Canada and the United States, but she does not call attention to her disregard for American-imposed national boundaries; rather, she forges links among Native women as a means for surviving present-day conditions of poverty, imprisonment, sexism (within Native communities as well outside them), and homophobia, and it is these issues that conjoin the contributors. Even when Brant mentions that the book's contributors come from forty different nations, her stress is on their common grounding as Indian women. As she puts it, "Our spirit is making a little bit of Indian country wherever we travel or live,"[64] and, "We are a community. We are a nation" (15). For Brant, "Indian country" and nationhood are tied less to specific land claims than to psychic bonds that conjoin Native women. The shift in emphasis, then, from *A Gathering of Spirit* to *Returning the Gift*, is consonant with the shift from a politics of identity to a politics of location. The interconnections between these politics, however, and the continuing urgency of Brant's concerns in *A Gathering of Spirit*, are evidenced in *Returning the Gift*. Brant's poem in this later collection, "Telling," maintains a focus on crimes against Indian women, and on ways they can work together to survive them. Brant's expression of gratitude in *A Gathering of Spirit* to Bruchac and Hobson also suggests the correspondences and compatibility of their and the two anthologies' political visions.

Returning the Gift and, to a lesser extent, *A Gathering of Spirit*, challenge the gendered boundaries I have maintained in this study. In including Bruchac's anthology in this concluding chapter, I hope to call these boundaries into question, and to highlight the cultural, political, and historical contexts that contribute to different contemporary anthologizing practices and forms of feminism. Native women have long been pointing to these contexts in differentiating their feminist practices from those of other women, especially white women. In her 1986 collection of essays, *The Sacred Hoop: Recovering the Feminine in American Indian Traditions,* Paula Gunn Allen locates her feminism in her mother's Laguna Pueblo culture, a gynocracy wherein "Woman is the Supreme Being, the Great Spirit, the Great Mystery, the All-Being."[65] Indeed, one of the book's central contentions is that "traditional tribal lifestyles are more often gynocratic than not, and they are never patriarchal."[66] Gunn Allen attributes the oppression and degradation of (Native) women to Christianity and Western patriarchal politics and culture (a view her cousin Leslie Marmon Silko supports in her novel *Ceremony*), and argues that colonialism alone has made it necessary for American Indian women to define themselves politically as Indian women.[67] Because her feminism has "red roots," it is not predicated on a division from Native men.[68]

In *From a Native Daughter,* Trask similarly links the oppression and degradation of Native Hawaiian women to Western colonialism. Furthermore, she claims that Hawaiian women are at the forefront of resisting colonialism, and that their leadership powers emerge out of, not in opposition to, a Hawaiian world view. Trask underlines women's prominence in the sovereignty movements that have been gaining force since the 1970s: "And on the front lines, in the glare of public disapproval, are our women—articulate, fierce, and culturally grounded."[69] Trask accounts for her observation that "by any standard—public, personal, political—our sovereignty movement is led by women" (121) by explaining: "Our mother is our land, Papa-hānau-moku—she who births the islands. This means that Hawaiian women leaders are genealogically empowered to lead the nation" (122). Giving as examples Native historian Lilikalā Kameʻeleihiwa, poet and community organizer Dana Naone Hall, self-sufficiency activist LaFrance Kapaka, and Mililani Trask, Trask says that Hawaiian women have assumed a leadership that is not simply determined by genealogy, but also by *"mana,* exercised on behalf of the people" (123). Kameʻeleihiwa herself, in her groundbreaking history *Native Land and Foreign Desires,* argues for women's central and powerful position in Hawaiian history, culture, and politics.

Moreover, because the issue for both Hawaiians and Natives in the Americas is, as Gunn Allen points out, "survival, literal survival, both on a cultural and biological level" (189), and because their struggles are nationalist, not solely cultural nationalist ones, separation along gender lines makes less sense than it does for other marginalized groups of women. For both groups, ongoing histories of colonialism and genocidal policies and practices have led to poor health, low life expectancy, a high rate of enforced sterilization, drug and alcohol dependency, and relatively small and often dispersed populations. Thus, Native women activists often take colonialism as their main target and context, and work alongside men for their survival as a people. As Trask puts this, "to most Native people, women's concerns are part of the greater concern for our *lāhui*, our nation" (265).[70]

Gift-Giving Economies and Occasions

A community-building project, *Returning the Gift* reflects the emphases on Native men and women's shared struggles against colonialism and for self-determination. Both the festival, which, as Bruchac notes, "brought more Native writers together in one place than at any other time in history" (xix), and the anthology are organized with the explicit purpose of strengthening bridges among Native writers, and among Native writers and their communities. Festival historian Hobson emphasizes this focus, as his narrative about the conference and anthology invest both with a sense of their wider significances and communal purposes. As part of his narrative, Hobson tells of an address Chief Tom Porter of the Akwesasne Mohawk Nation gave to conference organizers that resulted in the festival's title: "He remarked that in our avocation as Native writers, involved as we are in taking our peoples' literature back to them in the form of stories and songs, we were actually returning the gift—the gift of storytelling, culture, continuance—to the people, the source from whence it had come" (xxv).

What orders the diverse offerings of *Returning the Gift* and holds them together is this sense of gift-giving. Running through the 171 pieces the anthology includes are references to the festival as a gift to writers and their communities. Bruchac presents the anthology as a gift he dedicates "to those who went before us and those yet to come." And individual contributors, having been asked for new material by Bruchac, in many instances responded with pieces that pay tribute to the Returning the Gift Festival—that, in effect, return (to) the gift. This continuation of the gift gives evidence of the communal ties and connections from which Native writing emerges, and keeps alive the festival site of Norman, Oklahoma, as a center from which the anthology's offerings and possibilities radiate. As Trask does in "Returning the Gift," Duane Niatum reflects on the Festival in his "North American Native Writers Journey to a Place Where the Air Is a Gift of Promise": "We have come to Oklahoma country in the belief that the mound builders of this land will give our blood a new dream path if we thank our elders in a way that links all things to our recovery of the ritual dance of words" (201). In "Recollecting the Gift," Barney Bush stresses the regional and cultural diversity of those who gathered in Oklahoma as he pays tribute to them and, in sharing jokes with them, conveys a sense of their community, its emotional sustenance, and its political aims: after joking that "Kathy Peltier / has some strange art deco plan that we will / surely hear when her dad comes home" (66), he thanks "all the grantors," telling them "Your gift is duly / noted and will be remembered long after / our country is free again" (67). Such recurring references to the festival, which locate the anthology, and encode in it the importance of this occasion, work to blur the lines between the text and event, between poet and poem, and also between written literature and Native oral storytelling traditions.

The anthology also includes more general mentions of storytelling and cultural continuity as gifts that Native writers/storytellers give to one another and to their communities. In "Wolf Warrior," Joy Harjo passes on a story that she calls a gift, telling her audience, "The / story now belongs to you, too, and much as pollen on the legs of a / butterfly is nourishment carried by the butterfly from one / flowering to another, this is an ongoing prayer for strength for us / all" (146). In highlighting these acts of gift-giving, and in presenting poems and stories as gifts that are not commodities or items of exchange, but communally shared experiences, the anthology (re)claims the term "Indian giver." (It also makes clear the cruel ironies that attend this term in its many references to broken treaties and stolen land.) In his untitled poem about a family reunion, Harold Littlebird make this reclamation explicit, as he also plays off the anthology and festival title: "Oh Grandfather! / In Love, for Giving / I give lovingly / For I am an Indian-Giver, returning . . ." (184).

Not only "for giving," but also "forgiving," the anthology offers its writings as gifts to non-Native readers as well. Some of the poems, and their respective gifts, are extended in particular to white readers, to remind and warn us against perpetuating a history of colonialism and attempted genocide. The dreamscape in Gloria Bird's prose poem, "History," uncannily captures a part of this history: in the piece, a man "dreams of beautiful, scantily dressed people baring [*sic*] gifts, but just as he reaches out to receive them they spill blood-soaked into his bed, thud like severed hands" (39). Other pieces warn non-Natives, whites in particular, against present-day forms of commodifying, or appropriating, Native gifts. In Chrystos' "Zenith Supplies," the speaker sees Sweet Grass Braids for sale as "Native Scents" and explains, "All night

I'm angry as I dream of selling eucharists on street corners / This sacred gift is never to be sold / but hippies don't care as they give themselves new names for the same old" (79).

While *Returning the Gift* is for sale, it attempts to resist this "same old" with its many-layered references to gift-giving. Some of these references, as in "Zenith Supplies," warn against appropriation or containment by non-Native readers. *Returning the Gift* contributors also oppose old and new forms of American colonialism and commodification "500 A.C." by locating the meaning of the anthology in exchanges among Native peoples that take place outside its bindings—in Norman, Oklahoma, or in contributors' own communities (or, in some cases, nations), where their poems and stories are communally shared events.[71]

Editable Words: Anthologies as Commodities

In an academy obsessed with identity and "difference," multi-genre anthologies by marginalized groups have become commodities as hot as "Native Scents." In "She Said They Say," the poem that precedes "Zenith Supplies," Chrystos addresses not only the commodification of Native cultures, but also the inescapability of Natives participating in their own commodification. As the speaker remarks, "This IS capitalism / even when we have other ideas / We're all selling out to stay alive" (78). In the concluding lines, this speaker tells someone (presumably Winona LaDuke, to whom the poem is dedicated), "Myself I'll definitely buy / any words you'd care to put on the table" (79). A few years earlier, in *Haciendo Caras,* Chrystos was raising questions about the ethics and purpose not of writing, but of publishing, of turning words into textual commodities (see "Not Editable"). "She Said They Say" can in some ways be seen as a response to "Not Editable," indicating as it does that if a capitalist economy is inescapable, there is room to sell words that will sustain those who buy them. And the fact that this later poetry appears in an anthology published by the University of Arizona Press suggests that Chrystos and her poetry have found a place in the academy, and have proven commercially viable. Likewise, Routledge's 1994 reissuing of *Compañeras: Latina Lesbians,* originally published in 1987 by the Latina Lesbian History Project, signals that such identity-based anthologies have gained institutional acceptance and recognition.

Such success can of course be costly. Not only can the identities that the anthologies put forth be bought and consumed as yet another colorful and exotic addition to what happy pluralists, profit-hungry corporations, and savvy politicians are calling the "salad bowl," but, as these anthologies have become more firmly located in the academy, the energy and tension produced by their in-between position, as well as the challenges they pose to the academy, have diminished. From their firmer grounding in the academy, editors and contributors no longer expect their anthologies to revolutionize the academy, or to transgress boundaries in a way that *This Bridge* and other anthologies of the 1980s did. For example, despite their reference points to *This Bridge*, editors to the 1993 anthology *Our Feet Walk the Sky: Women of the South Asian Diaspora* do not aim to foment revolution or resist the academy; rather, as they explain, "One of our main concerns throughout this process has been to create a balance of viewpoints."[72] Throughout the anthology, contributors strive to be understood within, rather than to transform, their South Asian communities and their university environments.

The journal *smell this*, established in 1990 by "women of color in coalition" at the University of California at Berkeley, serves as another example of the more circumscribed vision and goals of identity-based multi-genre collections. The cover of *smell this 2*, which pictures a woman of color with a huge basket on her back, links the journal's project to that of *This Bridge*, and evokes its central metaphor: a note explains that the basket "is representative of the baskets which were once used by women to carry wood, but in [artist Karyn Noble's] piece, the basket is supposed to be filled with the problems that women have to deal with in their lives and all of the 'burdens' they have to carry."[73] Significantly, however, in their translation of *This Bridge*'s guiding metaphor, the editors of *smell this* stress the oppressive weight placed on the backs of women of color rather than their roles as bridges between worlds and women. Furthermore, even as the metaphoric nature of the picture attempts to establish a connection between contributors and third world women whose burdens are more material than their own, it also suggests the distance between them.

At the same time, however, publications such as *Our Feet Walk the Sky* and *smell this* both suggest the important work that anthologies—both because of and in spite of their commodification—are doing in colleges and universities, which, after all, are far from homogeneous in their populations. Both publications are student-based ones which explicitly express their indebtedness to *This Bridge* and other anthologies. *Our Feet Walk the Sky* was started by a group of women who met as students at UC Berkeley, and its contributors were primarily students (some in high school, most in undergraduate and graduate programs at UC campuses). Editors and contributors to the student-based journal *smell this* acknowledged the help and inspiration of UC academics who were themselves contributors to *Making Waves, This Bridge, Haciendo Caras,* and other anthologies, and modelled *smell this* on anthologies of the 1980s, *This Bridge* in particular. The fact that such identity-based anthologies continue to be (re)produced by diverse feminist communities within universities, with and without the support of university or alternative presses, testifies to their impact, and points to their continuing importance for those—students as well as professional academics—who participate in the anthologies.[74] This participation, which is in fact enabled by the textual circulation—or commodification—of previous anthologies, engenders new coalitional communities and anthologies.[75] Anthologies also work to resist commodification and appropriation by highlighting the sites and occasions that lead to their production. This attention to location and occasion is enabled by, and linked to, anthology editors' and contributors' deployments of a politics of location (diasporic or indigenous), in which they foreground the connections among their locations, their identities, and their communities.

Eating Words and Just Desserts at the University of Hawai'i

At the University of Hawai'i, I have structured several of my freshman composition and sophomore writing-intensive literature courses around the reading and making of anthologies.[76] I ask students—whether or not they consider themselves Local—to contribute, then organize and structure, writing and art that in some way expresses their relationship to Hawai'i. My aim is to involve students in a project that they can claim and care about, and to enable them to become part of a lasting writing community. These anthologies, and the processes involved in their making, serve as intense sites of negotiation wherein students define themselves in relation to Hawai'i, the university, one another, and me.

In spring semester of 1995, when students in my composition classes were brainstorming titles for their anthologies, *Forrest Gump* had just won an Oscar. Of the dozen or so titles that students in one section proposed, "English 100 Is Like a Box of Chocolates" won hands down (in a class of twenty, mine was one of the two dissenting votes). So much, I thought, for my efforts to prompt students to give voice to their own locality and to their distinctive identities. At the same time, I felt a grim sense of appreciation for their choice: if the embrace of Forrest Gump signaled students' endorsement of or identification with mainstream American culture, it also, in the more immediate contexts of the course, could be viewed as an act of defiance. After all, students had entered the classroom expecting a mainlander's version of grammar and essay-writing instruction during which they would leave their locality, so to speak, at the door. Instead, they encountered politicized and polemical reading and writing assignments that asked them to reflect upon the place of Local language, identity, and literature in Hawai'i classrooms. I had hoped that I would learn a lot from such a focus, while providing students with a sense of authority and a subject that mattered to them. Some of them, however, told me that they felt cheated of their right to an education that would serve them as transport out of Hawai'i. Others seemed suspicious, unwilling to discuss Local issues in a university classroom taught by a haole fresh from the mainland. Maybe, I concluded, Gump's box of chocolates was my just desserts. So a few days after they selected the title, when Mahana, one of the students in charge of the cover art, came to my office to show me a picture he had extracted, via the internet, of Tom Hanks as Forrest Gump, I tried my best to share his excitement.

This story, however, does not end here, or with me. When the group in charge of organizing the anthology—creating subheadings and deciding which pieces to place where—received the cover art and the anthology's contents, there were rumblings about the anthology title and the Gump photo. The rumblings got louder, and after much spirited discussion, the group requested that those in charge of the cover art produce an additional cover. They wanted this cover to have the title "Pidgin Is One Box Choclat, Li Dat," and to feature a picture of Bu La'ia, a self-styled "Hawaiian Supaman" who had just run for governor because, as he explains in "Day-Old, Day-Old Poi," a song off his wildly popular CD *False Crack???*: "Oh Mr. Haole man, steal our aina, / Haole come and forget to go home. / Das why Bu'La'ia run for govenor."[77] Having asked for a second Bu La'ia cover, the organizational group proceeded to divide the class's contributions into two piles—the Gump, or haole-style, pile, and the "Bradda Bu," or Local pile. They then placed the Gump selections upside down and in reverse order from the Bu La'ia ones.

Their divisions suggest the complexities of questions pertaining to race, class, ethnicity, and nation in Hawai'i, and the challenges Local categorizations of identity pose to those on the continental United States. Haoles' writing about surfing and a piece by a Filipino transfer student from San Francisco about the volcano goddess Pele were placed in the Bu La'ia section. A Local sansei, writing rap music lyrics under the pseudonym "Rice Cube" in protest of the imprisonment of Japanese Americans during World War II, was relegated to the Gump section. Students responsible for this decision claimed that concentration camps,

rap, and the positioning of Japanese Americans as oppressed racial minorities were "not local." This student, who didn't appreciate being
placed in the Gump section, pointed out, though to no avail, the popularity of rap music among Local students, and the fact that his grandparents had been interned in Hawai'i during World War II.

Although in the Gump/Bu class students regarded the subject matter as more important than the author's identity in determining what,
or who, was Local, in other classes students were not nearly so consis-
tent. What the classes did have in common, though, was a tendency to
organize the anthologies by ethnic and/or by Local versus non-Local
categories of belonging, and to use food metaphors as a way to resist or
reinscribe racial and ethnic divisions and hierarchies—and, in the case
of the women's studies classes, gendered ones as well. Of the six anthologies students have produced, four have employed food in their titles: in addition to "Box of Choclats," these titles include "Rice, Potatoes and Poi," and, from two sections of sophomore literature taken in
combination with a women's studies course, "We Ate Mother Goose for
Dinner," and "Bye Bye Miss American Pie."

In the class working on "Rice, Potatoes and Poi," the group in charge
of organization decided to categorize each student's writing as either
"Rice Dish Specials," "Poi 'Da Local style' Entrees," "Potatoe [sic] Salads 'Western Style,'" or "Dazzling Desserts: 'A Little Something of Everything.'" Earlier in the semester, we had read *The Best of Bamboo Ridge*,
paying particular attention to Lum's introduction. Entitled "Local Literature and Lunch," this introduction compares Local literature to a
plate lunch, a Hawai'i specialty that reflects the island's ethnic diversity
and is consumed by Locals of all classes. In setting up their menu, then,
the "Rice, Potatoes and Poi" organizers played off of Lum's food
metaphor, but used their own to demarcate differences among contributors, rather than to demonstrate the presence of a multi-ethnic Local
community. They designed the table of contents as a menu, and presented each student's contribution as a food dish (e.g., "'The Birth of
Pā'ū' Plate Lunch").

There was much joking among these organizers, who included the
only Hawaiians in the class, about the primary position of "Poi," which
contained their own entries (or entrees), along with a few others by
Asian Locals that focused on Hawaiian culture. Their centering of
"Poi" resonated with students' earlier criticisms concerning the lack of
any reference to Hawaiian food in "Local Literature and Lunch." The
"Rice Dish Specials" were writings by Asian Locals about their particular Asian cultural traditions. The "Potatoe Salads 'Western Style'"

category featured writings about Hawai'i legends from students born in Argentina and Okinawa; poems by an African American student, one an address to black men everywhere, the other about her father's home in Moloka'i; and a description by a Japanese Local of a Honolulu rock concert. Also appearing in the "Potatoes" section were pieces by the only two haoles in the class and a story by their roommate, a student of Filipino and Japanese descent. The "Dessert" section contained essays debating the place of Pidgin in the schools.

Virtually everyone protested their classification—some felt they were more "Rice" than "Poi," others objected to being "Potatoes," especially the three roommates, who had written autobiographical accounts in Pidgin about growing up Local, and an essay in celebration of the great Hawaiian and American folk heroes, Bu La'ia and Rush Limbaugh(!). Throughout the semester, this threesome had done their best to dominate the class, and, despite everything that I could think of, they and I had done most of the talking. The two Hawaiian women in the class, both of them from outer islands and attending the University of Hawai'i at tremendous personal and economic sacrifice (one had a child at home whom she could rarely afford to see), had been particularly bothered by this trio's disrespectful behavior, and had not been comfortable in the class to begin with. Although they almost never spoke in class, they had plenty to say in their group journals, especially about the "haole" and "male" behavior of these men. When the men loudly objected to being classified as "suckin' haole Potatoes," the women in the organizing group spoke up for the first time, and an argument ensued regarding who was and was not Local, the place of Hawaiians in University of Hawai'i classrooms, and the purpose of studying American literature. After this argument, the three roommates did not entirely cease their obnoxious behavior, the two women did not become at ease in class, and no one decided to become an English major. However, a decided shift did occur: these men spoke with greater self-consciousness, and the women in the organizing group, and others in the class as well, participated with greater freedom.

In all of the classes, putting together the anthologies involved complex negotiations that resulted in shifting alliances, and transformations in classroom dynamics and power relations (student-student as well as student-teacher). Students met both outside and inside of class to make their anthologies; they began phoning and emailing each other and me. Struggles over titling the anthologies involved them in heated discussions of the purpose of women's studies, or classes in composition. Fights erupted over whether or not to pay for colored xeroxes, what information contributors' notes should include, and whether or not everybody had to read their anthology piece out loud. Through these various arguments, students worked through power struggles that had been present all semester that involved interrelated issues of gender, class (particularly their histories of attending public versus private high schools), race, language, birthplace (Hawai'i or not-Hawai'i, city or country, O'ahu or outer island), Local belonging, the right to claim Hawai'i as home, and (especially in the women's studies classes) sexuality. Students followed up on others whose attendance had dropped to obtain a contributor's note or a story from them, and ended up helping them through personal problems. A strong, if contentious, sense of community developed in the classroom.

Students' interrelations with one another and with me clarified for me the significance and multiple layers of any given location and also the inseparability of location from deployments of identity politics and questions of race, ethnicity, class, nation, political allegiances, and cultural alliances. In addition to reminding me that "the academy" is not simply a single locale or institution of abstraction, such classroom experiences also have confirmed for me the importance of anthologies as agents to negotiate still-pressing issues of identity politics, and to formulate communities that can serve as sites of struggle and emotional sustenance. If anthologies have moved largely into the academy, it is this site-specific work they can do in particular classrooms that speaks most powerfully to me of their ongoing relevance.

This account of anthology-making in the classroom sounds more productive and uplifting than my own, and certainly many students', experiences of it were at the time. In writing this conclusion, and in turning through the pages of the student anthologies, I have realized that, as much as participating in the making of the anthologies, the effort of narrating and reflecting upon this process consolidates and sustains a sense of coalition-building and community. Throughout *Writing Women's Communities,* I have been insisting on the importance of the process of anthology-making, an importance impressed upon me by reading anthology editors' and contributors' accounts of this process. Paradoxically, however, it was not until I engaged in this process with my students, and began reflecting upon it, that I realized the importance of the product, of the material reality of the book itself, and the narratives it engenders.

In the foreword to the second edition of *This Bridge,* Cherríe Moraga remarks, "The *idea* of Third World feminism has proved to be much easier between the covers of a book than between real live women."[78] This quote has stayed with me since I first read it, when I found it not only indicative of the difficulties of forging political movements and communities, but also suggestive of the limitations of *This Bridge* and other anthologies. I think differently now, in large part because of my experiences with the student anthologies. While these experiences support the idea that community might be easier to realize textually than in "real life," I do not want to discount the importance of producing a book that carries with it a sense of community, one that its participants, as well as those to whom they in various ways speak, can access at any time. If the forms of community that reside in the identity-based anthologies are not as physically tangible as those we participate in through the course of our daily interactions, they nevertheless can be sustaining, and even transformative in terms of what we work towards in the communities we participate in, and create.

Notes

Chapter 1. Introduction: Writing across Communities

1. Movements and conferences influenced by *This Bridge* include, for example, UC Berkeley's Empowering Women of Color Conference and the student journal *smell this*, edited by the group "women of color in coalition."

2. See Barbara Christian's "A Rough Terrain: The Case of Shaping an Anthology of Caribbean Women Writers," in *The Ethnic Canon: Histories, Institutions, and Interventions*, ed. David Palumbo-Liu (Minneapolis and London: University of Minnesota Press, 1995).

3. The fact that three panels for the 1996 MLA Convention focus on either multiethnic or African American anthologies suggests that this may be changing.

4. I also found an outpouring of anthologies of fiction or poetry organized around writers' specific racial, ethnic, class, and/or sexual identities. In addition, educational publishers are rapidly producing multi-genre multicultural anthologies as textbooks for composition courses. Because these anthologies do not explicitly theorize community-building, nor make it their project to challenge the literary academy through genre crossings, I am differentiating them from the anthologies in this book. I also do not address the interrelations among these different kinds of anthologies, although it would be interesting to do so, particularly as part of a study of the commercialization of identity politics and multiculturalism.

5. Henry Louis Gates, Jr., *Loose Canons: Notes on the Culture War* (New York and Oxford: Oxford University Press, 1992), pp. 31–32.

6. Ibid., p. 33.

7. Kenneth Warren, "The Problem of Anthologies, or Making the Dead Wince," *American Literature* 65. 2 (June 1993): 341.

8. M. H. Abrams, "Preface to the Fifth Edition," *The Norton Anthology of English Literature*, vol. 2, ed. M. H. Abrams (Norton, 1986), p. xl.

9. Carby makes this point in "The Multicultural Wars," in *Black Popular Culture*, a project by Michele Wallace, ed. Gina Dent (Seattle: Bay Press, 1992): 187–199. See also John Guillory's discussion, albeit from a decidedly more conservative political perspective, of the tenuous relationship between the representation of minorities in the canon and their political power and place in the university, in *Cultural Capital: The Problem of Literary Canon Formation* (Chicago and London: University of Chicago Press, 1993), esp. pp. 3–19.

10. James E. Miller, ed., preface to *Heritage of American Literature: Beginnings to the Civil War,* vol. 1 (Harcourt Brace Jovanovich, 1991), p. vii.

11. Elizabeth Abel, "Black Writing, White Reading: Race and the Politics of Feminist Interpretation," *Critical Inquiry* 19 (spring 1993): 478.

12. Women (mostly white) usually make up about 10 percent of the most recent editions of canonical anthologies. For example, in volume 2 of the 1986 *Norton Anthology of English Literature,* writings by white women occupy 233 of the anthology's 2433 pages; even in volume 2 of the more progressive 1987 *The Harper American Literature,* in which editor Don McQuade claims to "have worked to extend the conventional boundaries of the American literary tradition" (xxxiii), 39 of the 142 contributors are women and 27 are people of color, only 10 of whom are women of color.

13. *The Norton Anthology of American Literature,* vol. 2, ed. Nina Baym (New York: Norton, 1985), p. 1507.

14. Mitsuye Yamada and Sarie Sachie Hylkema, eds., *Sowing Ti Leaves: Writings by Multi-Cultural Women* (Irvine, CA: Multi-Cultural Women Writers of Orange County, 1990), p. 9.

15. Beth Brant (Degonwadonti), ed., *A Gathering of Spirit: A Collection by North American Indian Women* (Ithaca, NY: Firebrand, 1988), p. 12.

16. Eric Sundquist, *To Wake the Nations: Race in the Making of American Literature* (Cambridge and London: Harvard University Press, Belknap Press, 1993), p. 18.

17. Jo Cochran, J. T. Stewart, and Mayumi Tsutakawa, eds., *Gathering Ground: New Writing and Art by Northwest Women of Color* (Seattle: The Seal Press, 1984), p. 15.

18. See, for example, Nina Auerbach's *Communities of Women: An Idea in Fiction* (Cambridge: Harvard University Press, 1978), or Dorothy Allison's "Weaving the Web of Community" *Quest: A Feminist Quarterly* 4 (1978): 78.

19. See, for example, Iris Marion Young's "The Ideal of Community and the Politics of Difference," in *Feminism/Postmodernism,* ed. Linda Nicholson (New York and London: Routledge, 1990), pp. 300–302.

20. The Dartmouth Collective, introduction to *Feminist Readings: French Texts/American Contexts, Yale French Studies* 62 (1981): 2. I am grateful to Elizabeth Abel for directing my attention to this introduction in *YFS.*

21. Jane Gallop, "The Monster in the Mirror," in *Around 1981* (New York and London: Routledge, 1992), p. 195. Gallop's focus in *Around 1981* is primarily on the problems models of white middle-class homogeneity pose for their members, rather than on what or whom such models exclude. Hereafter cited in the text.

22. Gloria Anzaldúa, foreword to second edition of *This Bridge Called My Back: Writings by Radical Women of Color,* ed. Cherríe Moraga and Gloria Anzaldúa (New York: Kitchen Table: Women of Color Press, 1981), p. 170. Hereafter cited in the text.

23. Significantly, nine years after writing her article on *YFS* 62, Gallop probes her differences with Marianne Hirsch and Nancy Miller in *Conflicts in Feminism,* showing a movement away from a relational model dependent upon sameness. (See Gallop, Hirsch, and Miller, "Criticizing Feminist Criticism," in *Conflicts in*

Feminism, ed. Hirsch and Evelyn Fox Keller [New York: Routledge, 1990], pp. 349–369). I would argue that this movement is influenced by models of feminist community put forth by feminists of color as well as necessitated by the increasingly apparent fissures among white feminists themselves. However, although they set out to explore their differences, Gallop, Hirsch, and Miller end up unifying around their anxieties about feeling inadequate in their response to women of color and issues of race.

24. Barbara Smith, introduction to *Home Girls: A Black Feminist Anthology,* ed. Barbara Smith (New York: Kitchen Table: Women of Color Press, 1983), p. xlix.

25. AnaLouise Keating and Alvina E. Quintana have recently made related arguments about the multi-genre form. In *Women Reading Women Writing: Self Invention in Paula Gunn Allen, Gloria Anzaldúa, and Audre Lorde* (Philadelphia: Temple University Press, 1996), Keating says that Gunn Allen, Anzaldúa, and Lorde all "invent what I would call threshold theories, theories that cross genres and mix codes, combining language with action, activism with aesthetics, and individual identity formation with collective cultural change" (15). Keating's analysis differs from mine in that she focuses on the relationship between individual writer (and individually authored text) and reader rather than on writing women's communities. Quintana's concerns in *Home Girls: Chicana Literary Voices* (Philadelphia: Temple University Press, 1996) also pertain more to models for individual development, or female subjectivity, than (textual) communities, as she argues for the importance of genre-crossing works that include *This Bridge* as well as single-author texts.

26. Gloria Anzaldúa, ed., *Making Face, Making Soul/Haciendo Caras* (San Francisco: Aunt Lute, 1990), p. xvii. Hereafter cited in the text.

27. Peggy Kamuf and Nancy Miller, "Parisian Letters: Between Feminism and Deconstruction," in *Conflicts in Feminism,* p. 122. Hereafter cited in the text.

28. Diane Elam and Robyn Wiegman, "Contingencies," in *Feminism Beside Itself,* ed. Diane Elam and Robyn Wiegman (New York and London: Routledge, 1995), p. 1. I would like to thank Dale Bauer for calling my attention to this anthology and other academic feminist anthologies of the 1990s, and for urging me to think about how these anthologies relate to this project.

29. Jenny Bourne, "Homelands of the Mind: Jewish Feminism and Identity Politics," *Race and Class: A Journal for Black and Third World Liberation* 29.1 (summer 1987): 1. Diana Fuss remarks upon the intensity of debates over identity in *Essentially Speaking,* her 1989 book given over to this topic: "In fact, at no other time in the history of feminist theory has identity been at once so vilified and so sanctified" (*Essentially Speaking: Feminism, Nature, and Difference* [New York and London: Routledge, 1989], p. 102). I will return to Fuss's book later in the introduction. Further references to it appear in the text.

30. Norma Alarcón suggests the interrelations, and also the earlier roots, of these movements in the United States: "In the United States even as Jacques Derrida was addressing the French Philosophical Society in January 27, 1968, with his ground-breaking theorization of 'Différance,' people of Mexican de-

scent, under the recodified name Chicano, signaling *différance*, mobilized in Los Angeles for the school walkouts of March 1968. In brief with broad strokes, I am attempting to convey the convergence of discourses of identity-in-difference as linked to the 'essence-experience' binary" ("Conjugating Subjects: The Heteroglossia of Essence and Resistance," in *An Other Tongue: Nation and Ethnicity in the Linguistic Borderlands,* ed. Alfred Arteaga [Durham and London: Duke University Press, 1994], p. 127). While for Alarcón it is poststructuralist theory that disrupts the hegemony of white feminism, and thus enables women of color and their "politics of identity-in-difference" to be heard (see p. 127), I would attribute the disruption not only to postmodernism, but, perhaps more importantly, to the pressure women of color themselves placed upon a hegemonic model of feminism by way of works including *This Bridge.*

31. For an acute explanation and analysis of the essentialism that underwrites poststructuralist thought, see Fuss, *Essentially Speaking.*

32. Norma Alarcón, herself a contributor to *This Bridge* and *Making Face* (and a publisher of other such anthologies), remarks upon this distinction between women of color and their model of what she calls "identity-in-difference" and poststructuralist thinkers in "Conjugating Subjects." While she claims these women's revolutionary politics were "dramatically documented in *This Bridge Called My Back,*" she focuses on articulations of "identity-in-difference" in the work of Chela Sandoval and other theorists (127). My emphasis differs from Alarcón's in that I see what she calls the resulting "new subject of history" and new politics as intimately connected to, rather than simply documented by, multi-genre experimental writing that is collectively produced.

33. Henry Giroux, "Resisting Difference: Cultural Studies and the Discourse of Critical Pedagogy," in *Cultural Studies,* ed. Lawrence Grossberg, Cary Nelson, and Paula A. Treichler (New York and London: Routledge, 1992), p. 208.

34. Avtar Brah, "Difference, Diversity and Differentiation," in *"Race," Culture, and Difference,* ed. James Donald and Ali Rattansi (London: Sage, 1992), pp. 135–136. For other thorough critiques, see Liz Bondi's "Locating Identity Politics" and other essays in Michael Keith and Steve Pile's *Place and the Politics of Identity* (London and New York: Routledge, 1993), Giroux's "Resisting Difference," and E. San Juan, Jr.'s "Beyond Identity Politics: The Predicament of the Asian American Writer in Late Capitalism," in *American Literary History* 3.3 (fall 1991), esp. p. 553. See also Shane Phelan's *Identity Politics: Lesbian Feminism and the Limits of Community* (Philadelphia: Temple University Press, 1989), especially her final chapter, "Rethinking Identity Politics." The guiding principle of Werner Sollers' *The Invention of Ethnicity* (New York: Oxford University Press, 1989) is that identity "is not a thing but a process—and it requires constant detective work from readers, not a settling on a fixed encyclopedia of supposed cultural essentials" (xiv–xv). Critiques of identity politics continue. Reviewing abstracts of academic journal articles called up on my computer by the keywords *identity politics,* I came across over forty entries for the period between 1992 and 1995, and all of these mounted attacks against it.

35. Cornel West, "The New Cultural Politics of Difference," in *Out There: Marginalization and Contemporary Cultures,* ed. Russell Ferguson, Martha Gever, Trinh T. Minh-ha, and Cornel West (Cambridge and London: MIT Press, 1990), pp. 34–35. For a helpful gloss on "the new cultural politics of difference," see Edward Soja and Barbara Hooper, "The Spaces That Difference Makes: Some Notes on the Geographical Margins of the New Cultural Politics," in the book edited by Keith and Pile, *Place and the Politics of Identity,* pp. 183–205.

36. Grossberg, Nelson, and Treichler, introduction in *Cultural Studies,* p. 18. Contributors throughout *Cultural Studies* make evident their investment in such a project, which they define in opposition to identity politics. See, for example, the essays by Henry A. Giroux, Angie Chabram-Dernersesian, Stuart Hall, and Kobena Mercer. Other theorists engaged in a move beyond identity politics include Teresa de Lauretis, Henry Louis Gates, Jr., and Ernesto Laclau and Chantal Mouffe, who are influential to many of the theorists in the *Cultural Studies* volume.

37. Reading the 1995 collection edited by John Rajchman, *The Identity in Question* (New York and London: Routledge, 1995), reinforced this position for me. As an unnamed woman of color remarks in one of the "Discussion" sections, in their meditations on identity (virtually all of which include a castigation of identity politics), none of the contributors address their own position, or the fact that the symposium does not include a single woman of color (142). The published account of this symposium, which includes additional essays, does nothing to address this situation: of the book's thirteen contributors, the four women are white, and only three contributors are men of color.

38. Rosaura Sánchez, "Calculated Musings: Richard Rodríguez's Metaphysics of Difference," in *The Ethnic Canon,* ed. Palumbo-Liu, p. 156.

39. Suparna Bhaskara, "Physical Subjectivity and the Risk of Essentialism," in *Our Feet Walk the Sky: Women of the South Asian Diaspora,* ed. The Women of South Asian Descent Collective (San Francisco: Aunt Lute, 1993), p. 196.

40. In the last year, more in-depth and richly contextualized writings on Anzaldúa have been published. These include Keating's *Women Reading Women Writing* and Quintana's *Home Girls.* However, although Quintana does include a brief analysis of the importance of *This Bridge* in chapter 6 of her book, both she and Keating focus predominantly on *Borderlands* (and, in the case of Quintana, on Moraga's *Loving in the War Years*).

41. Fuss's edited collection *Inside/Out* (New York and London: Routledge, 1991) maintains the focus on gender and sexuality as the only axes of difference. Of this collection, whose contributors are predominantly white, and which contains little discussion of how sexuality articulates with race or class, Fuss explains, "On the cover of this book is not a face (no attempt was made to select 'representative' gay and lesbian bodies, as if such a thing were possible) but a figure, a knot, a figure-eight knot or four knot to be precise." Of this figure, Fuss says, "The undecidability of this simple topology may be its greatest appeal," as "it visualizes for us . . . the contortions and convolutions of any sexual

identity formation . . . The figure-eight or four knot is intended as a twist or variation on Lacan's famous Borromean knot which . . . demonstrates how the unconscious itself has neither an inside nor an outside" (7). In her avoidance here of representation, Fuss falls into it anyway—the combination of abstraction, Lacanian play, and an exclusive focus on gender and sexual difference suggests a white middle-class academic subject (and audience) whose only perceived marks of difference are gendered or sexual ones. My point here is that we can't escape identity politics; the question is, how self-consciously do we employ it?

42. Norma Alarcón, "Conjugating Subjects," p. 132.

43. I am referring, of course, to *All the Women Are White, All the Blacks Are Men, But Some of Us Are Brave: Black Women's Studies,* ed. Gloria T. Hull, Patricia Bell Scott, and Barbara Smith (Old Westbury, NY: The Feminist Press, 1982). Furthermore, as Norma Alarcón remarks, Fuss's treatment of race as a black and white issue reinforces bipolar understandings of it.

44. While in the chapter "Lesbian and Gay Theory: The Question of Identity Politics," Fuss speaks as part of a lesbian and gay "we," in "Erasing 'Race'?" her defense of anti-essentialism also frees her from reflecting on her own position as white. While at one point she refers to white poststructuralist critics, it is only to distance herself from them, instead aligning herself with Baker against African American critic Kwame Anthony Appiah (Fuss, *Essentially Speaking,* p. 93).

45. In her review of *Essentially Speaking,* bell hooks further points out that black feminist theorists are far more diverse in their positioning than Fuss's chapter allows. See bell hooks, "Essentialism and Experience," *American Literary History* 3.1 (spring 1991): 172–183. Hereafter cited in the text.

46. I find the equation in this chapter of essentialism and experience a problematic one; while I understand an essence to be that which stands outside of time and history, I understand experience to be entirely context-bound, or constructed. For me, then, experience exists at odds with essentialism at the same time as it can be allied with it. As Gayatri Spivak so incisively puts this: "Experience makes the strongest bond and also produces the greatest impatience with antiessentialism as a battle cry" ("In a Word," *Outside in the Teaching Machine* [New York and London: Routledge, 1993], p. 11).

47. See Spivak's interview with Rooney, "In a Word," where she claims essence as a necessary strategy, but not a theory. Throughout this interview she insists upon differentiating theory from strategy, explaining, "I really do believe in undermining the vanguardism of theory" (15). If strategy is not theory, Spivak occupies the realm of theory (she theorizes about strategy). And if she privileges strategy over theory, the academy in which she is situated does not. And in this Anglo-American academy, Spivak is one of the reigning theorists, with a critical industry all of her own. (The interview in which she presents this position is but one of many signs in *Outside in the Teaching Machine* of her position as a master theorist; others include her own citations of people citing or addressing

her work.) So why the privileging of strategy? And why the opposition between theory and strategy? For me the distinction between theory and strategy is far from clear, and it's odd to me that Spivak is willing to let such a distinction stand, given the relentlessness of her deconstructive mode. What motivates this opposition?

48. This situation, of course, does not apply only to white feminists in the academy. As Michael Awkward puts it in his foray into black feminist theory and criticism, *Negotiating Difference: Race, Gender, and the Politics of Positionality* (Chicago and London: University of Chicago Press, 1995), "boundary transgression—interpretive movement across putatively fixed biological, cultural, or ideological lines in order to explore, in a word, difference—has come to require either extreme theoretical naiveté or perhaps unprecedented scholarly daring" (4).

49. For example, when I began this project in the late 1980s, invoking the phrase "as a white middle-class woman" seemed to me urgent, important, and revelatory. Today this phrase strikes me as empty, formulaic and predictable, often delivering as little as do unfulfilled promises in introductions to address the "triumvirate" of race, class, and gender (and sometimes sexuality). Furthermore, as Michael Awkward points out, "self-referentiality is not necessarily a sign of the intense self-investigation that minimizes or eliminates the dangers of hegemonic self-interest. In fact, this critical practice can be used expressly to mask more sinister, more tyrannizing intentions" (*Negotiating Difference*, p. 84). Nevertheless, in revising this project, I found myself unable to edit out phrases beginning "as a . . . ," even though they often struck me as inadequate and clichéd. Although such phrases have become less than arresting, and can operate as nothing more than (duplicitous) gestures of good faith or glib authorizations to say anything, I do not believe that they are ones with which we can dispense. Rather I believe that we must strive in the work that follows such formulations to inhabit our positions with honesty and responsibility.

50. Spivak, "In a Word," p. 3.

51. See Alarcón's "Conjugating Subjects" and her essay in *Haciendo Caras*, "The Theoretical Subject(s) of *This Bridge Called My Back* and Anglo-American Feminism." See also Chela Sandoval's "U.S. Third World Feminism: The Theory and Method of Oppositional Consciousness in the Postmodern World," in *Genders* 10 (spring 1991): 1–24. Sandoval's theory of "Oppositional Consciousness" has been circulating since 1979.

52. Sandoval, "U.S. Third World Feminism," p. 23.

53. Throughout her brilliant and exciting book *Tango and the Political Economy of Passion* (Boulder: Westview, 1995), Marta Savigliano, too, likens her position as an intellectual to that of Che Guevara's as guerrilla soldier, as she simultaneously casts Guevara as an intellectual and theorist.

54. This contrasts to the recent poststructuralist move to evoke identity at the very moment that this identity is disavowed or disowned. Spivak often engages in self-identification as she depersonalizes such a move. She explains this pro-

cess in "In a Word": "I believe that the way to save oneself from either objective, disinterested positioning or the attitude of there being no author (and these two opposed positions legitimize each other), or yet *the* story of one's life, is to 'recognize' oneself as also an instantiation of historical and psychosexual narratives that one can piece together, however fragmentarily, in order to do deontological work in the humanities. When one represents oneself in such a way, it becomes, curiously enough, a deidentification of oneself, a claiming of an identity from a text that comes from somewhere else" (6). Similar moments occur in work by Fuss and Judith Butler. Both play with and undermine the positions they speak from (and the positions which authorize their speech), and utilize personal narrative as they claim their distance from it. Butler, for example, makes statements such as, "Here is something like a confession which is meant merely to thematize the impossibility of confession" ("Imitation and Gender Insubordination," in *Inside/Out*, p. 20). I call this having your cake and eating it too.

55. See Douglas Crimp's "Mourning and Militancy," in *Out There,* for an eloquent and moving exploration of the importance of a politics that respects our psychic experiences. And Savigliano makes crucial interventions on behalf of the importance of passion, while maintaining an insistence on strategic positioning that is politically efficacious, in *Tango and the Political Economy of Passion.*

56. As I do so, I hope, along with Elizabeth Abel, that "if we produce our readings cautiously and locate them in a self-conscious and self-critical relation to black feminist criticism, these risks, I hope, would be counterbalanced by the benefits of broadening the spectrum of interpretation, illuminating the social determinants of reading, and deepening our recognition of our racial selves and the 'others' we fantasmatically construct—and thereby expanding the possibilities of dialogue across as well as about racial boundaries" ("Black Writing, White Reading," p. 498).

57. See Paul Gilroy's *Black Atlantic: Modernity and Double Consciousness* (Cambridge: Harvard University Press, 1993) for his theorizing on the ways in which twentieth-century American literature and music is importantly shaped by transatlantic exchanges between writers and musicians. However, as Gauri Viswanathan has pointed out to me, Gilroy tends to see influence moving from Britain across to the United States; what I am positing is an exchange that works in both directions.

58. As Ernesto Laclau and Chantal Mouffe state, in order to combat the separatism that supports rather than opposes hegemony, "We must concentrate not only on the plurality of forms of struggle but also on the relations which they establish among themselves and on the unifying effects which follow from them" (*Hegemony and Socialist Strategy: Towards a Radical Democratic Politics* [London: Verso, 1985], p. 10). For, as they conclude, "nothing can consolidate antiracist struggles more than the construction of stable forms of overdetermination among such contents as anti-racism, anti-sexism and anti-capitalism" (141). Placing the anthologies in this study in dialogue with one another provides a way to begin constructing "forms of overdetermination," if not the stable forms

called for by Laclau and Mouffe. I am not, in fact, sure that such stable forms are possible; instead I agree with Avtar Brah when she states in "Difference, Diversity, and Differentiation" that "the search for grand theories specifying the interconnections between racism, gender and class has been less than productive. They are best construed as historically contingent and context-specific relationships" (138).

59. See, for example, Anzaldúa's review of *Gathering of Spirit* in *Conditions: Ten* (1984): 145–153 and Barbara Smith's review of *Gathering Ground* in *Conditions: 11/12* (1985): 175–184.

60. In their movements, the contributors to these anthologies engage in the political practice Inderpal Grewal advocates in "Autobiographic Subjects and Diasporic Locations: *Meatless Days* and *Borderlands*" (in *Scattered Hegemonies: Postmodernity and Transnational Feminist Practices*, ed. Inderpal Grewal and Caren Kaplan [Minneapolis and London: University of Minnesota Press, 1994]), when she states that, "for those termed minorities, it is not the resolution of identity that is necessary for political action, but oppositional mobilization and coalitional, transnational, feminist practices" (251).

61. Gallop does make a passing reference to *Home Girls* in her discussion of the black feminist anthology *Conjuring*, noting that Gloria Hull's essay in that collection originally appeared in *Home Girls* (158).

62. While feminist theory is founded upon making evident the presence of the personal in all arenas, much of it nevertheless maintains, at least most of the time, a level of discourse that keeps the identity and experiences of the writer at some remove. When academic feminists depart from this language, they usually mark this move as something out of the ordinary, signal it as a departure from their usual form of academic discourse (see Nancy Miller's *Getting Personal*, and, more recently, the phenomenon of memoirs coming out of the Duke English Department). Jane Gallop constitutes an exception to this generalization; her theory frequently contains moments of audacious self-disclosure which convey or illuminate her theoretical formulations. I would argue that this accounts, in large part, for the fact that, as Gallop herself puts it, "I have, throughout my career as an academic feminist, enjoyed the role of bad girl" (*Around 1981*, p. 238).

Chapter 2. Another 1981: From *This Bridge Called My Back* to *Making Face, Making Soul/Haciendo Caras*

1. The following are a few examples of anthologies that have noted *This Bridge*'s influence: In *Home Girls: A Black Feminist Anthology.* (New York: Kitchen Table: Women of Color Press, 1983), editor Barbara Smith expresses the belief that "more than any other single work, *This Bridge* has made the vision of Third World feminism real" (xlii). And in Anzaldúa's *Making Face, Making Soul/Haciendo Caras*, Papusa Molina says that for the group Women Against Racism, "*This Bridge* became our bible" (327). In *Gathering Ground*, editors Cochran, Stewart, and Tsuta-

kawa, and also other contributors, make constant references to, and differentiate themselves from, the women in *This Bridge*. In *A Gathering of Spirit*, in letters
between "Raven," a woman in jail who is sentenced to die, and herself, the editor Beth Brant writes, "I am sending you a book called *This Bridge Called My
Back*. I think you will understand everything. It was written by women like you
and me. . . . It is a book that made a great change in my life" (223). Critics in
academic journals and books also note *This Bridge* as a feminist landmark. In
Technologies of Gender (Bloomington: Indiana University Press, 1987), Teresa de
Lauretis claims that *This Bridge* has contributed to a "shift in feminist consciousness" (10). Or, as Sandoval states in "U.S. Third World Feminism," "The
publication of *This Bridge Called My Back* in 1981 made the presence of U.S. third
world feminism impossible to ignore on the same terms as it had been throughout the 1970s" (p. 5).

2. Donna Haraway comments upon this relationship in *Simians, Cyborgs, and
Women* (London: Free Association Books, 1991); she links the development in
the early 1980s of Kitchen Table, Women of Color Press to publications by women
"writing into consciousness the stories of their constructions" in a variety of
genres, and destabilizing, among other discourses, the "canons of Western feminism" (144).

3. The Women of South Asian Descent Collective, eds., *Our Feet Walk the Sky*,
p. iv.

4. Barbara Smith gives an important account of the founding of Kitchen Table
in "A Press of Our Own: Kitchen Table: Women of Color Press," *Frontiers* 10.3
(1989): 11–13. See also Jaime M. Grant's "Building Community-Based Coalitions from Academe: The Union Institute and the Kitchen Table: Women of
Color Press Transition Coalition" (*Signs* 21.4 [summer 1996]: 1024–1033), a report which accounts for the important work Kitchen Table continues to do and
describes its coalitional work with the Union Institute Center for Women. And
in "Coming to the Table: The Differential Politics of *This Bridge Called My Back*"
(in *Genders* 20 [New York and London: New York University Press, 1994]: 3–
44), Kayann Short provides an excellent and detailed history of Kitchen Table.

5. Joan Pinkvoss, Aunt Lute Catalogue (spring 1993), p. 4.

6. Maureen Brady, Spinsters Ink Catalogue (fall 1993), p. 9.

7. Pinkvoss, Spinsters Catalogue (spring 1993), p. 1.

8. Brady, Spinsters Catalogue (spring 1993), p. 1.

9. Through the course of the 1980s, such enterprises in fact have proved to be
economically viable, if not profitable. Aunt Lute, started in 1982, became Aunt
Lute Foundation, a nonprofit in 1991. It saw a 34 percent growth in earned income between 1992 and 1993 alone, and has been the recent recipient of large
NEA grants, and other grants as well. Despite the fact that the staff still work
second jobs to support themselves, the press has proved that a market exists for
works by and about a range of women. (Their work is comparable to what Toni
Morrison did from the center, not the margins of publishing, by publishing *The
Black Book* as an editor at Random House, and, through its sales, proving the ex-

istence of a large black readership.) The fact that more mainstream or established presses are publishing and marketing anthologies by marginalized groups of writers demonstrates the influence of these smaller presses in establishing diverse groups of readers. Beacon, a more established and commercial press, reissued expanded versions of *The Tribe of Dina* and *Nice Jewish Girls* as part of its new Jewish feminist line. They also published *Making Waves*. In 1993, *Charlie Chan Is Dead* was the first Asian American anthology to be published by a mainstream publisher (Penguin Books).

10. These anthologies also could be compared profitably with those of the Harlem Renaissance. Both James Weldon Johnson's *The Book of American Negro Poetry* (1922), and Alain Locke's *The New Negro: Voices of the Harlem Renaissance* (1925) were important in defining a distinctly black aesthetic, and a social movement. In his 1992 introduction to *The New Negro* (New York: Atheneum, 1992 rpt.), Arnold Rampersad states, "Even today, it [*The New Negro*] remains a reliable index to the black American sensibility at that point where art and politics meet, as well as to the events in Harlem and elsewhere among blacks in the 1920s" (xxiii).

11. Gates, *Loose Canons*, p. 30.

12. See Angie Chambram-Dernersesian's feminist critique of La Raza movement, "I Throw Punches for My Race, But I Don't Want to Be a Man: Writing Us—Chica-nos (Girl, Us)/Chicanas—into the Movement Script," in *Cultural Studies*, ed. Grossberg, Nelson, and Treichler, pp. 81–95.

13. Janice Mirikitani, Buriel Clay II, Janet Campbell Hale, Alejandro Murguia, and Roberto Vargas, eds., *Time to Greez! Incantations from the Third World* (San Francisco: Glide Publications, 1975), p. v.

14. Chela Sandoval, "U.S. Third World Feminism," *The Oxford Companion to Women's Writing in the United States*, ed. Cathy N. Davidson and Linda Martin-Wagner (New York and Oxford: Oxford University Press, 1995), p. 880. Sandoval also notes that in 1981, the same year as the publication of *This Bridge*, the National Women's Studies Association held the first U.S. conference on the troubled relationship between white and third world women, "Women Respond to Racism." Three hundred women of color attended and established the first "National Alliance of US Third World Feminists," along with a statement of purpose arguing for the different structure of organizations for third world feminism and hegemonic U.S. feminism (881).

15. Cade's multi-genre anthology, "a collection of poems, stories, essays, formal, informal, reminiscent, that seem to best reflect the process of the contemporary Black woman in this country," looks forward to the multi-genre anthologies of the 1980s (*The Black Woman*, ed. Cade [New York: New American Library, 1970], p. 11). However, as its title indicates, *The Black Woman* is more focused on defining the individual black woman than on exploring relations among black women; most of the contributors critique the negative stereotypes that oppress them without putting forth a positive self-definition or sense of black women's community. Contributors also concentrate on analyzing and

healing divisions between black men and women, and the anthology is strongly heterosexual in orientation, in marked distinction from the anthologies which follow it.

16. Cade, *The Black Woman*, p. 12.

17. Robin Morgan, introduction to *Sisterhood Is Powerful: An Anthology of Writings from the Women's Liberation Movement*, ed. Robin Morgan (New York: Vintage, 1970), p. xii. Hereafter cited in the text.

18. Though Morgan's stress in the anthology is on women's commonalities, individual pieces by Gene Damon and Elizabeth Sutherland give voice to sexual and racial tensions the anthology attempts to elide. Furthermore, *Sisterhood*'s bibliography, the "Drop Dead List of Books to Watch Out For," a list of works harmful to women, includes books by women authors, thus suggesting the divisions that exist among women.

19. In fact, in the preface to her edition of *Sisterhood Is Global: The International Women's Movement Anthology* (Garden City, NY: Anchor, 1984), Morgan comments that "an international perspective began to surface during my compilation of that earlier anthology, which includes articles by women of many different cultures within the United States" (xiii).

20. The omission in *This Bridge* of reference to *Sisterhood is Powerful* also seems related to the need in *This Bridge* to establish dichotomies between white women and women of color, a subject I explore at length later in this chapter. For another critique of *Sisterhood Is Powerful*, see Judith Roof's "How to Satisfy a Woman 'Every Time,'" in *Feminism Beside Itself*, ed. Elam and Wiegman, pp. 57–61. While this article takes *Sisterhood* to task for the relentless heterosexism of its "sisterly familial narrative" (57), its complete inattentiveness to questions of race suggests the ongoing need for *This Bridge*'s critiques.

21. For example, Gloria T. Hull's "Reading Literature by U.S. Third World Women" (Wellesley, MA: Center for Research on Women, 1984) draws heavily on Fisher's work in suggesting ideas for curricula on third world women.

22. For another illuminating discussion of the political importance as well as the problematics of the terms "women of color" and "third world women," see Chandra Talpade Mohanty's introduction to *Third World Women and the Politics of Feminism*, ed. Chandra Talpade Mohanty, Ann Russo, and Lourdes Torres (Bloomington and Indianapolis: Indiana University Press, 1991).

23. In the announcement Moraga and Anzaldúa make in *Conditions: Five, The Black Women's Issue* (1979), her name still links her to her father and her Anglo roots: "Cher'ríe Moraga-Lawrence, Gloria Anzaldúa, and friends are compiling a list of Third World Women writers, artists, scholars, performers, and political activists" (n.p.).

24. In *Women Reading Women Writing: Self Invention in Paula Gunn Allen, Gloria Anzaldúa, and Audre Lorde* (Philadelphia: Temple University Press, 1996), in a chapter entitled "Writing the Body/Writing the Soul: Gloria Anzaldúa's Mestizaje Écriture," Keating provides an extended and compelling comparison between Anzaldúa and Cixous. Her argument concerns the ways Anzaldúa

transforms her readers and herself through her writing in *Borderlands;* my own interest lies more in viewing this writing as a means for constructing (textual) community that is attentive to material considerations.

25. In her introduction to *Haciendo Caras,* Anzaldúa speaks to *This Bridge's* representative status, and to the subsequent demands on her own energies: "I got tired of hearing students say that *Bridge* was required in two or three of their women's studies courses; tired of being a resource for teachers and students who asked me what texts by women of color they should read or teach and where they could get these writings" (xvi).

26. See Savigliano's *Tango and the Political Economy of Passion* for an incisive analysis of the position of women of color in the academy, particularly the chapter entitled "From Exoticism to Decolonization." In this chapter she contends that "there are no ears ready for Third World women's voices. We continue to be carefully inspected as untrustworthy candidates for feminism and for our own cultures. Is she brown enough? Is she poor enough? Is she thirdworldish enough—usually meaning picturesque and untheoretical enough—for her voice to be legitimate, her words to be taken seriously, her claims to deserve respect? Either too exotic or not exotic enough, too Westernized or not Westernized enough, there seems to be no legitimate place for our conflictive, unfit protests" (229).

27. Katie King, "Producing Sex, Theory, and Culture: Gay/Straight Remappings in Contemporary Feminism," in *Conflicts in Feminism,* ed. Hirsch and Keller, p. 88. Barbara Christian makes a similar argument about the status and function of theory in the academy in her essay "The Race for Theory" (*Cultural Critique* 6 [spring 1987]).

28. Here, in addition to building on King's argument, I am drawing on Paul Lauter's "The Two Criticisms—or, Structure, Lingo, and Power in the Discourse of Academic Humanists" (in *Canons and Contexts* [New York: Oxford University Press, 1991]). In this essay, Lauter states, "Theory as a mode of literary discourse . . . has primarily succeeded in reestablishing academic privilege—ironically, not for the study of literature in the academy, but for those who practice theory within the literary profession" (141). The present study, with its recognizable academic form, results in part from my efforts to challenge the containment of *This Bridge.*

29. Alarcón, "The Theoretical Subject(s)," p. 357. Also, as Sandoval comments in "U.S. Third World Feminism: The Theory and Method of Oppositional Consciousness": "But soon the writings and theoretical challenges of U.S. third world feminists were marginalized into the category of what Allison Jaggar characterized in 1983 as mere 'description,' and their essays deferred to what Hester Eisenstein in 1985 called 'the special force of poetry,'" while their theoretical contribution has been "bypassed and ignored" (5). Recent work by critics such as Keating, Quintana, Kayann Short, and Biddy Martin suggests that this may be changing.

30. In general, anthologies published in the late 1980s and early 1990s turn

more to a coalitional model than a communal one in portraying relations among contributors. I will return to this point, and to the concept of "coalitional community," in later chapters.

31. Gloria Anzaldúa, "Bridge, Drawbridge, Sandbar, or Island: Lesbians-of-Color *Hacienda Alianzas*," in *Bridges of Power: Women's Multicultural Alliances*, ed. Lisa Albrecht and Rose M. Brewer (Santa Cruz and Philadelphia: New Society, 1990), p. 230.

32. Since then, Anzaldúa has participated as a keynote speaker (along with Melanie Kaye/Kantrowitz) in a 1994 conference organized by the Berkeley Hillel entitled "Claiming Our Place: Jews in a Multicultural Community." However, she began her address by stating that she was initially puzzled about why she was asked to speak, and uncertain of what to say, but then realized that "just as there's a white man in my head, there's a Jew in my head. So I'm here as an ally." The associative link she makes here between a white man and a (implicitly male-gendered) Jew sets forth this alliance in less than friendly terms, and the speech that followed did nothing to explain this statement, nor did Anzaldúa engage with any specificity (or even much generality) in issues pertaining to Jewish identity or anti-Semitism.

33. See, for example, Kaye/Kantrowitz's "To Be a Radical Jew in the Late Twentieth-Century," in *The Tribe of Dina: A Jewish Women's Anthology*, ed. Melanie Kaye/Kantrowitz and Irena Klepfisz (Boston: Beacon Press, 1989), esp. pp. 303–310 (most of the material in this volume originally appeared in nos. 29/30 of the journal *Sinister Wisdom* [1986]). Also, while white Jewish women in the 1981 edition of *Nice Jewish Girls* stress the similarity of their oppression to that experienced by women of color, the 1989 revised addition shows the same contributors much more willing to probe the differences between anti-Semitism and racism; these contributors have shifted their focus from assertions of sameness to alliance-building.

34. bell hooks, "Keeping a Legacy of Shared Struggle," *Z Magazine* (September 1992), p. 25.

35. In their reviews in *Bridges: A Journal for Jewish Feminists and Our Friends* 2.1 (spring 1991), both Clarke and Mennis are critical of *Haciendo Caras* on other grounds. Clarke expresses a sense of wariness regarding Anzaldúa's reliance "on notions that 'the blood' (mestiza, queer, or other) determines thought, action, history, and revolution" (131). She also critiques the relative invisibility of contributors' lesbianism, and the absence of writings on sex. Mennis finds "too much theory" (136) in the anthology that estranges her as a reader.

36. Mennis does, however, develop the ways in which the organizational structure of *Haciendo Caras* leads her to think about the themes that recur throughout *The Tribe of Dina*, and she also compares the way both anthologies establish the relationship of language to identity, voice, and visibility.

37. Elly Bulkin, Minnie Bruce Pratt, and Barbara Smith undertake just such a project in *Yours in Struggle: Three Feminist Perspectives on Anti-Semitism and Racism* (Ithaca, NY: Firebrand, 1984).

38. Perhaps this helps to account for the way lesbianism is less of a focus in *Haciendo Caras* than it is in *This Bridge*. Although many of the contributors highlight their lesbianism elsewhere, as Cheryl Clarke notes, lesbian sexuality is de-emphasized in *Haciendo Caras*, and in the contributors' biographies, only two women (Audre Lorde and Andrea Canaan) identify themselves explicitly as lesbians.

39. Alarcón, in "The Theoretical Subject(s)," explores the theoretical underpinnings of *This Bridge* and emphasizes that its multi-genre format (and by extension, that of *Haciendo Caras* as well) rests on theoretical constructions. Alarcón finds, "By giving voice to such experiences, each according to her style, the editors and contributors [of *This Bridge*] believed they were developing a theory of subjectivity and culture that would demonstrate the considerable differences between them and Anglo-European women, as well as between them and Anglo-European men and men of their own culture" (356). Perhaps Alarcón's distance here, though she is a participant in *This Bridge* and also translated it into Spanish, attests to the difficulties attached to this project.

40. What this analysis must hold in suspension, due to the anonymity of the readers' reports, are how the readers' different positions contribute to their responses. While one of the earlier readers marked herself as a woman of color, the other readers did not mark their identities, racially or otherwise.

Chapter 3. Coming Out and Staying Home: *Nice Jewish Girls* and *Home Girls*

1. Barbara Johnson, "Home," a talk delivered at UC Berkeley on 3/1/92.

2. Evelyn Torton Beck, introduction to *Nice Jewish Girls: A Lesbian Anthology*, rev. ed., ed. Evelyn Torton Beck (Boston: Beacon Press, 1989), p. xxxii. Hereafter cited in the text.

3. In *The Tribe of Dina*, ed. Kaye/Kantrowitz and Klepfisz, Kaye/Kantrowitz gives some insight into the dismissal of anti-Semitism in her "To Be a Radical Jew in the Late Twentieth-Century" when she claims, "The way Jews have been met with 'not you too,' the way anti-Semitism becomes the one issue too many, suggest that many white women are angry and resistant to dealing with racism but are too frightened to express that anger openly; suggest further how little our movement has taught us to see struggles against racism as life-giving, nourishing; as our own" (314).

4. Daniel Boyarin and Jonathan Boyarin, "Diaspora: Generation and the Ground of Jewish Identity" *Critical Inquiry* 19 (summer 1993): 721.

5. *The Tribe of Dina*, a collection that contains more contributions by Holocaust survivors, presents a different conception of being Jewish, one not characterized by choice or the ability to pass. The anthology serves as a reminder of the importance of contextualizing formulations of Jewish invisibility.

6. One indication within *Nice Jewish Girls* of the difficulties in extending the Jewish lesbian community beyond the anthology occurs when Beck claims, "We exist as part of a rapidly growing grassroots movement of Jewish lesbian-femi-

nists, creating an informal network of local consciousness-raising, support and study groups. We have even produced two issues of a Jewish lesbian newsletter *Shehechiyatnu,* the editorship of which is intended to rotate from city to city" (xxxiii). A footnote suggests that this newsletter did not last beyond two issues.

7. At the time *Nice Jewish Girls* was published, such questions may have proven too destabilizing to the Jewish lesbian identity contributors were working to assert. Four years later, in *The Tribe of Dina,* some of the *Nice Jewish Girls* contributors (for example, Klepfisz and Kaye/Kantrowitz) do articulate these questions directly, and explicitly struggle with them.

8. For a brief treatment of how a racial definition of Judaism has been developed and used by white supremacists, past and present, see Minnie Bruce Pratt's "The Maps in My Bible" (in *Bridges: A Journal for Jewish Feminists and Our Friends,* 2.1 [spring 1991]: 102–103).

9. In *The Tribe of Dina,* editors Kaye/Kantrowitz and Klepfisz include far more entries by Jewish women of color/Sephardic Jews, and their own essays explore the contradictions and complexities of the relationship between anti-Semitism and racism.

10. Barbara Smith, "Towards a Black Feminist Criticism," *All the Women Are White, All the Men Are Black, But Some of Us Are Brave,* ed. Hull, Scott, and Barbara Smith, p. 173.

11. Barbara Smith and Lorraine Bethel, introduction to *Conditions: Five, The Black Women's Issue* (1979), p. 13. Hereafter cited in the text.

12. Hull, Scott, and Barbara Smith, eds., introduction to *All the Women Are White, All the Men Are Black, But Some of Us Are Brave.*

13. Beverly Smith, "The Wedding," in *Home Girls,* ed. Barbara Smith, p. 176. Hereafter cited in the text.

14. For example, Hull's essay on Toni Cade Bambara, "What It Is I Think She's Doing Anyhow," is a traditional enough academic essay to be included in *Conjuring, Black Women, Fiction, and Literary Tradition,* ed. Marjorie Pryse and Hortense J. Spillers (Bloomington: Indiana University Press, 1985).

15. Initially published in *This Bridge Called My Back,* this epigraph, from "Across the Kitchen Table: A Sister-to-Sister Dialogue," also serves as a bridge between *This Bridge* and *Home Girls.*

16. Joyce Hope Scott, "From Foreground to Margin: Female Configuration and Masculine Self-Representation in Black Nationalist Fiction," in *Nationalisms and Sexualities,* ed. Andrew Parker, Mary Russo, Doris Sommer, and Patricia Yaeger (New York and London: Routledge, 1992), p. 304.

17. Quoted in Scott, "From Foreground to Margin," p. 305.

18. In *Women Reading Women Writing,* Keating makes a similar argument about Audre Lorde's strategy in *Zami:* "By thus naturalizing her lesbian identity, Lorde subtly challenges the homophobia in black communities and in dominant U.S. culture that condemns same-sex desire as unnatural" (84).

19. Scott makes a similar argument in "From Foreground to Margin." She looks to literary texts to demonstrate "a paradoxical movement of the black fe-

male from her earlier vocality and centrality to the [nationalist] movement to a position of silence as the phallocentric and patriarchal vision of Black Power advocates relocate the black woman in the margins of the struggle for freedom and equality in the United States" (299).

20. Cheryl Clarke, in "The Failure to Transform: Homophobia in the Black Community," is one of the few to do so. She condemns not only black men for their misogyny, but also feminist writers Michele Wallace, Mary Helen Washington, and bell hooks for their failure to address lesbianism in their writing.

21. See, for example, Jewelle Gomez's wholly celebratory treatment of *The Color Purple*.

22. Audre Lorde, "Eye to Eye: Black Women, Hatred, and Anger," in *Sister Outsider* (Trumansburg, NY: The Crossing Press, 1984), p. 153.

23. For some of the difficulties involved in defining working-class identity, see chapter 5.

24. For other arguments about the uses of nostalgia, see Rob Wilson and Wimal Dissanayake's introduction to their edited collection, *Global/Local: Cultural Production and the Transnational Imaginary* (Durham and London: Duke University Press, 1996), where they claim, "Even nostalgia can be a critical tool if one is cognizant of the newer forces of domination and wary of sentimental idealizations" (9). See also Genaro M. Padilla's *My History, Not Yours: The Formation of Mexican American Autobiography* (Madison: University of Wisconsin Press, 1993).

25. Teresa de Lauretis, "Eccentric Subjects: Feminist Theory and Historical Consciousness," *Feminist Studies,* 16.1 (spring 1990): 139. In tracing the historical development of what she calls the "eccentric subject," de Lauretis pays close attention to the work of Barbara Smith and, in fact, claims "Smith's home girls" as examples, even exemplars, of this subject position (144). However, I believe that de Lauretis's advocacy for a position of displacement, or homelessness, leads her to overlook *Home Girls*'s resistance to displacement, and its insistence on creating a home for black lesbians.

26. While my position here is similar to Pratt's, I am more interested in the comforts of coalition than the necessary discomforts of home.

Chapter 4. The Making and Unmaking of Asian American Identity: *Making Waves* and *The Forbidden Stitch*

1. Asian Women United of California, eds., *Making Waves: An Anthology of Writing by and about Asian American Women* (Boston: Beacon Press, 1989), hereafter cited in the text; Shirley Geok-lin Lim, Mayumi Tsutakawa, and the Calyx Collective, eds., *The Forbidden Stitch: An Asian American Women's Anthology* (Corvallis, OR: Calyx Books, 1989), hereafter cited in the text; and Ronald Takaki, *Strangers from a Different Shore: A History of Asian Americans* (New York: Penguin, 1989).

2. While I would argue that feminist issues since have moved to the forefront in Asian American studies due to the continuing work of, among others, Elaine Kim and Lim, as well as more recent work by critics including King-Kok Cheung,

Cynthia Liu, Lisa Lowe, Susan Schweik, Karen Su, and Sau-ling Cynthia Wong, around the time of the publication of *Making Waves, The Forbidden Stitch,* and *Strangers,* far less attention was given to questions of feminism.

3. See *Making Waves,* p. ix, and *The Forbidden Stitch,* pp. 12, 15. As I explore later in this chapter, both anthologies fail to note that *Between the Lines: An Anthology of Pacific/Asian Lesbians* preceded them by two years.

4. While previous anthologies such as *Roots* (1971), *Aiiieeeee!* (1974) and *Counterpoint* (1976) focused primarily on Chinese and Japanese American populations and, to a lesser extent, Filipino and Korean American ones, *Making Waves* and *The Forbidden Stitch* register this diversification of the Asian American population, and also the increasingly blurred boundaries between Asian and Asian American identity.

5. These factors have resulted in a 577 percent increase in Asian Americans in the United States between 1965 and 1985. And whereas until 1960 this population was composed primarily of Japanese (52 percent), Chinese (27 percent), and Filipino (20 percent) Americans, and a small number of Korean and South Asian Americans (1 percent each), by 1985 the population had become more evenly divided between these groups, and inclusive as well of people of Vietnamese, Laotian, Cambodian, Samoan, Guamanian, and other origins. These figures are taken from Takaki's *Strangers from a Different Shore.* For a provocative analysis of the demographic shifts in the Asian American population, see Arif Dirlik's "Asians on the Rim: Transnational Capital and Local Community in the Making of Contemporary Asian America" (forthcoming).

6. See Sau-ling Cynthia Wong's "Denationalization Reconsidered: Asian American Cultural Criticism at a Theoretical Crossroads," in *Amerasia Journal* 21.1, 2 (1995): 1–27. While the term "denationalization" has previously been employed by scholars, including Armand Mattelart and Immanuel Wallerstein, I am here drawing on Wong's use of it.

7. Elaine Kim, forum in *Amerasia Journal* 16.2 (1990): 105.

8. For a brief history of AWU, see William Wei, *The Asian American Movement* (Philadelphia: Temple University Press, 1993).

9. Recent works that contrast to *Making Waves's* approach include *Between the Lines: An Anthology by Pacific/Asian Lesbians of Santa Cruz, California,* ed. C. Chung, A. Kim, and A. K. Lemeshewsky (Santa Cruz: Dancing Bird, 1987) and *Asian American Women's Journal: Moving the Mountains,* published out of UC San Diego in 1993 by alternative visions and Sisterhood across the Waves. In the preface to *Between the Lines,* the editors explain, "We are aware that none of the writers included are of Pacific Island heritage, yet we choose to call this a Pacific/Asian lesbian anthology. We do so, claiming the name as a political identity, as sisters in solidarity" (4). From my location in Hawai'i, the problems both of calling Pacific Islanders "Asian Americans," and of assuming any easy alliance between these groups, are especially glaring: Native Hawaiians' struggle for sovereignty gives them a decidedly different set of concerns than

those of Asian Americans in Hawai'i and the continental United States. I explore these differences in chapter 6.

10. Sucheta Mazumdar, "Race and Racism: South Asians in the United States," in *Frontiers of Asian American Studies: Writing, Research, and Commentary,* ed. Gail M. Nomura, Russell Endo, Stephen H. Sumida, and Russell C. Leong (Pullman: Washington State University Press, 1989), p. 30.

11. For discussions of some of these differences, see Oscar Campomanes' "Filipinos in the United States and Their Literature of Exile," in *Reading the Literatures of Asian America,* ed. Shirley Geok-lin Lim and Amy Ling (Philadelphia: Temple University Press, 1992), as well as E. San Juan, Jr.'s, extensive writings analyzing the relationship of Filipinos to other Asian Americans. See also Jonathan Okamura, "Why There Are No Asian Americans in Hawai'i: The Continuing Significance of Local Identity," *Social Process in Hawaii* 35 (1994): 161–178.

12. The growing awareness and importance of these differences is clearly registered in *The State of Asian America: Activism and Resistance in the 1990s,* ed. Karin Aguilar-San Juan (Boston: South End, 1994). In this collection, class divisions constitute a primary concern.

13. Gary Y. Okihiro, introduction to *Reflections on Shattered Windows: Promises and Prospects of Asian American Studies,* ed. Gary Y. Okihiro, Shirley Hune, Arthur A. Hansen, and John M. Liu (Pullman: Washington State University Press, 1988), p. xvii. For an excellent account of the founding of Asian American studies, see Glenn Omatsu's "The 'Four Prisons' and the Movements of Liberation: Asian American Activism from the 1960s to the 1990s," in Aguilar-San Juan's *The State of Asian America.*

14. In *Asian American Literature: An Introduction to the Writings and Their Social Context* (Philadelphia: Temple University Press, 1982), Elaine Kim provides an excellent overview of the rush of journals, newspapers, pamphlets, and anthologies concerned with Asian American community that emerged from Asian American studies programs in the 1970s. See esp. pp. 312–314.

15. Michael Omi, "It Just Ain't the Sixties No More: The Contemporary Dilemmas of Asian American Studies," in *Reflections,* ed. Okihiro et al., p. 34.

16. For another exploration of the many facets of silence, see King-Kok Cheung's *Articulate Silences: Hisaye Yamamoto, Maxine Hong Kingston, Joy Kogawa* (Ithaca, NY: Cornell University Press, 1993).

17. That such a strategy is not possible for *This Bridge* or *Home Girls* accounts in large part for these anthologies' more oppositional tone. Also, the (related) fact that many Asian Americans have come to the United States largely through choice, or because it offers a place of refuge, makes their relationship to this country more ambivalent than that of other minority groups.

18. For an assessment of the dangers of utilizing access to mainstream success and influence, see *The State of Asian America*'s trenchant critiques (particularly Omatsu's) of the neoconservatism that may accompany such a position.

19. Bruce Iwasaki, introduction to the section on "Asian American Litera-

ture," in *Counterpoint*, ed. Emma Gee (Los Angeles: Asian American Studies Center, 1976), p. 458.

20. Garrett Hongo critiques the ideological narrowness that he thinks limits understandings of Asian American literature in his introduction to *The Open Boat* (New York: Anchor, 1993), p. xxxiv. However, despite Hongo's plea for, and claim to, openness in *The Open Boat*, the anthology excludes any explicitly feminist work. Though Hongo includes feminist poets such as Janice Mirikitani and Nellie Wong, the work of theirs that he selects does not reflect their feminism. The anthology also excludes poetry presenting an explicitly gay or lesbian point of view.

21. Kim, *Asian American Literature*, p. 250.

22. See Takaki's *Strangers from a Different Shore* for specific histories of racial discrimination Asian American men have experienced. See also Donald C. Goellnicht's "Tang Ao in America: Male Subject Positions in *China Men*," in *Reading the Literatures of Asian America*, ed. Lim and Ling.

23. Kim, *Amerasia Journal* forum, p. 109.

24. See Cristy Chung, Aly Kim, Zoon Nguyen, and Trinity Ordoña, with Arlene Stein, "In Our Own Way: A Roundtable Discussion," *Amerasia Journal* 20.1 (1994): 137–147.

25. Dana Y. Takagi remarks the necessity to address the topic of sexualities in Asian American studies in "Maiden Voyage: Excursion into Sexuality and Identity Politics in Asian America," *Amerasia Journal* 20.1 (1994): 1–17. Recent Asian American publications are beginning to do so, including the issue of *Amerasia* entitled "Dimensions of Desire," in which Takagi's article occurs, and *The Very Inside: An Anthology of Writings by Asian and Pacific Islander Lesbian and Bisexual Women*, ed. Sharon Lim-Hing (Ontario: Sister Vision, 1994), discussed in detail in chapter 6. In editing *Charlie Chan Is Dead*, Jessica Hagedorn also includes fiction that foregrounds issues of sexuality. See also Shawn Wong's novel *American Knees* (New York: Simon and Schuster, 1995).

26. Perhaps for this reason, in the first Asian Canadian women's anthology, a special issue of *Fireweed: A Feminist Quarterly* (issue 30, entitled *Asian Canadian Women*), lesbian contributors cite the influence of *This Bridge* and writers such as Gloria Anzaldúa rather than *Making Waves* or its individual contributors.

27. Chung, Kim, and Lemeshewsky, *Between the Lines*, p. 6.

28. Kim, *Amerasia* forum, p. 109. AWU is currently engaged in putting together *Making Waves 2* (its working title). Perhaps this anthology will bring AWU closer to such a goal, for their work provides a model for change that happens not through rupture, but step by step, with one work paving the way for subsequent ones. As Kim herself says regarding AWU's projects in "Room for a View from a Marginal Sight," "What is not entirely satisfactory can make possible the development of something else" (*Critical Mass* 1. 2 [spring 1994]: 12).

29. Kim, foreword to *Reading the Literatures of Asian America*, ed. Lim and Ling, p. xi.

30. Other critics to remark this sea change include Amy Ling, in *Between Worlds: Women Writers of Chinese Ancestry* (New York: Pergamon, 1990), p. xiii; Sau-ling Cynthia Wong, in *Reading Asian American Literature: From Necessity to Extravagance* (Princeton: Princeton University Press, 1993), p. 3; Sylvia Watanabe, in *Home to Stay: Asian American Women's Fiction*, ed. Sylvia Watanabe and Carol Bruchac (New York: Greenfield Review Press, 1990), p. xi; Stephen Sumida, in "Asian/Pacific American Literature in the Classroom," in *American Literature* 65. 2 (June 1993): 352; and Garrett Hongo, in *The Open Boat* (New York: Anchor, 1993), p. xvii. For an outstanding bibliography of recent literary studies, fiction, poetry, and literary anthologies, cultural events, and awards received by Asian American writers, see the introduction and the bibliography to *Reading Asian American Literature*. So well-documented and accepted is this cultural "arrival" that it is now beginning to be critiqued. See, for example, the "Editors' Note" to the first issue of *Critical Mass*, which questions the arrival its name announces. Moreover, this journal changed its name in 1995 to "Hitting Critical Mass." While this was done to avoid potential conflict with an existing registered publication, the change further qualifies this arrival.

31. In the face of this new activity, Chan et al.'s focus on Chinese and Japanese American literature in *The Big Aiiieeeee!*, their 1991 follow-up to *Aiiieeeee!*, at once makes their project more precise and specific and, at the same time, appropriates the field of Asian American literature for Chinese and Japanese American literature through their totalizing claims: in *The Big Aiiieeeee!*, the editors use "Asian American" interchangeably with "Chinese and Japanese American." *The Big Aiiieeeee!* does, however, move away from *Aiiieeeee!*'s expression of contempt for foreign-born Chinese and Chinese culture, reflecting the blurring between Chinese Americans and Chinese in China: while in *Aiiieeeee!*, the editors express contempt for Asians and Asian culture, in the follow-up they claim and celebrate this culture, and connect themselves to Asian history.

32. Oscar V. Campomanes, "Filipinos in the United States and Their Literature of Exile," in *Reading the Literatures of Asian America*, p. 72.

33. For example, while Edith Eaton, who wrote under the pseudonym Sui Sin Far to claim her Chinese origins, has long been included in Asian American anthologies, her sister Winnifred Eaton, who among other things wrote *The Diary of Delia* in Irish American dialect under the Japanese name Onoto Watanna, has only recently been acknowledged by Asian American critics.

34. Lim's paradoxical making and unmaking of Asian American identity and literature in *The Forbidden Stitch* characterizes much of the prodigious amount of work she has undertaken in the last few years. In addition to her books of poetry and her short fiction, Lim has helped to pioneer the study of Asian American literature. Works she has edited include *Approaches to Teaching Kingston's "The Woman Warrior"* (1991), the 1992 collection *Reading the Literatures of Asian America*, with Amy Ling, and the journal *Asian America*. In all of these projects she has insistently called attention to and demonstrated the shifting and het-

erogeneous definition of Asian American identity and literature as she has emphasized the political importance of such categories.

35. This approach is consonant with Tsutakawa's work in co-editing *Gathering Ground*. In "Listening In: A Conversation with the Editors of *Gathering Ground*," she states, "I think it's important in terms of what we're doing to define the aspects of the Third World woman in this country. A really strong definition is needed" (*Gathering Ground*, p. 24).

36. In *Between Worlds*, Amy Ling tells how, "In 1980, when I began my research, there was no listing for 'Chinese American authors'" (xiii). Describing the difficulty she had finding books, Ling explains that the few books that were available were shelved as sociology or children's literature (xiii).

37. Sau-ling Cynthia Wong, *Reading Asian American Literature*, p. 13.

38. This is not Lim's stand elsewhere, though it is consonant with Tsutakawa's in *Gathering Ground*. While in *Making Waves*, eleven women provide information about their husbands, in *The Forbidden Stitch* only one contributor does so.

39. See Cynthia Liu's review of *The Forbidden Stitch* in *Amerasia* 15.2 (1989): 205–208.

40. The introduction to *Between the Lines* echoes themes of namelessness and invisibility: "Understandably, for personal and political reasons, there are some of us who chose to use first names only or pen names. There are others who chose not to appear at all, either in written form or in photographs" (4).

41. Shirley Geok-lin Lim, preface to *Asian America: Journal of Culture and the Arts* 1 (winter 1992): 7. Hereafter cited in the text.

42. Responses to the L.A. uprisings in *Why L.A. Happened: Implications of the '92 Los Angeles Rebellion*, ed. Haki R. Madhubuti (Chicago: Third World Press, 1993) underline these divisions. In "From Slavery to Rodney King: Continuity and Change," Tony Martin distinguishes between African Americans and "Ethnic Americans," a group that for him includes "Jews, Italians, Greeks, Chinese, Arabs and now East Indians and Koreans," all of whom have "stepped on the necks of African-American communities on their way up" (32). And in Anderson Thompson's "The Los Angeles Rebellion: Seizing the Historical Moment," he follows a section on white supremacy with one entitled "Asian Supremacy," where he claims, "Africa has had an Asian problem for *thousands* of years. Black anger in Los Angeles has its roots in a 4000 year-old battle against a well-known adversary" (53). While these constitute the most dramatically anti-Asian American moments in *Why L.A. Happened*, the book's overall tenor evidences the pressures currently being exerted on the coalitional identity "Third World."

Chapter 5. (Un)Common Class Identities in the United States and Britain: *Calling Home* and *The Common Thread*

1. I have drawn most of these figures from *Why L.A. Happened*, ed. Madhubuti.

2. Wendy Brown, "Wounded Attachments: Late Modern Oppositional Polit-

ical Formations," in *The Identity in Question*, ed. John Rajchman (New York and London: Routledge, 1995), p. 206. Hereafter cited in the text.

3. See, for example, Stanley Aronowitz' "Reflections on Identity" and Cornel West's "A Matter of Life and Death," both in the book edited by Rajchman, *Identity in Question*, and Constance Coiner's introduction to *Radical Teacher* 46 (spring 1995), a special issue on working-class studies.

4. Janet Zandy, ed., *Calling Home: Working-Class Women's Writings* (New Brunswick, NJ, and London: Rutgers University Press, 1990). Hereafter cited in the text.

5. June Burnett, Julie Cotterill, Annette Kennerly, Phoebe Nathan, and Jeanne Wilding, eds. *The Common Thread: Writings by Working-Class Women* (London: Mandarin, 1989). Hereafter cited in the text.

6. Lauter, "Working-Class Women's Literature," in *Opportunities for Women's Studies in Language and Literature*, ed. Joan E. Hartman and Ellen Messer-Davidow, vol. 1 of *Women in Print* (New York: Modern Language Association of America, 1982), p. 110.

7. As Susan Estabrook Kennedy asserts in *If All We Did Was to Weep at Home: A History of White Working-Class Women in America* (Bloomington and London: Indiana University Press, 1979): "So consistently has tenure in the working class been regarded as a temporary condition that working-class women have generally not developed a sense of their own place or of their history as a collective entity" (xiii). *Working-Class Women in the Academy: Laborers in the Knowledge Factory*, ed. Michelle M. Tokarczyk and Elizabeth A. Fay (Amherst: University of Massachusetts Press, 1993), also contains many essays addressing what contributor Pam Annas terms "the peculiarly American denial of social class and the fervent belief in social mobility" (in "Pass the Cake: The Politics of Gender, Class, and Text in the Academic Workplace," p. 171).

8. E. P. Thompson, *The Making of the English Working Class* (New York: Vintage, 1966), p. 9. That I find myself so often turning to British theorists of class to make such claims is itself symptomatic of the absence of class theory in the U.S.

9. Paul Gilroy, *"There Ain't No Black in the Union Jack": The Cultural Politics of Race and Nation* (Chicago: University of Chicago Press, 1987), p. 20.

10. As Gareth Stedman Jones explains in *Languages of Class: Studies in English Working Class History, 1832–1982* (Cambridge: Cambridge University Press, 1983): "Because there are different languages of class, one should not proceed upon the assumption that 'class' as an elementary counter of official social description, 'class' as an effect of theoretical discourse about distribution or productive relations, 'class' as the summary of a cluster of culturally signifying practices or 'class' as a species of political or ideological self-definition, share a single reference point in anterior social reality" (quoted in Cora Kaplan, *Sea Changes: Culture and Feminism* [London: Verso, 1986], p. 163).

11. For an account of the racialization of the working class as white, see Michael Omi and Howard Winant's *Racial Formation in the United States* (New York and London: Routledge, 1986). Their focus on male forms of working-class culture also attests, unwittingly, to the gendering of class.

12. For example, in "Beyond the Double Day: Work and Family in Working-Class Women's Lives," Sandra Morgen reviews three such studies of women's work cultures—Louise Lamphere's *From Working Daughters to Working Mothers: Immigrant Women in a New England Industrial Community,* Karen Sacks's *Caring by the Hour: Women, Work, and Organizing at Duke Medical Center,* and Patricia Zavella's *Women's Work and Chicano Families: Cannery Workers of the Santa Clara Valley*—in *Feminist Studies* 16. 1 (spring 1990): 53–67.

13. For an account of the university's inattention to class and its assumption of a middle-class norm, see, for example, Saundra Gardner's "What's a Nice Working-Class Girl Like You Doing in a Place Like This?" in *Working-Class Women in the Academy,* ed. Tokarczyk and Fay, p. 51.

14. For a discussion of the New Class, see Alvin Gouldner, *The Future of Intellectuals and the Rise of the New Class* (New York: Oxford University Press, 1979). For a discussion of the professional-managerial class, see Barbara Ehrenreich and John Ehrenreich, "The Professional-Managerial Class," in *Between Labor and Capital,* ed. Pat Walker (Montreal: Black Rose, 1979). Guillory's *Cultural Capital* builds on Pierre Bourdieu's attention to the relationship between class and culture, and also on Gouldner's and the Ehrenreichs' formulations.

15. Lillian Robinson, *Sex, Class, and Culture* (Bloomington: Indiana University Press, 1978), p. 29.

16. Sharon O'Dair, "Vestments and Vested Interests: Academia, the Working Class, and Affirmative Action," in *Working-Class Women in the Academy,* ed. Tokarczyk and Fay, p. 247.

17. Jake Ryan and Charles Sackrey, *Strangers in Paradise: Academics from the Working Class* (Boston: South End, 1984), p. 113 (emphasis in the original).

18. Zandy, "The Complexities and Contradictions of Working-Class Women's Writing," *Radical Teacher* 46 (spring 1995): 5.

19. See Monique Wittig, "One Is Not Born a Woman," *Feminist Issues* 2 (winter 1981): 47–54; and Christine Delphy, *Close to Home: A Materialist Analysis of Women's Oppression,* trans. and ed. Diana Leonard (Amherst: University of Massachusetts Press, 1984). While such analyses are becoming increasingly rare, they are nevertheless perpetuated in, for example, Naomi Wolf's highly influential book *The Beauty Myth* (New York: Doubleday, 1991).

20. For example, in the introduction to *Working-Class Women in the Academy,* as the editors Tokarczyk and Fay worry about "unrepresented voices" in the collection, they explain: "Articles by women of color were particularly hard to find. Numerous queries from us were unanswered" (19). Their difficulties in obtaining these articles seem, in part, as they themselves suggest, due to some women of color's lack of identification with a working-class identity. I will have more to say about this later in this chapter in relation to Zandy's *Liberating Memory: Our Work and Our Working-Class Consciousness* (New Brunswick, NJ: Rutgers University Press, 1995), a collection of writings by intellectuals from the working class.

21. In addition to *Calling Home,* such projects, which have begun to emerge in the early 1990s, include Valerie Miners' *Rumors from the Cauldron,* Tokarczyk and Fay's *Working-Class Women in the Academy,* and Zandy's *Liberating Memory.*

22. For commentary on Marxist literary criticism's inadequate treatment of working-class literature, see Tim Libretti's "Is There a Working Class in U.S. Literature? Race, Ethnicity, and the Proletarian Literary Tradition," in *Radical Teacher* 46 (spring 1995): 22–26.

23. Joann Maria Vasconcellos supports this perception in *Liberating Memory.* When she stages a dialogue between "Academic Joann" and "[working-class] Joann" in "For Laughing Out Loud," it is "Academic Joann" who quotes Anzaldúa (127).

24. The MLA's marginalization of working-class literature continues. As Zandy notes in the introduction to *Liberating Memory,* her "recent efforts to petition the Program Committee of the Modern Language Association for a Discussion Group on 'Working-Class Literature' have failed. The Program Committee decided that 'a discussion group on the proposed topic was not needed'" (15).

25. In *Liberating Memory,* Zandy makes a similar move in an introductory section entitled "Organic Intellectuals" when she evokes Gramsci's concept of the organic intellectual in relation to the book's contributors without laying claim to this term for them: "Whether these voices are labeled as 'organic intellectuals' is less important than how they use intellectual space in their own work and how they make room for other democratic intellectuals, especially those outside the academy" (12).

26. For example, current criteria for literary excellence have been importantly shaped by critics such as T. S. Eliot (to cite just one of many possible examples), whose aesthetic criteria emerged from his desire to make literature the province of the elite, and to defend against, and separate himself from, American culture, which was coded as lower class in relation to English culture.

27. Lauter, *Canons and Contexts,* p. 77. From a similar perspective, Lillian Robinson suggests that "whatever we have been taught, cliches or sentimentality need not be signals of meretricious prose" (*Sex, Class, and Culture,* p. 252).

28. In addition, only one contributor (Margaret Randall) is mentioned in Zandy's acknowledgements. *Calling Home* thus marks a contrast to the other anthologies in this study, which largely consist of new materials and give evidence of close interrelations between the editors and contributors. The 1993 *Working-Class Women in the Academy,* co-edited by *Calling Home* contributor Tokarczyk, suggests that a stronger sense of working-class women's community is being forged in the academy.

29. Such critics include Robinson, in *Sex, Class, and Culture,* and Lauter, in *Canons and Contexts.*

30. Sherna Berger Gluck and Daphne Patai, introduction to *Women's Words: The Feminist Practice of Oral History,* ed. Sherna Berger Gluck and Daphne Patai (New York and London: Routledge, 1991), pp. 2–3. See also Anne Goldman's *Take My Word: Autobiographical Innovations of Ethnic American Working Women*

(Berkeley: University of California Press, 1996) for an insightful discussion of the politics of collaborative autobiographies.

31. Sherry Thomas, who gathers the stories of rural women in *We Didn't Have Much, But We Sure Had Plenty: Stories of Rural Women* (Garden City, NY: Anchor, Doubleday, 1981), provides a glimpse of the sort of dynamics that shape oral narratives in her introduction, and also explains the interventions involved in the narratives she publishes (see p. xvi). By including illustrations of the narrators alongside many of the narratives in her book, Thomas further highlights the way these narratives become, in some sense, her creations.

32. *Home Girls* makes a similar movement to honor black working-class women and their political struggles (see chapter 3), but the distinctly African American movements and traditions, as well as the women referred to by the anthology do not appear in *Calling Home*. A comparison of these two anthologies thus points to intersections between class- and race-based struggles, but also suggests the extent to which race divides working-class women, and the racial biases of the movements *Calling Home* claims on behalf of all working-class women. I will return to this issue later in the chapter.

33. Lauter, *Canons and Contexts*, p. 68.

34. That her next edited collection, *Liberating Memory*, is dedicated to her father, and includes men contributors, underlines her commitment to working-class men and women.

35. Sue Doro, commentary on "Focus," in *Liberating Memory*, p. 47.

36. See Deborah King's article "Multiple Jeopardy, Multiple Consciousness: The Context of a Black Feminist Ideology," in *Signs* 14. 1 (1988): 42–72, for a historical overview of the sexism and racism in organized labor movements.

37. If *Calling Home* provides but little space for lesbian (and gay) concerns, *Liberating Memory* provides no space at all.

38. Omi and Winant, *Racial Formation in the United States*, p. 65. Also, Deborah King points out the ways in which working-class politics have excluded black women in "Multiple Jeopardy," and Kennedy remarks on the ethnic divisions between members of the working-classes in *If All We Did Was to Weep at Home* (p. 115). In *Iron Cages* and *Strangers from a Different Shore*, Takaki addresses the American labor movement's exclusion of Asian Americans and instances of anti-Asian violence on the part of white workers. For insightful discussions about the structural necessity of working-class racism to the functioning of capitalist societies, see Etienne Balibar and Immanuel Wallerstein's *Race, Nation, Class* (London and New York: Verso, 1991).

39. In "Beyond the Double Day," her review of three such studies, Sandra Morgen finds that the works she reviews all "show that to the extent that women's work cultures in multiethnic or multiracial workplaces reflect rather than undermine occupational segregation, ethnic prejudice, and racism, they reinforce the management-promoted 'divide and conquer' strategies that have been so detrimental to workplace organizing in this country" (57).

40. For example, Aida Hurtado, in "Relating to Privilege: Seduction and Sub-

ordination of White Women and Women of Color," states, "When I discuss feminists of Color I will treat them as working class unless I specifically mention otherwise. When I discuss white feminists, I will treat them as middle class" (in *Signs: Journal of Women in Culture and Society* 14. 4 [1989]: 837).

41. Anzaldúa, introduction to *Making Face, Making Soul/Haciendo Caras,* p. xxi.

42. Omi and Winant, *Racial Formation,* p. xi.

43. For example, in "Black Women's Life Stories: Reclaiming Self in Narrative Texts" (in *Women's Words,* ed. Gluck and Patai), Gwendolyn Etter-Lewis points to the different determinants of class identity for blacks and whites (p. 49).

44. See, for example, the essays by Barbara Fox, Maxine Scates, Pat Wynne, and Carole Tarlen.

45. That Zandy focuses largely on academics in *Liberating Memory* (as did Anzaldúa when she followed up *This Bridge* with *Haciendo Caras*) supports this argument.

46. Zandy's words here echo Anzaldúa's and Moraga's in *This Bridge,* and those of Barbara Smith and Beverly Smith in *Home Girls.*

47. Margaret Llewelyn Davies, ed., *Life as We Have Known It, by Co-operative Working Women* (London: Virago, 1977), p. xxix–xxx. Hereafter cited in the text.

48. Nor did *Life* by 1977: in the Virago edition Anna Davin's introduction precedes Woolf's, and her use of a working-class women's "us" contrasts with Woolf's "them."

49. Thompson, *The Making of the English Working Class,* p. 194.

50. Raphael Samuel, introduction to *Patriotism: The Making and Unmaking of British National Identity,* vol. 2 of *Minorities and Outsiders,* ed. Raphael Samuel (London and New York: Routledge, 1989), p. xxxiii. What my discussion here neglects are the ways in which the working-class in Britain was also historically constructed in relation to Britain's racist imperial history. I discuss interrelations between race and class later in this chapter.

51. Mike Featherstone, "Localism, Globalism, and Cultural Identity," in *Global/ Local: Cultural Production and the Transnational Imaginary,* ed. Rob Wilson and Wimal Dissanayake (Durham and London: Duke University Press, 1996), p. 50.

52. As Featherstone notes in "Localism, Globalism, and Cultural Identity," in accounts such as Hoggart's in *The Uses of Literacy,* and, more recently, Brian Jackson's *Working Class Community* (1968) and B. Williamson's *Class, Culture and Community* (1982), "we get a strong sense of a distinctive working-class way of life with its occupations' homogeneity, strictly segregated gender roles with male group ties and the 'mateship' code of loyalty dominant both in work and leisure (drinking, gambling, sport)—women were largely confined to the separate home sphere" (48).

53. Jean Gaffin and David Thoms, *Caring and Sharing: The Centenary History of the Co-operative Women's Guild* (Manchester: Co-operative Union, 1983), p. 1.

54. Ibid., p. 73.

55. Paul Willis, *Learning to Labour: How Working-Class Kids Get Working-Class Jobs* (Farnborough, England: Saxon House, 1977), p. 12.

56. This section, one of the anthology's shortest, consists primarily of entries by Collective members, and an additional two entries by Sie Jalloh which celebrate her identity as black.

57. Jeanne Wilding's letters to a feminist bookshop Collective stands as the only interaction between working-class and middle-class feminists in *The Common Thread,* and these letters stress their class divisions over their commonalities. In these letters, Wilding protests the renaming of the "Working-Class Women" section of the bookstore to a section entitled "Community." Wilding's letters, which are endorsed by The Common Thread and her working-class lesbian group, are addressed "Dear Sisters." This address points to the sameness of The Common Thread Collective's concerns and the (middle-class) bookstore collective's as it ironizes their relationship, and calls attention to the divisions between them. Although Wilding's letters resulted in the bookstore readopting the "Working-Class Women" section, the bookstore collective refused Wilding permission to publish the letters they wrote to her in return. Therefore, while the letters to the bookstore produced the desired effects, the bookstore collective's refusal to include their responses in *The Common Thread,* and *The Common Thread*'s announcement of this refusal, undercuts the sense that their dialogue produced the possibility of friendship, community, or any radical shift in consciousness (or behavior) on the part of the bookstore collective.

58. Paul Gilroy, "Steppin' Out of Babylon—Race, Class, and Autonomy," in *The Empire Strikes Back: Race and Racism in 70s Britain,* ed. The Centre for Contemporary Cultural Studies (London: Hutchinson, 1982), p. 304.

59. Gilroy, *"There Ain't No Black in the Union Jack,"* p. 12. In "Black to Front and Black Again: Racialization through Contested Times and Spaces" (in *Place and the Politics of Identity,* ed. Keith and Pile), Barnor Hesse concurs: "The politics of 'race' in general and Black politics in particular does not appear to have a theoretically defined status in the literature which constitutes the field of 'radical' social and political thought in Britain" (165).

60. Avtar Brah, "Difference, Diversity, and Differentiation," *"Race," Culture, and Difference,* ed. James Donald and Ali Rattansi (London: Sage, 1992,) p. 127.

61. Ibid. For another discussion of the evolution of Black identity in Britain, see Stuart Hall's "Old and New Identities, Old and New Ethnicities," in *Culture, Globalization, and the World-System: Contemporary Conditions for the Representation of Identity,* ed. Anthony D. King (Department of Art and Art History: State University of New York at Binghamton, 1991).

62. These different contexts point to the specificity with which any struggle concerning racism must be waged: whereas in the United States, multiculturalism serves as a concept deployed by racial and ethnic minorities (with some significant reservations), in Britain, it has served to divide and subjugate ethnic and racial minorities.

63. See, for example, Amina Mama, "Black Women, the Economic Crisis, and the British State," in *Feminist Review* 17 (July 1984): 23. Brah, in "Difference, Diversity, and Differentiation," also explains that the term "black" met with crit-

icism in the late 1980s on the grounds that it denies Asian cultural identity, and conceals the needs of cultural groups who are not African-Caribbean in origin (pp. 127–130).

64. See Gilroy's *"There Ain't No Black in the Union Jack,"* esp. pp. 19–35, for an extended analysis of how race is destabilizing class in Britain.

65. Stuart Hall, "The Local and the Global: Globalization and Ethnicity," in *Culture, Globalization, and the World-System*, p. 24.

66. Shabnam Grewal, Jackie Kay, Liliane Landor, Gail Lewis, and Pratibha Parmar, eds., *Charting the Journey: Writings by Black and Third World Women* (London: Sheba Feminist Publishers, 1988), p. 4. Hereafter cited in the text.

Chapter 6. Around 1996: Re-Placing Identity Politics from the "Racial Paradise" of Hawai'i

1. In my spelling of Hawaiian words and names, I use the 'okina (glottal stop) and kahakō (macron, signaling elongated vowels) except when they are not present in texts from which I am quoting, and when I am using Anglicized words (i.e., *Hawaii's*, or *Hawaiian*).

2. Bamboo Ridge's conceptualization of "Local" is far from the only one, and while they primarily publish pieces by Asians, this press also publishes work by "haoles" (a Hawaiian word for "foreigners" that in its current usage most commonly refers to white people) and writers of Puerto Rican, Portuguese, and Hawaiian descent. In its contemporary and most general usage, a Local identity is a panethnic one for people living in Hawai'i who have a shared commitment to and appreciation for this place—for its land, peoples, and cultures. However, in ways this chapter later suggests, precisely who can claim a Local identity is far from clear—its class, racial, and ethnic parameters are contested ones, as are the importance of factors such as being Hawai'i-born (versus being a long-time resident), and whether or not one speaks Pidgin, also known as Hawaiian Creole English. For arguments about Local identity that also give an outline of its historical development and a sense of its complexities, see Jonathan Y. Okamura, "Why There Are No Asian Americans in Hawai'i: The Continuing Significance of Local Identity," in *Social Process in Hawaii* 35 (1994): 161–178, and Candace Fujikane, "Between Nationalisms: Hawaii's Local Nation and Its Troubled Racial Paradise," in *Critical Mass* 1.2 (spring/summer 1994): 23–57.

3. The figure 8 percent comes from the university's report of the number of enrolled students who defined themselves as Hawaiian in the spring of 1996. This number is by no means an undisputed or purely "factual" one. Not only do such statistics vary depending on the political agendas of those who provide them and how they define "Hawaiian," but the numbers of people who identify as Hawaiian at a given time fluctuates; since most Hawaiians have mixed ethnic origins, the decision to identify as Hawaiian on a census form, or any other form, has much to do with the current political climate, and with ever-

changing decrees from the U.S. government about what percentage of Hawaiian blood makes one Native Hawaiian.

4. Rodney Morales, "Pirates Yes They Rob I," a talk given at the Hawai'i Literature Conférence in Honolulu, on March 12, 1994.

5. Bondi, "Locating Identity Politics," p. 98. Keith and Pile, the editors of *Place and the Politics of Identity,* concur. In their conclusion they proclaim: "This is a moment in which spatiality appears about to take its place alongside historicity as one of the key terms in theories of conjuncture and situated knowledges" (223). Indeed, the appearance of this stylish Routledge book of radical postmodern geographers itself helps evidence Bondi's and Keith and Pile's claims, as does the new attention in the academy to Marxist geographers such as Edward Soja and David Harvey.

6. By embedding the date in this title, Adrienne Rich insists on the importance of time as well as place. The fact that Rich's attention to time goes unremarked in the many discussions of this essay that I have seen speaks to the difficulty of keeping both time and space in play as critical terms. "Notes towards a Politics of Location (1984)" appears in Rich's *Blood, Bread, and Poetry: Selected Prose 1979–1985* (London: Virago, 1987), p. 167–187. Further references to this essay are cited in the text.

7. For a nuanced assessment of the competing and contradictory uses of emergent versus residual regionalisms, as well as a discussion of regionalism's relationship to "the local," see Paul Lyons, "Larry Brown's *Joe* and the Uses and Abuses of the Region Concept," forthcoming in *Studies in American Fiction* (spring 1997).

8. Eric J. Sundquist, introduction to "American Literary History: The Next Century," *American Literature* 67.4 (December 1995): 793.

9. While Porter's main focus is on the challenges issued by Chicano/a studies, related ones have been issued in the fields of Asian American studies (see, for example, Sau-ling Cynthia Wong's "Denationalization Reconsidered" or Arif Dirlik's "The Asia-Pacific in Asian-American Perspective," in *What Is in a Rim?,* ed. Arif Dirlik [Boulder: Westview, 1993]: 305–329), Native American studies (e.g., writings by Vine Deloria and Ward Churchill, as well as Leslie Marmon Silko's massive and amazing novel *Almanac of the Dead,* which brilliantly conjures the current lay of the land), and African American Studies (e.g., Gilroy's *Black Atlantic,* and essays by Vévé Clark and Hortense Spillers).

For a different revisionary project that nonetheless reflects in its title a preoccupation with spatialization, see *Redrawing the Boundaries: The Transformation of English and American Literary Studies,* ed. Stephen Greenblatt and Giles Gunn (New York: Modern Language Association of America, 1992), especially Philip Fisher's essay, "American Literary and Cultural Studies since the Civil War" (pp. 232–250). This essay, offered in the spirit of revision, repackages a familiar narrative about American literary studies; in ways that Carolyn Porter delineates, Fisher's "redrawing" reinscribes the status quo.

10. See Gregory Jay, "The End of 'American' Literature: Toward a Multicultural Practice," *College English* 53 (1991): 264–281.

11. For a particularly incisive articulation of this last point, see Arif Dirlik's "The Postcolonial Aura: Third World Criticism in the Age of Global Capitalism," in *Critical Inquiry* 20.2 (winter 1994): 328–356.

12. Arif Dirlik, "The Global in the Local," in *Global/Local: Cultural Production and the Transnational Imaginary,* ed. Rob Wilson and Wimal Dissanayake (Durham and London: Duke University Press, 1996), p. 22.

13. Joan Dayan, "'A Receptacle for That Race of Men': Blood, Boundaries, and Mutations of Theory," *American Literature* 67.4 (December 1994): 811.

14. Ibid., p. 812.

15. One of the finest examples of site-specific work that I have seen is Annette Fuentes and Barbara Ehrenreich's pamphlet entitled "Women in the Global Factory" (INC Pamphlet no. 2, ed. Holly Sklar and Gloria Jacobs [Boston: South End, 1983]). This pamphlet is also noteworthy for the way in which it makes gender integral to its global/local analysis: it makes clear women workers' particular urgency to forge transnational links, given their new role in the spread of transnational and multinational corporations. Thanks to Laura Lyons for giving me a copy of this pamphlet.

16. Sharon Lim-Hing, ed., *The Very Inside: An Anthology of Writing by Asian and Pacific Islander Lesbian and Bisexual Women* (Toronto: Sister Vision, 1994). Joseph Bruchac, ed., *Returning the Gift: Poetry and Prose from the First North American Native Writer's Festival* (Tucson and London: University of Arizona Press, 1994).

17. For a discussion of the ongoing force of nationalism, see R. Radhakrishnan, "Nationalism, Gender, and the Narrative of Identity," in *Nationalisms and Sexualities,* ed. Andrew Parker, Mary Russo, Doris Sommer, and Patricia Yaeger (New York and London: Routledge, 1992): 77–95. See also Hall's comments in "The Local and the Global," where he remarks, "The erosion of the nation-state, national economies and national cultural identities is a very complex and dangerous moment. Entities of power are dangerous when they are ascending and when they are declining and it is a moot point whether they are more dangerous in the second or the first moment. The first moment, they gobble up everybody and in the second moment they take everybody down with them" (25).

18. Indeed, in "A Borderless World? From Colonialism to Transnationalism and the Decline of the Nation-State" (*Critical Inquiry* 19 [summer 1993]: 726–751), Masao Miyoshi claims that the most crucial question that theorists the world over face pertains to the relation of globalization (or transnationalization) and the local: "How then to balance the transnationalization of economy and politics with the survival of local culture and history—without mummifying them with tourism and in museums" (747).

19. Mitsuhiro Yoshimoto, "Real Virtuality," in *Global/Local,* ed. Wilson and Dissanayake, p. 107.

20. Hall, "The Local and the Global," p. 33.

21. Hall, "Old and New Identities," p. 52.

22. See Dirlik's "The Global in the Local," esp. pp. 22–23.

23. Frederick Buell makes this point in *National Culture and the New Global System* (Baltimore and London: Johns Hopkins University Press, 1994): "The insurgency within the borders of the United States occurred in sync with the anticolonial struggles going on outside them; this interrelationship, moreover, had been in place for some time, culturally in the interactions between movements like *négritude* and the Harlem Renaissance, and politically in the involvement of African-Americans like W. E. B. Du Bois in the struggle of African nationalism" (154).

24. As Hall remarks in "The Local and the Global," "We suffer increasingly from a process of historical amnesia in which we think that just because we are thinking about an idea it has only just started" (20).

25. Gilroy, *Black Atlantic*, p. 207.

26. It seems to me no accident that only recently have I seen mention of Nancy Cunard's 1934 anthology *Negro* (the 1996 MLA is featuring a panel on the anthology). If a race-based identity politics might dismiss this work, edited as it is by a white woman who exoticizes blacks, its appeal is apparent now, given its diasporic focus.

27. Bondi, "Locating Identity Politics," pp. 98–99.

28. Caren Kaplan, "The Politics of Location as Transnational Feminist Critical Practice," in *Scattered Hegemonies*, ed. Inderpal Grewal and Caren Kaplan (Minneapolis and London: University of Minnesota Press, 1994), p. 139. Hereafter cited in the text.

29. The binary Kaplan establishes here is problematic in other ways as well. After all, it is not clear to me that hooks and Wallace are more clearly marginalized than Meese and Miller (for example, while bell hooks might have a harder time than Elizabeth Meese catching a cab, hooks might receive more conference invitations, or be a more highly sought-after job candidate). Furthermore, hooks's own self-positioning is not in and of itself unproblematic, since to choose the margin, as hooks herself argues, puts one in a different location than those marginalized by material circumstances and a lack of choices. (To continue with the cab analogy: as hooks herself would be the first to acknowledge, she can afford to flag one.) Despite hooks's firm assertion in *Yearning* (Boston: South End, 1990) that she makes a "definite distinction between that marginality which is imposed by oppressive structures and that marginality one chooses as a site of resistance" (153), critics often quote hooks out of context, with the result that they romanticize imposed marginality by equating it with chosen marginality, or romanticize (and appropriate) chosen marginality by leaving behind its connections to experiences of domination, material deprivation, and struggle as they claim a position in the margins for themselves.

30. In part, this might be because Kaplan and Grewal's introduction to *Scattered Hegemonies* addresses their collaborative work. However, even in their introduction, the racial politics of this collaboration goes unmentioned, as do the locations from which they edited the book. (While they say that they did the

work 3,000 miles apart, only the acknowledgments suggest their specific geographic and institutional locations.)

31. Kaplan and Grewal's term "scattered *hegemonies*" does convey this more complex vision of each location itself being a site of struggle, but in Kaplan's article (and in the introduction, as well), the dynamics of particular hegemonic sites drop from consideration. Furthermore, the term "scattered hegemonies" itself fails to convey a sense of the connections among hegemonies.

32. Laura Lyons, introduction to *Writing in Trouble: Protest and the Cultural Politics of Irish Nationalism*, photocopy.

33. The Routledge edition of *Compañeras* suggests the institutional acceptance and the marketability in the 1990s of these anthologies and the identities they promote. I will return to the significance of this near the end of this chapter.

34. The importance of Hawai'i is, in fact, being noted with increasing frequency in global/local studies, and in studies of Asian American and multiethnic U.S. literatures. However, if Hawai'i signifies a depopulated island paradise to vacationers who know it only from the Hawaii Visitor's Bureau, academics sometimes fall into their own forms of romanticization. Bonnie Tu Smith, for example, miscasts Hawai'i as a racial paradise. Drawing on Stephen Sumida's work, in her conclusion to *All My Relatives: Community in Contemporary Ethnic American Literatures* (Ann Arbor: University of Michigan Press, 1994), she posits Hawai'i as an example of a multiculturalism that works—that maintains unity in diversity and puts forth a happy pluralism (see p. 190). Such celebrations fail to take into account Jonathan Okamura's insights in "The Illusion of Paradise: Multiculturalism in Hawai'i" (a paper presented at the conference on "Reconfiguring Minority-Majority Discourse: Problematizing Multiculturalism," August 11–13, 1994, East-West Center, Honolulu, Hawai'i) that, in the context of Hawai'i, multiculturalism works to keep the status quo in place, and therefore acts as a repressive ideology for Hawaiians working to have their sovereignty recognized. Other continentally based critics to take up Hawai'i in a perhaps still-idealizing, but more enabling and knowledgeable way include Dirlik, who uses Hawai'i to exemplify a place where postmodern consciousness creates the condition for a contemporary localism, and also produces it (Dirlik's "The Global in the Local"). Reflecting the influence of Rob Wilson, a locally based fierce and exuberant advocate of Hawai'i as a site of critical regionalism, Hawai'i is similarly remarked upon by other contributors to his and Dissanayake's *Global/Local*.

35. In her groundbreaking essay "Between Nationalisms," Fujikane uses the phrase "between nationalisms" mainly to explore the relationship between Hawaiian nationalism and what she advances as a Local form of cultural nationalism.

36. Arif Dirlik, "Asians on the Rim" (photocopy, p. 21). In "The Asia-Pacific in Asian-American Perspective," Dirlik provides a context for this discussion. In this article, he says that the hegemonic paradigm of the expanding western frontier is being challenged by Asian American historiography, which is re-

vealing "that there was an eastern frontier as well, with a significant Asian presence on its outposts" (319).

37. In the U.S. academy, this split has been registered, on both sides, by Asian and Asian American studies departments since their inception.

38. Dirlik, "Asians on the Rim," p. 14.

39. Ibid., pp. 14–15. Arjun Appadurai makes a related argument in "Patriotism and Its Futures," *Public Culture* 5. 3 (1993): 411–430.

40. Dirlik, "Asians on the Rim," p. 20.

41. Miyoshi, "A Borderless World?" p. 742.

42. "Kānaka Maoli" is Hawaiian for "true" or indigenous people and a term some contributors to *The Very Inside* prefer to "Hawaiian" or "Native Hawaiian." Outside Hawai'i, this term can be especially useful, as it serves more clearly to differentiate Native Hawaiians from those who simply live in the state of Hawai'i and are thus assumed to be Hawaiian. In my discussion, I use "Hawaiian," "Native Hawaiian," and "Kānaka Maoli" interchangeably. In this chapter, I also follow the lead of *The Very Inside* and *Returning the Gift* in capitalizing "Native" and "Islander."

43. See, for example, Epeli Hau'ofa's "Our Sea of Islands," in *A New Oceania: Rediscovering Our Sea of Islands*, ed. Eric Waddell, Vijay Naidu, and Epeli Hau'ofa (Suva, Fiji: University of the South Pacific, 1993). See also Paul Sharrad's "Making Beginnings: Johnny Frisbie and Pacific Literature," in *New Literary History* 25 (1994): 121–136.

44. They also implicitly provide a challenge to the use of the term "Queer Nation."

45. Sau-ling Cynthia Wong, "Denationalization Reconsidered," p. 17.

46. For a related lesbian subversion of that which is traditionally feminine, see the section "Cravings," in *Piece of My Heart*. By interweaving erotic lesbian poetry that is full of food imagery with recipes that involve the same foods as the poems do, editor Silvera takes women and their food creations from the kitchen into the bedroom.

47. Hall, "The Local and the Global," p. 28.

48. See, for example, Leolani M.'s description to Joyoti Grech of the international attendance at the first Asian Pacifica Sisters retreat held in Santa Cruz (Lim-Hing, *The Very Inside*, pp. 370–371).

49. In fact, if *The Very Inside* seems to offer a global perspective in comparison to the 1987 *Between the Lines* and its six contributors from Santa Cruz, there are also ways in which *The Very Inside*, too, is tied to Santa Cruz by way of the annual retreats there that have conjoined so many of its contributors.

What shifts between *Between the Lines* and *The Very Inside* is the nature of the Asian and Pacific coalition established. Chung, Kim, and Lemeshewsky, the editors of *Between the Lines*, state in their introduction: "We are aware that none of the writers included are of Pacific Island heritage, yet we choose to call this a Pacific/Asian lesbian anthology. We do so, claiming the name as a political identity, as sisters in solidarity" (4). In comparison to that of *The Very Inside*, this coalitional gesture reads as more strictly symbolic, and empty. However, in pointing this out, I do not mean to condemn *Between the Lines* 's coalitional politics; to do so would entail ignoring the editors' precarious and marginalized position within both lesbian and Asian American communities. That *Between the Lines* contains only six Santa Cruz contributors (three of them the editors) suggests the fragility and tenuousness of the community that the editors are working towards, and means that their claim to be speaking for/as Asian/ Pacific lesbians can only be read as a strategic effort to open up a space for the articulation of this identity, and for an anthology such as *The Very Inside*.

50. *The Very Inside*, to sketch out one possible example of this challenge, offers an alternative to the model for nation-making Doris Sommer discovers in "Irresistable Romance: The Foundational Fictions of Latin America," in *Nation and Narration*, ed. Homi K. Bhabha (London and New York: Routledge, 1990), her study of Latin American fiction. Sommer suggests that "natural and familial grounding, along with its rhetoric of productive sexuality, provides a model for apparently non-violent national consolidation during periods of internecine conflict. To paraphrase another foundational text, after the creation of the new nations, the domestic romance is an exhortation to be fruitful and multiply" (76). If, as Sommer suggests, a heterosexual reproductive model has worked in the service of national consolidation, non-heteronormative sexuality in *The Very Inside* works to establish new alliances (both ethnic and sexual) that further unfix already-eroding national identities, as they uncouple sexuality and reproduction.

51. Khachig Tölöyan, "The Nation-State and Its Others: In Lieu of a Preface," *Diaspora* 1.1 (1991): 5.

52. Keith and Pile, "Introduction Part 1: The Politics of Place," in *Place and the Politics of Identity*, p. 20.

53. Daniel Boyarin and Jonathan Boyarin, "Diaspora: Generation and the Ground of Jewish Identity," *Critical Inquiry* 19 (summer 1993): 723. Hereafter cited in the text.

54. Haunani-Kay Trask, *From a Native Daughter: Colonialism and Sovereignty in Hawai'i* (Monroe, ME: Common Courage Press, 1993), n.p.

55. It is ironic that the Boyarins, in this article, strongly argue against universalizing Jewish identity since, in promoting a form of diaspora anchored in Jewish history, they themselves replicate this problem. While in relation to Hawaiian sovereignty the Boyarins' arguments appear self-serving and politically reprehensible, from their own position as Jewish studies scholars, and in relation to debates regarding Zionism, their arguments serve a more progressive function.

56. Jonathan Y. Okamura compellingly addressed many of these issues in his paper "The Illusion of Paradise: Multiculturalism in Hawai'i." *The Very Inside* also provides a few glimpses of these issues. For example, in "'Asian Pacific Islander': Issues of Representation and Responsibility," J. Kehaulani Kauanui and Ju Hui 'Judy' Han ask, "How many Japanese Americans would acknowl-

edge the imperialist projects and the impact of multi-national Japanese corporations on the 'development' of Hawai'i or the dumping of nuclear waste in the Pacific?" (378). While Han and Kauanui themselves demonstrate the possibilities for an effective "Asian Pacific" coalition, their article is also one of the few in the anthology that asserts that such a relationship cannot move beyond the coalitional. Its purpose is to identify the tensions that exist among these groups from the perspective of Hawai'i.

The Very Inside also suggests tensions that may exist between Native Hawaiians living in Hawai'i and those on the North American continent who are claiming a diasporic Hawaiian identity and working in alliance with Asian Americans or Asian Canadians. In an interview with Joyoti Grech, Leolani M., a founding member of the San Francisco group Asian Pacifica Sisters, tells of the first APS retreat in Santa Cruz. She says, "We had K. come from Hawaii. She too was in the political movement. And of course she corrected us in a lot of Hawaiian statements—because we had this T-shirt made of different languages, saying 'For the Love of Women.' And of course we didn't know Hawaiian, right, so we just stated the line 'Ke Aloha o Wahini.' . . . But it was wrong! But I don't care—being that it was from our heart. There was a deadline to make this T-shirt and we did the best we could. So she came and she said, that's not how it's supposed to be. [But] it was from our hearts . . ." (372). As K's response to Leolani M. suggests, Hawaiians living off-island can have different priorities and conceptions of community and activism than those on-island. For many politically active Hawaiians living in Hawai'i, accurate rendering of, if not fluency in, the Hawaiian language might seem more crucial, especially given the links between the revival of the Hawaiian language (under siege since the United States forcibly annexed Hawai'i in 1898) and the movement to reclaim ancestral lands. Furthermore, assertions of "Hawaiian at heart" are charged ones in Hawai'i, where they are usually made by non-Hawaiians—see Haunani-Kay Trask's comment that the phrase "Hawaiians at heart" "speaks worlds about how grotesque the theft of things Hawaiian has become" (*From a Native Daughter: Colonialism and Sovereignty in Hawai'i* [Monroe, ME: Common Courage, 1993], p. 3).

57. Joseph Balaz, "Da Mainland to Me," in *Asia/Pacific as Space of Cultural Production*, ed. Rob Wilson and Arif Dirlik (Durham and London: Duke University Press, 1995), pp. 175–176.

58. For example, as I am writing this, Ian Zabarte, a lawyer and counselor to the Chief and member of the Western Shoshone nation is in Hawai'i at the invitation of the Hawai'i Coalition Against Nuclear Testing (HCANT). He is here to raise awareness of the situation in the Shoshone territory of *Newe Segobia*, where the United States has conducted 935 nuclear tests. *The Honolulu Weekly*, one of Honolulu's few alternative newspapers, organized and published a discussion in their 17 July 1996 issue (pp. 8–10) that included, among others, Zabarte and Hawaiian activists from Ka Pakaukau (a coalition of organizations seeking peaceful decolonization of the Pacific), the Nuclear Free and Indepen-

dent Pacific (NFIP) and HCANT. Participants linked the nuclear testing on Shoshone land to the situation in Hawai'i. (A series of twelve atomic tests was conducted in the Hawaiian Archipelago in the atmosphere above Kalama Island [Johnston Island] between 1958–1962. During these tests, a Thor missile blew up on the launch pad, contaminating the area with plutonium from the warhead. The island currently houses facilities for the incineration of chemical weapons). Mino'aka Fitzsimmons established connections among native land struggles, destruction of the land, nuclear mining and testing, and the military buildup to protect land stolen from native peoples, explaining, "We believe, in NFIP, that de-nuclearization means the same thing as de-colonization" (8).

59. Ka Lāhui has 23,000 registered citizens, an elected legislature, and a constitution.

60. However, particularly as the U.S. government is trying to contain the force of sovereignty movements in Hawai'i by trying to set and control the conditions for recognition of sovereignty (e.g., the plebiscite vote), many Native Hawaiians, including Trask, are, along with Native American activists such as Churchill, calling attention to the inadequacy of the American Indian Model of sovereignty, wherein those belonging to Indian nations remain wards of the state.

61. There is also a film about this ten-day event entitled *The Tribunal*. This 1994 film was produced by Nā Maka o ka 'Āina.

62. Bruchac's and other conference organizers' criteria for writers to be considered "Native" were "provable Native heritage, self-identification as a Native person, and affiliation with the tribal community" (xx). The Festival sponsored 220 invited Native writers and 47 student writers from dozens of different tribal nations; another 101 Native writers came on their own, as did non-Native writers, scholars, publishers, and translators.

63. The alliances Trask establishes can also be traced in the promotional literature to her book of poetry, *Light in the Crevice Never Seen*, which includes blurbs from *Returning the Gift* participants Bruchac, Linda Hogan, and Joy Harjo.

64. Brant, *A Gathering of Spirit*, p. 11. Hereafter cited in the text.

65. Paula Gunn Allen, *The Sacred Hoop: Recovering the Feminine in American Indian Traditions* (Boston: Beacon Press, 1986), p. 264.

66. Ibid., p. 2.

67. Ibid., p. 30. See also Laura Coltelli's *Winged Words: American Indian Writers Speak* (Lincoln and London: University of Nebraska Press, 1990), pp. 13–14.

68. Gunn Allen in fact claims "red roots" for white feminism as well—see her essay "Who Is Your Mother? Red Roots of White Feminism," in *The Sacred Hoop*, pp. 209–221. While Gunn Allen's views are by no means uncontested ones, and are increasingly being challenged as essentialist and/or overly generalizing of Native cultures (see Greg Sarris's 1993 *Keeping Slug Woman Alive: A Holistic Approach to American Indian Texts*), they nevertheless are widely influential, and critiques of them have not been in the service of claiming Native women's need for a separatist feminist movement.

69. Trask, "Women's *Mana* and Hawaiian Sovereignty," *From a Native Daughter,* p. 121. Hereafter cited in the text.

70. Trask amplifies her position on the relationship between gender and colonialism in "Feminism and Indigenous Hawaiian Nationalism," her article in *Signs* 21.4 (summer 1996): 906–919. She explains, "The request for this article occasioned the first moment in many years that I have seriously considered the relationship between feminist theory and feminist praxis. More than a feminist, I am a nationalist, trained by my family and destined by my genealogy to speak and work on my people's behalf, including our women" (915).

71. In thinking through the relationship of printed, widely circulating texts to stories that are located in a particular location and community, I am indebted to Jacqueline Shea Murphy's unpublished manuscript, "Denaturalizing the National, Replacing the Regional: Abenaki Tales and 'Jewett's' Coastal Maine."

72. The Women of South Asian Descent Collective, eds., *Our Feet Walk the Sky,* p. xvii.

73. women of color in coalition, eds., *smell this,* vol. 2 (Berkeley: The Center for Racial Education, 1991), p. 3.

74. The influence of the multi-genre anthologies also arguably extends to the increasing frequency with which academics are engaging in projects that adopt a more personal or narrative style, and that focus on their marginalized and previously invisible identities in the academy. See, for example, *Working-Class Women in the Academy,* ed. Tokarczyk and Fay; *Unsettling Relations: The University as a Site of Feminist Struggles,* by Himani Bannerji, Linda Carty, Kari Dehli, Susan Heald, and Kate McKenna (Boston: South End, 1991); or *People of the Book: Thirty Scholars Reflect on Their Jewish Identity,* ed. Jeffrey Rubin-Dorsky and Shelly Fisher Fishkin (Madison: University of Wisconsin Press, 1996).

The women's anthologies of the 1980s also have spawned a few men's anthologies. While an anthology such as Robert Bly's 1992 *The Rag and Bone Shop of the Heart: Poems for Men* borrows from and responds to movements on the part of women and people of color, and constitutes a reaction to the perceived threat of being marginal, of losing masculine identity and power in the face of multiculturalism and various feminist movements, anthologies by men of color have worked more in solidarity with women of color and their anthologies. The journal for UC Berkeley men of color, *in your face,* for example, presents itself in coalition with *smell this.*

75. A related example of the kind of work that anthologies—and the events that surround their production—can do in the academy can be found in June Jordan's Poetry for the People. Jordan teaches a course by this title at UC Berkeley that as many as a hundred students sign up for at a time. In this course, students read from the work of a wide range of published poets, and write, perform, and anthologize their own poetry. Class readings, which can last as long as four hours, draw students' friends and family members by the hundreds, including those who say they have never set foot on the Berkeley campus before. Additional readings take place each semester in jails, high schools, churches,

and other community sites, as well as on public radio, and the anthologies students produce circulate widely. In 1995, Lauren Muller and the Blueprint Collective wrote and published *June Jordan's Poetry for the People: A Revolutionary Blueprint* with Routledge, with the idea of taking Poetry for the People to other parts of the country.

76. I have been able to contact some, but far from all, of the students in these classes to ask them about including a discussion of their anthologizing practices in this book. Because students did not produce their writings or anthologies with the expectation that they would be discussed in a context such as this one (a discussion I did not foresee), I am not including any quotations from the anthologies beyond title references, nor do I include details that would identify students I was unable to reach.

77. Bu La'ia, "Day-Old, Day-Old Poi," *False Crack???* (Pig Poi Records, 1995). The parodic force of this song is intensified by the fact that it is sung to the tune of "The Banana Boat Song." The lines I have cited are deceptively simple in terms of the racial politics they suggest. Bu La'ia focused much of his campaign against candidate Ben Cayetano, who, upon winning, became Hawaii's first Filipino governor. Cayetano, who premised his campaign on his dedication to Local people and interests and played up his Local working-class origins, is currently under fire for his perceived betrayal of Local people and interests.

78. Moraga, "Refugees of a World on Fire: Foreword to the Second Edition," *This Bridge Called My Back*, n.p.

Works Cited

Abel, Elizabeth. "Black Writing, White Reading: Race and the Politics of Feminist Interpretation." *Critical Inquiry* 19 (spring 1993): 470–498.

Abrams, M. H., ed. *The Norton Anthology of English Literature*. Vol. 2. New York: Norton, 1986.

Aguilar-San Juan, Karin, ed. *The State of Asian America: Activism and Resistance in the 1990s*. Boston: South End, 1994.

Alarcón, Norma. "Conjugating Subjects: The Heteroglossia of Essence and Resistance." In *An Other Tongue: Nation and Ethnicity in the Linguistic Borderlands,* edited by Alfred Arteaga. Durham and London: Duke University Press, 1989.

Alarcón, Norma, Ana Castillo, and Cherríe Moraga, eds. *Third Woman: The Sexuality of Latinas*. Berkeley: Third Woman, 1989.

Allison, Dorothy. "Weaving the Web of Community." *Quest: A Feminist Quarterly* (fall 1978): 75–92.

Anzaldúa, Gloria. *Borderlands/La Frontera: The New Mestiza*. San Francisco: Spinsters/Aunt Lute, 1987.

Anzaldúa, Gloria. "Bridge, Drawbridge, Sandbar, or Island: Lesbians of Color Hacienda Alianzas." In *Bridges of Power: Women's Multicultural Alliances,* edited by Lisa Albrecht and Rose M. Brewer. Santa Cruz and Philadelphia: New Society, 1990.

Anzaldúa, Gloria, ed. *Making Face, Making Soul/Hacienda Caras*. San Francisco: Aunt Lute, 1990.

Anzaldúa, Gloria. Review of *Gathering of Spirit*. *Conditions Ten* (1984): 145–153.

Appadurai, Arjun. "Patriotism and Its Futures." *Public Culture* 5.3 (1993): 411–430.

Arkeketa, Annette. "Quincentennial Ghostdance Song." In *Returning the Gift: Poetry and Prose from the First North American Native Writers' Festival,* edited by Joseph Bruchac. Tuscon and London: University of Arizona Press, 1994.

Asian Women United of California, eds. *Making Waves: An Anthology of Writing By and About Asian American Women*. Boston: Beacon Press, 1989.

Auerbach, Nina. *Communities of Women: An Idea in Fiction*. Cambridge: Harvard University Press, 1978.

Aunt Lute Catalogue (spring 1993).

Awkward, Michael. *Negotiating Difference: Race, Gender, and the Politics of Positionality.* Chicago and London: University of Chicago Press, 1995.

Balaz, Joseph. "Da Mainland to Me." In *Asia/Pacific as Space of Cultural Production,* edited by Rob Wilson and Arif Dirlik. Durham and London: Duke University Press, 1995.

Balibar, Etienne, and Immanuel Wallerstein. *Race, Nation, Class.* London and New York: Verso, 1991.

Bannerji, Himani, Linda Carty, Kari Dehli, Susan Heald, and Kate McKenna. *Unsettling Relations: The University as a Site of Feminist Struggles.* Boston: South End, 1991.

Beck, Evelyn Torton, ed. *Nice Jewish Girls: A Lesbian Anthology.* rev. ed. Boston: Beacon Press, 1989.

Bhaskara, Suparna. "Physical Subjectivity and the Risk of Essentialism." In *Our Feet Walk the Sky: Women of the South Asian Diaspora,* edited by The Women of South Asian Descent Collective. San Francisco: Aunt Lute, 1993.

Bly, Robert, ed. *The Rag and Bone Shop of the Heart: Poems for Men.* New York: Harper and Row, 1993.

Bondi, Liz. "Locating Identity Politics." In *Place and the Politics of Identity,* edited by Michael Keith and Steve Pile. London and New York: Routledge, 1993.

Boone, Joseph Allen. *Tradition Counter Tradition.* Chicago: University of Chicago Press, 1987.

Borland, Katherine. " 'That's Not What I Said': Interpreting Conflict in Oral Narrative Research." In *Women's Words: The Feminist Practice of Oral History,* edited by Sherna Berger Gluck and Daphne Patai. New York and London: Routledge, 1991.

Bourne, Jenny. "Homelands of the Mind: Jewish Feminism and Identity Politics." *Race and Class: A Journal for Black and Third World Liberation* 29.1 (summer 1987): 1–24.

Boyarin, Daniel, and Jonathan Boyarin. "Diaspora: Generation and the Ground of Jewish Identity." *Critical Inquiry* 19 (summer 1993): 693–725.

Brah, Avtar. "Difference, Diversity and Differentiation." In *"Race," Culture, and Difference,* edited by James Donald and Ali Rattansi. London: Sage, 1992.

Brant, Beth (Degonwadonti), ed. *A Gathering of Spirit: A Collection by North American Indian Women.* Ithaca, NY: Firebrand, 1988.

Brown, Wendy. "Wounded Attachments: Late Modern Oppositional Political Formations." In *The Identity in Question,* edited by John Rajchman. New York and London: Routledge, 1995.

Bruchac, Joseph, ed. *Returning the Gift: Poetry and Prose from the First North American Native Writers' Festival.* Tucson and London: University of Arizona Press, 1994.

Buell, Frederick. *National Culture and the New Global System.* Baltimore and London: Johns Hopkins University Press, 1994.

Bulkin, Elly, Minnie Bruce Pratt, and Barbara Smith. *Yours in Struggle: Three Feminist Perspectives on Anti-Semitism and Racism.* Ithaca, NY: Firebrand, 1984.

Burnett, June, Julie Cotterill, Annette Kennerley, Phoebe Nathan, and Jeanne Wilding, eds. *The Common Thread: Writings by Working-Class Women*. London: Mandarin, 1989.

Butler, Judith. "Imitation and Gender Insubordination." In *Inside/Out: Lesbian Theories, Gay Theories*, edited by Diana Fuss. New York and London: Routledge, 1991.

Cade, Toni, ed. *The Black Woman*. New York: New American Library, 1970.

Campomanes, Oscar V. "Filipinos in the United States and Their Literature of Exile." In *Reading the Literatures of Asian American*, edited by Shirley Geoklin Lim and Amy Ling. Philadelphia: Temple University Press, 1992.

Carby, Hazel. "The Multicultural Wars." In *Black Popular Culture*, edited by Gina Dent. Seattle: Bay Press, 1992. From a project by Michele Wallace.

Carmen, Gail, Shaila, and Pratibha. "Becoming Visible: Black Lesbian Discussions." *Feminist Review* 17 (July 1984): 53–72.

Chambram-Dernersesian, Angie. "I Throw Punches for My Race, But I Don't Want to Be a Man: Writing Us—Chica-nos (Girl, Us)/Chicanas—into the Movement Script." In *Cultural Studies*, edited by Lawrence Grossberg, Cary Nelson, and Paula Treichler. New York and London: Routledge, 1992.

Chan, Jeffery Paul, Frank Chin, Lawson Fusao Inada, and Shawn Wong, eds. *The Big Aiiieeeee!: An Anthology of Chinese and Japanese American Literature*. New York: Meridian, 1991.

Chin, Frank, Jeffery Paul Chan, Lawson Fusao Inada, and Shawn Wong, eds. *Aiiieeeee!: An Anthology of Asian American Writers*. New York: Mentor, 1991 (rprt.).

Chock, Eric, and Darrell H. Y. Lum, eds. *The Best of Bamboo Ridge*. Honolulu: Bamboo Ridge Press, 1986.

Christian, Barbara. "The Race for Theory." *Cultural Critique* 6 (spring 1987): 51–63.

Christian, Barbara. "A Rough Terrain: The Case of Shaping an Anthology of Caribbean Women Writers." In *The Ethnic Canon: Histories, Institutions, and Interventions*, edited by David Palumbo-Liu. Minneapolis and London: University of Minnesota Press, 1995.

Chung, C., A. Kim, and A. K. Lemeshewsky, eds., *Between the Lines: An Anthology by Pacific/Asian Lesbians of Santa Cruz, California*. Santa Cruz: Dancing Bird, 1987.

Chung, Christy, Aly Kim, Zoon Nguyen, and Trinity Ordoña, with Arlene Stein. "In Our Own Way: A Roundtable Discussion." *Amerasia Journal* 20.1 (1994): 137–147.

Clarke, Cheryl. Review of *Making Face, Making Soul/Haciendo Caras*. *Bridges: A Journal for Jewish Feminists and Our Friends* 2.1 (spring 1991): 128–133.

Cochran, Jo, J. T. Stewart, and Mayumi Tsutakawa, eds. *Gathering Ground: New Writing and Art by Northwest Women of Color*. Seattle: The Seal Press, 1984.

Coiner, Constance. Introduction to *Radical Teacher* 46 (spring 1995): 2–4.

Coltelli, Laura. *Winged Words: American Indian Writers Speak*. Lincoln and London: University of Nebraska Press, 1990.

Crimp, Douglas. "Mourning and Militancy." In *Out There: Marginalization and Contemporary Cultures,* edited by Russell Ferguson, Martha Gever, Trinh T. Minh-ha, and Cornel West. Cambridge and London: MIT Press, 1990.

Cunard, Nancy, ed. *Negro: An Anthology,* edited by Hugh Ford. New York: Frederick Ungar, 1970. Abridged edition.

The Dartmouth Collective. Introduction to *Feminist Readings: French Texts/ American Contexts. Yale French Studies* 62 (1981).

Davies, Margaret Llewelyn, ed. *Life as We Have Known It, by Co-operative Working Women.* London: Virago, 1977.

Dayan, Joan. "'A Receptacle for That Race of Men': Blood, Boundaries, and Mutations of Theory." *American Literature* 67.4 (December 1994): 801–813.

De Lauretis, Teresa. "Eccentric Subjects: Feminist Theory and Historical Consciousness." *Feminist Studies* 16.1 (spring 1990): 115–150.

De Lauretis, Teresa. *Technologies of Gender.* Bloomington: Indiana University Press, 1987.

Delphy, Christine. *Close to Home: A Materialist Analysis of Women's Oppression.* Translated and edited by Diana Leonard. Amherst: University of Massachusetts Press, 1984.

Dirlik, Arif. "Asians on the Rim: Transnational Capital and Local Community in the Making of Contemporary Asian America." Photocopy, forthcoming.

Dirlik, Arif. "The Asia-Pacific in Asian-American Perspective." In *What Is in a Rim: Critical Perspectives on the Pacific Region Idea,* edited by Arif Dirlik. Boulder, CO: Westview, 1993.

Dirlik, Arif. "The Global in the Local." In *Global/Local: Cultural Production and the Transnational Imaginary,* edited by Rob Wilson and Wimal Dissanayake. Durham and London: Duke University Press, 1996.

Dirlik, Arif. "The Postcolonial Aura: Third World Criticism in the Age of Global Capitalism." *Critical Inquiry,* 20.2 (winter 1994): 328–356.

Doro, Sue. Commentary on "Focus." In *Liberating Memory: Our Work and Our Working-Class Consciousness,* edited by Janet Zandy. New Brunswick, NJ: Rutgers University Press, 1995.

Ehrenreich, Barbara, and John Ehrenreich. "The Professional-Managerial Class." In *Between Labor and Capital,* edited by Pat Walker. Montreal: Black Rose, 1979.

Elam, Diane, and Robyn Wiegman. "Contingencies." In *Feminism Beside Itself,* edited by Diane Elam and Robyn Wiegman. New York and London: Routledge, 1995.

English 100 Students, University of Hawai'i at Mānoa. "English 100 Is Like a Box of Chocolates/Pidgin Is One Box Choclats Li Dat." Self-published anthology. Spring 1995.

English 250 Students, University of Hawai'i at Mānoa. "Rice, Potatoes, and Poi." Self-published anthology. Fall 1994.

English 255 Students, University of Hawai'i at Mānoa. "We Ate Mother Goose for Dinner." Self-published anthology. Fall 1995.

English 255 Students, University of Hawai'i at Mānoa. "Bye Bye Miss American Pie." Self-published anthology. Spring 1996.

Etter-Lewis, Gwendolyn. "Black Women's Life Stories: Reclaiming Self in Narrative Texts." In *Women's Words: The Feminist Practice of Oral History,* edited by Sherna Berger Gluck and Daphne Patai. New York and London: Routledge, 1991.

Featherstone, Mike. "Localism, Globalism, and Cultural Identity." In *Global/Local: Cultural Production and the Transnational Imaginary,* edited by Rob Wilson and Wimal Dissanayake. Durham and London: Duke University Press, 1996.

Fuentes, Annette, and Barbara Ehrenreich. "Women in the Global Factory." INC Pamphlet 2, edited by Holly Sklar and Gloria Jacobs. Boston: South End, 1983.

Fujikane, Candace. "Between Nationalisms: Hawaii's Local Nation and Its Troubled Racial Paradise." *Critical Mass* 1.2 (spring/summer 1994): 23–57.

Fuss, Diana. *Essentially Speaking: Feminism, Nature, and Difference.* New York and London: Routledge, 1989.

Fuss, Diana, ed. *Inside/Out: Lesbian Theories, Gay Theories.* New York and London: Routledge, 1991.

Gaffin, Jean, and David Thoms. *Caring and Sharing: The Centenary History of the Co-operative Women's Guild.* Manchester: Co-operative Union, 1983.

Gallop, Jane. *Around 1981.* New York and London: Routledge, 1992.

Gates, Henry Louis, Jr. *Loose Canons: Notes on the Culture War.* New York and Oxford: Oxford University Press, 1992.

Gilroy, Paul. *Black Atlantic: Modernity and Double Consciousness.* Cambridge: Harvard University Press, 1993.

Gilroy, Paul. "Steppin' Out of Babylon—Race, Class, and Autonomy." In *The Empire Strikes Back: Race and Racism in 70s Britain,* edited by The Centre for Contemporary Cultural Studies. London: Hutchinson, 1982.

Gilroy, Paul. *"There Ain't No Black in the Union Jack": The Cultural Politics of Race and Nation.* Chicago: University of Chicago Press, 1987.

Giroux, Henry. "Resisting Difference: Cultural Studies and the Discourse of Critical Pedagogy." In *Cultural Studies,* edited by Lawrence Grossberg, Cary Nelson, and Paula A. Treichler. New York and London: Routledge, 1992.

Gluck, Sherna Berger, and Daphne Patai, eds. Introduction to *Women's Words: The Feminist Practice of Oral History.* New York and London: Routledge, 1991.

Goellnicht, Donald C. "Tang Ao in America: Male Subject Positions in *China Men.*" In *Reading the Literatures of Asian America,* edited by Shirley Geok-lin Lim and Amy Ling. Philadelphia: Temple University Press, 1992.

Gouldner, Alvin. *The Future of Intellectuals and the Rise of the New Class.* New York: Oxford University Press, 1979.

Grant, Jaime M. "Building Community-Based Coalitions from Academe: The

Union Institute and the Kitchen Table: Women of Color Press Transition Coalition." *Signs* 21.4 (summer 1996): 1024–1033.

Greenblatt, Stephen, and Giles Gunn, eds. *Redrawing the Boundaries: The Transformation of English and American Literary Studies.* New York: Modern Language Association of America, 1992.

Grewal, Inderpal. "Autobiographic Subjects and Diasporic Locations: *Meatless Days* and *Borderlands.*" In *Scattered Hegemonies: Postmodernity and Transnational Feminist Practices,* edited by Inderpal Grewal and Caren Kaplan. Minneapolis and London: University of Minnesota Press, 1994.

Grewal, Inderpal, and Caren Kaplan, eds. *Scattered Hegemonies: Postmodernity and Transnational Feminist Practices.* Minneapolis and London: University of Minnesota Press, 1994.

Grewal, Shabnam, Jackie Kay, Liliane Landor, Gail Lewis, and Pratibha Parmar, eds. *Charting the Journey: Writings by Black and Third World Women.* London: Sheba Feminist Publishers, 1988.

Grossberg, Lawrence, Cary Nelson, and Paula Treichler, eds. *Cultural Studies.* New York and London: Routledge, 1992.

Guillory, John. *Cultural Capital: The Problem of Literary Canon Formation.* Chicago and London: University of Chicago Press, 1993.

Gunn Allen, Paula. *The Sacred Hoop: Recovering the Feminine in American Indian Traditions.* Boston: Beacon Press, 1986.

Hagedorn, Jessica, ed. *Charlie Chan Is Dead: An Anthology of Contemporary Asian American Fiction.* New York: Penguin, 1993.

Hall, Stuart. "The Local and the Global: Globalization and Ethnicity." In *Culture, Globalization, and the World-System: Contemporary Conditions for the Representation of Identity,* edited by Anthony King. Department of Art and History: State University of New York at Binghamton, 1991.

Hall, Stuart. "Old and New Identities, Old and New Ethnicities." In *Culture, Globalization, and the World-System: Contemporary Conditions for the Representation of Identity,* edited by Anthony D. King. Department of Art and History: State University of New York at Binghamton, 1991.

Haraway, Donna. *Simians, Cyborgs, and Women.* London: Free Association Books, 1991.

Hau'ofa, Epeli. "Our Sea of Islands." In *A New Oceania: Rediscovering Our Sea of Islands,* edited by Eric Waddell, Vijay Naidu, and Epeli Hau'ofa. Suva, Fiji: University of the South Pacific, 1993.

Hesse, Barnor. "Black to Front and Black Again: Racialization through Contested Times and Spaces." In *Place and the Politics of Identity,* edited by Michael Keith and Steve Pile. London and New York: Routledge, 1993.

Hirsch, Marianne, and Evelyn Fox Keller, eds. *Conflicts in Feminism.* New York: Routledge, 1990.

Hongo, Garrett, ed. *The Open Boat.* New York: Anchor, 1993.

hooks, bell. "Essentialism and Experience." *American Literary History* 3.1 (spring 1991): 172–183.

hooks, bell. "Keeping a Legacy of Shared Struggle." *Z Magazine* (September 1992): 23–25.

hooks, bell. *Yearning*. Boston: South End, 1990.

Hull, Gloria T. "Reading Literature by U.S. Third World Women." Wellesley, MA: Center for Research on Women, 1984.

Hull, Gloria T., Patricia Bell Scott, and Barbara Smith, eds. *All the Women are White, All the Men are Black, But Some of Us are Brave: Black Women's Studies*. Old Westbury, NY: The Feminist Press, 1982.

Hurtado, Aida. "Relating to Privilege: Seduction and Subordination of White Women and Women of Color." *Signs: Journal of Women in Culture and Society* 14.4 (1989): 833–855.

Iwasaki, Bruce. Introduction to "Asian American Literature" section in *Counterpoint*, ed. Emma Gee (Los Angeles: Asian American Studies Center, 1976).

Jay, Gregory. "The End of 'American' Literature: Toward a Multicultural Practice." *College English* 53 (1991): 264–281.

Johnson, Barbara. "Home." Talk delivered at the University of California at Berkeley, 3/1/92.

Jones, Gareth Stedman. *Languages of Class: Studies in English Working Class History, 1832–1982*. Cambridge and New York: Cambridge University Press, 1983.

Kame'eleihiwa, Lilikalā. *Native Land and Foreign Desires*. Honolulu: Bishop Museum Press, 1992.

Kaplan, Caren. "The Politics of Location as Transnational Feminist Critical Practice." In *Scattered Hegemonies*, edited by Inderpal Grewal and Caren Kaplan. Minneapolis and London: University of Minnesota Press, 1994.

Kaplan, Cora. *Sea Changes: Culture and Feminism*. London: Verso, 1986.

Kaye/Kantrowitz, Melanie. "To Be a Radical Jew in the Late Twentieth Century." In *The Tribe of Dina: A Jewish Women's Anthology*, edited by Melanie Kaye/Kantrowitz and Irena Klepfisz. Boston: Beacon Press, 1989.

Kaye/Kantrowitz, Melanie. "Some Notes on Jewish Lesbian Identity." In *Nice Jewish Girls: A Lesbian Anthology*, edited by Evelyn Torton Beck. Boston: Beacon Press, 1989 (rev. ed.).

Keating, AnaLouise. *Women Reading Women Writing: Self Invention in Paula Gunn Allen, Gloria Anzaldúa, and Audre Lorde*. Philadelphia: Temple University Press, 1996.

Keith, Michael, and Steve Pile, eds., *Place and the Politics of Identity*. London and New York: Routledge, 1993.

Kennedy, Susan Estabrook. *If All We Did Was to Weep at Home: A History of White Working-Class Women in America*. Bloomington and London: Indiana University Press, 1979.

Kim, Elaine. *Asian American Literature: An Introduction to the Writings and Their Social Context*. Philadelphia: Temple University Press, 1982.

Kim, Elaine. "Room for a View from a Marginal Sight." *Critical Mass* 1.2 (spring 1994): 3–22.

Kim, Elaine. Forum in *Amerasia Journal* 16.2 (1990): 101–111.

Kim, Elaine, and Janice Otani. *With Silk Wings: Asian American Women at Work.* San Francisco: Asian Women United of California, 1983.

King, Deborah K. "Multiple Jeopardy, Multiple Consciousness: The Context of a Black Feminist Ideology." *Signs* 14.1 (1988): 42–72.

King, Katie. "Producing Sex, Theory, and Culture: Gay/Straight Remappings in Contemporary Feminism." In *Conflicts in Feminism,* edited by Marianne Hirsch and Evelyn Fox Keller. New York: Routledge, 1990.

Laclau, Ernesto, and Chantal Mouffe. *Hegemony and Socialist Strategy: Towards a Radical Democratic Politics.* London: Verso, 1985.

La'ia, Bu. "Day-Old, Day-Old Poi." *False Crack???* Pig Poi Records, 1995.

Lauter, Paul. *Canons and Contexts.* New York and Oxford: Oxford University Press, 1991.

Lauter, Paul. "Working-Class Women's Literature." In *Opportunities for Women's Studies in Language and Literature,* edited by Joan E. Hartman and Ellen Messer-Davidow. Vol.1 of *Women in Print.* New York: Modern Language Association of America, 1982.

Leong, Russell, ed. Forum on *Strangers from a Different Shore. Amerasia* 16.2 (1990): 62–131.

Libretti, Tim. "Is There a Working Class in U.S. Literature? Race, Ethnicity, and the Proletarian Literary Tradition." *Radical Teacher* 46 (spring 1995): 22–26.

Lim, Shirley Geok-lin. Preface to *Asian America: Journal of Culture and the Arts* 1 (winter 1992).

Lim, Shirley Geok-lin, and Amy Ling, eds. *Reading the Literatures of Asian America.* Philadelphia: Temple University Press, 1992.

Lim, Shirley Geok-lin, Mayumi Tsutakawa, and Margarita Donnelly, eds. *The Forbidden Stitch: An Asian American Women's Anthology.* Corvallis, OR: Calyx Books, 1989.

Lim-Hing, Sharon, ed. *The Very Inside: An Anthology of Writings by Asian and Pacific Islander Lesbian and Bisexual Women.* Toronto: Sister Vision, 1994.

Ling, Amy. *Between Worlds: Women Writers of Chinese Ancestry.* New York: Pergamon, 1990.

Liu, Cynthia. Review of *The Forbidden Stitch.* In *Amerasia* 15.2 (1989): 205–208.

Locke, Alain. *The New Negro: Voices of the Harlem Renaissance.* New York: Atheneum, 1992. Reprint.

Lorde, Audre. "Eye to Eye: Black Women, Hatred, and Anger." In *Sister Outsider.* Trumansburg, NY: The Crossing Press, 1984.

Lyons, Laura. *Writing in Trouble: Protest and the Cultural Politics of Irish Nationalism.* Photocopy.

Madhubuti, Haki R., ed. *Why L.A. Happened: Implications of the '92 Los Angeles Rebellion.* Chicago: Third World Press, 1993.

Mazumdar, Sucheta. "Race and Racism: South Asians in the United States." In *Frontiers of Asian American Studies: Writing, Research, and Commentary,* edited by Gail M. Nomura, Russell Endo, Stephen H. Sumida, and Russell C. Leong. Pullman: Washington State University Press, 1989.

Mennis, Bernice. Review of *Making Face, Making Soul/Haciendo Caras. Bridges: A Journal for Jewish Feminists and Our Friends* 2.1 (spring 1991): 133–138.

Mirikitani, Janice, Buriel Clay II, Janet Campbell Hale, Alejandro Murguia, and Robert Vargas, eds. *Time to Greez! Incantations from the Third World.* San Francisco: Glide Productions, 1975.

Miyoshi, Masao. "A Borderless World? From Colonialism to Transnationalism and the Decline of the Nation-State." *Critical Inquiry* 19 (summer 1993): 726–751.

Mohanty, Chandra Talpade. Introduction to *Third World Women and the Politics of Feminism,* edited by Chandra Talpade Mohanty, Ann Russo, and Lourdes Torres. Bloomington and Indianapolis: Indiana University Press, 1991.

Moraga, Cherríe. *Loving in the War Years.* Boston: South End, 1983.

Moraga, Cherríe, and Gloria Anzaldúa, eds. *This Bridge Called My Back: Writings by Radical Women of Color.* New York: Kitchen Table: Women of Color Press, 1981.

Moraga, Cherríe, and Gloria Anzaldúa. Untitled. *Conditions: Five, The Black Women's Issue* (1979): n.p.

Morales, Rodney. "Pirates Yes They Rob I." Paper read at Hawai'i Literature Conference, Honolulu, March 12, 1994.

Morgan, Robin, ed. *Sisterhood Is Global: The International Women's Movement Anthology.* Garden City, NY: Anchor, 1984.

Morgan, Robin, ed. *Sisterhood Is Powerful: An Anthology of Writings from the Women's Liberation Movement.* New York: Vintage, 1970.

Morgen, Sandra. "Beyond the Double Day: Work and Family in Working-Class Women's Lives." *Feminist Studies* 16.1 (spring 1990): 53–67.

Morrison, Toni, ed. *The Black Book.* New York: Random House, 1974.

Muller, Lauren, and the Blueprint Collective. *June Jordan's Poetry for the People: A Revolutionary Blueprint.* New York and London: Routledge, 1995.

Nomura, Gail M., Russell Endo, Stephen H. Sumida, and Russell C. Leong, eds. *Frontiers of Asian American Studies: Writing, Research, and Commentary.* Pullman: Washington State University Press, 1989.

O'Dair, Sharon. "Vestments and Vested Interests: Academia, the Working Class, and Affirmative Action." In *Working-Class Women in the Academy,* edited by Michelle M. Tokarczyk and Elizabeth A. Fay. Amherst: University of Massachusetts Press, 1993.

Okamura, Jonathan. "Why There Are No Asian Americans in Hawai'i: The Continuing Significance of Local Identity." *Social Process in Hawaii* 35 (1994): 161–178.

Okihiro, Gary Y. Introduction to *Reflections on Shattered Windows: Promises and Prospects of Asian American Studies,* edited by Gary Y. Okihiro, Shirley

Hune, Arthur A. Hansen, and John M. Liu. Pullman: Washington State University Press, 1988.

Omi, Michael. "It Just Ain't the Sixties No More: The Contemporary Dilemmas of Asian American Studies." In *Reflections on Shattered Windows: Promises and Prospects of Asian American Studies,* edited by Gary Y. Okihiro, Shirley Hune, Arthur A. Hansen, and John M. Liu. Pullman: Washington State University Press, 1988.

Omi, Michael, and Howard Winant. *Racial Formation in the United States.* New York and London: Routledge, 1986.

Padilla, Genaro M. *My History, Not Yours: The Formation of Mexican American Autobiography.* Madison: University of Wisconsin Press, 1993.

Phelan, Shane. *Identity Politics: Lesbian Feminism and the Limits of Community.* Philadelphia: Temple University Press, 1989.

Porter, Carolyn. "What We Know That We Don't Know: Remapping American Literary Studies." *American Literary History* 6.3 (fall 1994): 467–526.

Pratt, Minnie Bruce. "The Maps in My Bible." *Bridges: A Journal for Jewish Feminists and Our Friends,* 2.1 (spring 1991): 93–116.

Pryse, Marjorie, and Hortense J. Spillers, eds. *Conjuring, Black Women, Fiction, and Literary Tradition.* Bloomington: Indiana University Press, 1985.

Quintana, Alvina E. *Home Girls: Chicana Literary Voices.* Philadelphia: Temple University Press, 1996.

Radhakrishnan, R. "Nationalism, Gender, and the Narrative of Identity." In *Nationalisms and Sexualities,* edited by Andrew Parker, Mary Russo, Doris Sommer, and Patricia Yaeger. New York and London: Routledge, 1992.

Rajchman, John, ed. *The Identity in Question.* New York and London: Routledge, 1995.

Ramos, Juanita, ed. *Compañeras: Latina Lesbians.* New York and London: Routledge, 1994.

Rich, Adrienne. "Notes towards a Politics of Location (1984)." In *Blood, Bread, and Poetry: Selected Prose 1979–1985.* London: Virago, 1987.

Robinson, Lillian. *Sex, Class, and Culture.* Bloomington: Indiana University Press, 1978.

Romano-V., Octavio Ignacio, and Hermino Rios C., eds. *El Espejo—The Mirror: Selected Chicano Literature.* Berkeley: Quinto Sol, 1969, 1972.

Roof, Judith. "How to Satisfy a Woman 'Every Time.'" In *Feminism Beside Itself,* edited by Diane Elam and Robyn Wiegman. New York and London: Routledge, 1995.

Rubin-Dorsky, Jeffrey, and Shelly Fisher Fishkin, eds. *People of the Book: Thirty Scholars Reflect on Their Jewish Identity.* Madison: University of Wisconsin Press, 1996.

Ryan, Jake, and Charles Sackrey. *Strangers in Paradise: Academics from the Working Class.* Boston: South End, 1984.

Samuel, Raphael. Introduction to *Patriotism: The Making and Unmaking of British*

National Identity, edited by Raphael Samuel. Vol. 2 of *Minorities and Outsiders.* London and New York: Routledge, 1989.

Sánchez, Rosaura. "Calculated Musings: Richard Rodríguez's Metaphysics of Difference." In *The Ethnic Canon: Histories, Institutions, and Interventions,* edited by David Palumbo-Liu. Minneapolis and London: University of Minnesota Press, 1995.

Sandoval, Chela. "U.S. Third World Feminism: The Theory and Method of Oppositional Consciousness in the Postmodern World." *Genders* 10 (spring 1991): 1–24.

Sandoval, Chela. "U.S. Third World Feminism." *The Oxford Companion to Women's Writing in the United States,* edited by Cathy N. Davidson and Linda Wagner-Martin. New York and Oxford: Oxford University Press, 1995.

San Juan, E., Jr. "Beyond Identity Politics: The Predicament of the Asian American Writer in Late Capitalism." *American Literary History* 3.3 (fall 1991): 542–565.

Savigliano, Marta. *Tango and the Political Economy of Passion.* Boulder, CO: Westview, 1995.

Scott, Joyce Hope. "From Foreground to Margin: Female Configuration and Masculine Self-Representation in Black Nationalist Fiction." In *Nationalisms and Sexualities,* edited by Andrew Parker, Mary Russo, Doris Sommer, and Patricia Yaeger. New York and London: Routledge, 1992.

Sharrad, Paul. "Making Beginnings: Johnny Frisbie and Pacific Literature." *New Literary History* 25 (1994): 121–136.

Shea Murphy, Jacqueline. "Denaturalizing the National, Replacing the Regional: Abenaki Tales and 'Jewett's' Coastal Maine." Photocopy.

Short, Kayann. "Coming to the Table: The Differential Politics of *This Bridge Called My Back.*" *Genders* 20 (New York and London: New York University Press, 1994): 3–44.

Showalter, Elaine. "A Feminist Critic in the Wilderness." *The New Feminist Criticism,* edited by Elaine Showalter. New York: Pantheon, 1985.

Silko, Leslie Marmon. *Almanac of the Dead.* New York: Penguin, 1991.

Silvera, Makeda, ed. *Piece of My Heart: A Lesbian of Colour Anthology.* Toronto: Sister Vision, 1991.

Sisterhood across the Waves. *Asian American Women's Journal: Moving the Mountains.* San Diego: University of California at San Diego, 1993.

Smith, Barbara. "A Press of Our Own: Kitchen Table: Women of Color Press." *Frontiers* 10.3 (1989): 11–13.

Smith, Barbara. Review of *Gathering Ground. Conditions* 11/12 (1985): 175–184.

Smith, Barbara. "Towards a Black Feminist Criticism." In *All the Women Are White, All the Men Are Black, But Some of Us Are Brave: Black Women's Studies,* edited by Gloria T. Hull, Patricia Bell Scott, and Barbara Smith. Old Westbury, NY: The Feminist Press, 1982.

Smith, Barbara. "The Truth That Never Hurts: Black Lesbians in Fiction in the

1980s." In *Third World Women and the Politics of Feminism,* edited by Chandra Talpade Mohanty, Ann Russo, and Lourdes Torres. Bloomington and Indianapolis: Indiana University Press, 1991.

Smith, Barbara, ed. *Home Girls: A Black Feminist Anthology.* New York: Kitchen Table: Women of Color Press, 1983.

Smith, Barbara, and Lorraine Bethel, eds. *Conditions: Five, The Black Women's Issue.* (1979).

Soja, Edward, and Barbara Hooper. "The Spaces That Difference Makes: Some Notes on the Geographical Margins of the New Cultural Politics." In *Place and the Politics of Identity,* edited by Michael Keith and Steve Pile. London and New York: Routledge, 1993.

Sollers, Werner, ed. *The Invention of Ethnicity.* New York: Oxford University Press, 1989.

Sommer, Doris. "Irresistible Romance: The Foundational Fictions of Latin America." In *Nation and Narration,* edited by Homi K. Bhabha. London and New York: Routledge, 1990.

Spinsters Ink Catalogue (fall 1993).

Spinsters Ink Catalogue (spring 1993).

Spivak, Gayatri. "In a Word." In *Outside in the Teaching Machine.* New York and London: Routledge, 1993.

Sumida, Stephen. "Asian/Pacific American Literature in the Classroom." *American Literature* 65.2 (June 1993): 348–353.

Sundquist, Eric J. Introduction to "American Literary History: The Next Century." *American Literature* 67.4 (December 1995): 93–94.

Sundquist, Eric. *To Wake the Nations: Race in the Making of American Literature.* Cambridge and London: Harvard University Press, Belknap Press, 1993.

Tachiki, Amy, Eddie Wong, and Franklin Odo, with Buck Wong, eds. *Roots: An Asian American Reader.* Los Angeles: UCLA Asian American Studies Center, 1971.

Takaki, Ronald. *Strangers from a Different Shore: A History of Asian Americans.* New York: Penguin, 1989.

Thomas, Sherry. *We Didn't Have Much, But We Sure Had Plenty: Stories of Rural Women.* Garden City, NY: Anchor, Doubleday, 1981.

Thompson, E. P. *The Making of the English Working Class.* New York: Vintage, 1966.

Tokarczyk, Michelle M., and Elizabeth A. Fay, eds. *Working-Class Women in the Academy: Laborers in the Knowledge Factory.* Amherst: University of Massachusetts Press, 1993.

Tölöyan, Khachig. "The Nation-State and Its Others: In Lieu of a Preface." *Diaspora* 1.1 (1991): 3–8.

Trask, Haunani-Kay. *From a Native Daughter: Colonialism and Sovereignty in Hawai'i.* Monroe, ME: Common Courage, 1993.

Trask, Haunani-Kay. "Feminism and Indigenous Hawaiian Nationalism." *Signs* 21.4 (summer 1996): 906–919.

Trask, Haunani-Kay. *Light in the Crevice Never Seen*. Corvallis, OR: Calyx Books, 1994.

The Tribunal. Video recording. Nā Maka o ka 'Āina, Producers. 1994.

Tu Smith, Bonnie. *All My Relatives: Community in Contemporary Ethnic American Literatures*. Ann Arbor: University of Michigan Press, 1994.

Warren, Kenneth. "The Problem of Anthologies, or Making the Dead Wince." *American Literature* 65.2 (June 1993): 338–342.

Watanabe, Sylvia, and Carol Bruchac, eds. *Home to Stay: Asian American Women's Fiction*. New York: Greenfield Review Press, 1990.

Wei, William. *The Asian American Movement*. Philadelphia: Temple University Press, 1993.

West, Cornel. "The New Cultural Politics of Difference." In *Out There: Marginalization and Contemporary Cultures*, edited by Russell Ferguson, Martha Gever, Trinh T. Minh-ha, and Cornel West. Cambridge and London: MIT Press, 1990.

Willis, Paul. *Learning to Labour: How Working-Class Kids Get Working-Class Jobs*. Farnborough, England: Saxon House, 1977.

Wilson, Rob, and Wimal Dissanayake, eds. *Global/Local: Cultural Production and the Transnational Imaginary*. Durham and London: Duke University Press, 1996.

Wittig, Monique. "One Is Not Born a Woman." *Feminist Issues* 2 (winter 1981): 47–54.

Wolf, Naomi. *The Beauty Myth*. New York: Doubleday, 1991.

women of color in coalition, eds. *smell this*. Vol. 2 (Berkeley: The Center for Racial Education, 1991).

The Women of South Asian Descent Collective, eds. *Our Feet Walk the Sky: Women of the South Asian Diaspora*. San Francisco: Aunt Lute, 1993.

Wong, Sau-ling Cynthia. "Denationalization Reconsidered: Asian American Cultural Criticism at a Theoretical Crossroads." *Amerasia Journal* 21.1, 2 (1995): 1–27.

Wong, Sau-ling Cynthia. *Reading Asian American Literature: From Necessity to Extravagance*. Princeton: Princeton University Press, 1993.

Wong, Shawn. *American Knees*. New York: Simon and Schuster, 1995.

Yamada, Mitsuye, and Sarie Sachie Hylkema, eds. *Sowing Ti Leaves: Writings by Multi-Cultural Women*. Irvine, CA: Multi-Cultural Women Writers of Orange County, 1990.

Yamamoto, Hisaye. *Seventeen Syllables and Other Stories*. Latham, NY: Kitchen Table: Women of Color Press, 1988.

Yoshimoto, Mitsuhiro. "Real Virtuality." In *Global/Local: Cultural Production and the Transnational Imaginary*, edited by Rob Wilson and Wimal Dissanayake. Durham and London: Duke University Press, 1996.

Young, Iris Marion. "The Ideal of Community and the Politics of Difference." In *Feminism/Postmodernism*, edited by Linda Nicholson. New York and London: Routledge, 1990.

Zandy, Janet. "The Complexities and Contradictions of Working-Class Women's Writing." *Radical Teacher* 46 (spring 1995): 5–8.

Zandy, Janet, ed. *Calling Home: Working-Class Women's Writings.* New Brunswick, NJ, and London: Rutgers University Press, 1990.

Zandy, Janet, ed. *Liberating Memory: Our Work and Our Working-Class Consciousness.* New Brunswick, NJ: Rutgers University Press, 1995.

Index